My Brother Ron

A Personal and Social History of Deinstitutionalization of the Mentally Ill

BOOKS BY CLAYTON E. CRAMER

By the Dim and Flaring Lamps: The Civil War Diary of Samuel McIlvaine (1990)

For the Defense of Themselves and the State: The Original Intent and Judicial Interpretation of the Right to Keep and Bear Arms (1994)

Firing Back: A Clear, Simple Guide to Defending Your Right to Keep and Bear Arms (1995)

Black Demographic Data, 1790-1860: A Sourcebook (1995)

Concealed Weapon Laws of the Early Republic:
Dueling, Southern Violence, and Moral Reform (1999)

Armed America: The Remarkable Story of How and Why Guns Became as American as Apple Pie (2006)

For my mother, who has watched out for Ron all these years

CONTENTS

ACKNOWLEDGMENTS

Every book represents the kind assistance of many people. This book, more than most, is a family project. I have spent many hours talking to my mother, my sisters Susan, Marilyn, and Carolyn, and to the extent that he is able to communicate effectively about the past, my brother Ron. Unsurprisingly, we have different perspectives on the past, and different views of the best way of solving the problems that deinstitutionalization created. I have done my best, where there were differing memories of these painful events involving Ron, to write a consensus account.

I also want to thank my daughter Hilary Cobb, LMSW, for many useful discussions of the problems of social policy and mental illness and the final edit of the book. My wife Rhonda Cramer has spent enormous amounts of time discussing these problems — and living through them with me — over the years. In the final stages of this book, she put her English faculty hat on, and provided many useful writing suggestions. John Simutis also assisted with final proofreading of the Kindle edition.

Thanks also to the regular readers of my blog who have contributed pointers to articles, and shared their own personal tragedies of family members with severe mental illness. It is for all of us that this book exists.

Clayton E. Cramer
June, 2012

INTRODUCTION

Every book has a starting point, the moment where the author finds himself saying, "This could be an interesting story to tell." Sometimes, if the issue is critical enough, you say, "This is a story that *must* be told." It may be five years or ten years, or even forty years from when you have that "Aha" moment to the day that you start researching it, but for *this* book, that moment was in 1977. I was not ready to write this book then — but I knew that something was terribly, terribly wrong, and something needed to be done. I just didn't know what.

I had gone looking for my older brother in a seedy hotel in downtown Los Angeles — what most people would have called a flophouse. In 1900, this was probably a first class hotel. As I walked through the halls, the smell of urine was nauseating. Sitting in the lobby, a group of men ranging in age from their 20s to their 60s passively sat in front of a television; most were smoking cigarettes. They had nowhere to go, and no reason to go anywhere, either.

As the month progressed, many of these residents of this hotel, including my brother, would run out of money and end up on the street. As depressing as this rundown hotel was, it was better than sleeping on park benches, or hoping to find one of the beds at the Salvation Army, or another rescue mission. Shortly after the first of the month, when Social Security Disability checks arrived at General Delivery in the nearest post office, these homeless people would again be solvent, and be back in a flophouse.

As a billboard for the Boise Rescue Mission says, "Not a bum — but someone's grandfather." True, but the full story is a bit more complicated than that. Except during the Depression, when many men (and some women) rode the rails, looking for work,[1] American society has traditionally seen "bums" or "hoboes" as lazy, or morally weak. It was easier to focus on those explanations, instead of learning how and why these people had ended up where they were. These homeless people — largely, but not exclusively men — were often homeless because they were mentally ill. Alcoholism or drug abuse often aggravated their mental illness and their financial problems.

Occasionally, popular songs or movies romanticized them as "free spirits," unwilling to be tied down to conventional stability. Think of Roger Miller's 1960s hit "King of the Road":

Third boxcar, midnight train
Destination...Bangor, Maine.
Old worn out clothes and shoes,
I don't pay no union dues,

I smoke old stogies I have found
Short, but not too big around
I'm a man of means by no means
King of the road.

Further romanticizing these "free spirits" was the counterculture of the 1960s, idolized in the movie *Easy Rider.* Unlike a generation who had the option of living free of conventional job and living arrangements but who settled down to fairly conventional lives in the 1970s, these homeless people had no choice.

In the 1980s, the homeless were reimagined again, not as lazy, and not as free spirits, but as victims of the heartlessness of capitalism, and specifically "Reaganomics," the label that liberals used to castigate President Reagan's supply side tax cut policies.[2] Only reluctantly did the activists who demanded that the government do more for the homeless admit that mental illness was widespread in this group — and even then, there was a strange inversion of causality, claiming that homelessness caused mental illness — not the other way around. (Although prolonged homelessness may aggravate existing or latent mental illness problems, the mental illness usually comes first.) Alcohol and drug abuse are additional layers that aggravate and sometimes cause mental illness.[3]

One of my own experiences illustrates the relationship between mental illness and criminal behavior. In the late 1990s, a rather strange character showed up at the church my wife and I attended in Rohnert Park, California. Jim had been sleeping in the fields on the edge of town with his dog, getting around by bicycle with a little trailer for his pet. He carried an impressive wad of cash, the fruits of a $600 a month Social Security disability check — and no rent to pay. Our pastor knew something was wrong, but he was not quite sure, so he asked me to talk to Jim.

Jim told a story of governmental oppression that for the first minute or two, while far-fetched, was not utterly impossible. His kids had been taken from him. His wife was locked up in a mental hospital. It was all a vast conspiracy! The more we talked, however, the more apparent it was that his thought processes, while not completely chaotic, were scattered and confused. Then Jim showed me the paperwork that had taken away his children. Jim was so confused that he did not realize what it revealed.

In one of California's Central Valley counties, Jim's wife had been committed to a mental hospital because she had physically abused their children, and been found not guilty by reason of insanity. After her hospitalization, Jim started showing pornographic films to his five year old and his three year old, then molesting them. Jim's parental rights had been permanently terminated by court order.

Why didn't the district attorney prosecute Jim? The documents provided no information, but my guess is that the prosecutor realized that a trial would require two small children to testify about sexual abuse by their father — having already lost their mother to mental illness. Under the best of conditions, such a criminal case would have been a hard case to win in court, and it would certainly have been traumatic for the children, certainly harder than terminating his parental rights in family court.

In 1950, Jim's mental illness would very likely have led to a commitment to a state mental hospital for the criminally insane. A judge would certainly have committed Jim based on the statements of police and the testimony of a psychiatrist, and the evidence of even a few minutes of conversation. Not today. Instead, Jim wandered the streets, telling his tale of woe. The best that we could hope for is that his mentally disordered thinking would be obvious to anyone talking to him; obvious enough that no one would put their children at risk by allowing Jim any contact.

For those of us who came of age in the 1970s and before, one of the most shocking aspects of the 1980s and 1990s was the rise of "spree killers": people who went into shopping malls, churches, schools, and restaurants, and murdered complete strangers, often ending in suicide. (Nor were these tragedies a uniquely American problem; they happened across the Western world.) What shocked people in 1984 when James Huberty did it in a McDonald's in San Ysidro, California no longer surprises us. Generally, these spree killers have histories of mental illness, and have already come to the attention of the criminal justice or mental health systems before they become headlines. For a while, it was fashionable to blame Prozac, or gun availability — and in some circles bizarre government conspiracy theories as well.[4]

The encounter with Jim was not the reason for this book, nor were the mentally ill spree killers. Had it not been for my brother, I might well have scratched my head at these seemingly isolated events and looked for meaning in the popular theories of the time. Similarly, the explosion of homelessness, and the ugly degradation of urban life that became so common in the 1980s, would have seemed like just another set of random bad news. Something had gone wrong in America — but what?

If not for my brother Ron, I suspect that I would be just as perplexed by these seemingly disconnected tragedies as most other Americans. As an adult, I met others who were mentally ill, but inevitably, most of these contacts were fleeting. For these other sufferers, I had less information from which to draw conclusions. Without my brother's suffering — and the shadows it cast in the lives of my parents and siblings — I rather doubt that I would ever have seen the patterns that have caused me to research this problem.

My brother put a face on this tragedy — that of someone whom I had grown up admiring and loving, who taught me to read, who took me on my first plane flight. He was part of the first generation to suffer a psychotic breakdown in the era of deinstitutionalization: the conscious decision that the severely mentally ill, with a few limited exceptions, would never again be hospitalized against their will.

1.   RON'S BREAKDOWN

My brother had always been a bit different. He was really smart — certainly smarter than me. But like some very smart people, he was quite introverted. From what we now know (or think we know) about the possible causes, he may have had a genetic predisposition towards schizophrenia.[1] While genetics predisposes some towards schizophrenia, it is not the only factor. If one identical twin has schizophrenia, there is a 48 percent chance that the other twin will have it as well. Similarly, a child of two schizophrenic parents has a 46 percent chance of developing schizophrenia. While this strongly suggests a genetic origin, it also means that a majority of those with genetics working against them will *not* come down with the disease. Other environmental factors almost certainly play some part.[2]

RON AT AGE 15

We had worried a bit about Ron when his draft notice came in
1966 — but when the Army saw his intelligence test results, they
gave him a rather remarkable opportunity: an honorable discharge
the day after they drafted him, conditional on volunteering. As a
draftee, he would almost certainly have gone to Vietnam. As a
volunteer, the recruiter could guarantee him a chance to go for
training as an electronics technician — and Ron made that choice.
While many other young men were dying and suffering in the
jungles of Southeast Asia, Ron went to Redstone Arsenal in
Huntsville, Alabama.   After completing electronics technician
school at the top of his class, instead of shipping out to Germany,
where he would have been repairing Nike-Hercules fire control
computers, the Army made him an instructor at the school he had
just completed.

At the time, it seemed a remarkable piece of good luck that
Ron, unlike many of his peers who were shipping out to Vietnam,
had a safe assignment. But that safety, in retrospect, was a little
deceptive.

RON AT MARCH AIR FORCE BASE, ABOUT TO LEAVE THE ARMY IN 1968

My brother's fall into schizophrenia was, I suspect, not so
different from many others of that time. Like many young people
of his generation, he used marijuana and LSD while he was in the
Army and afterwards.   This use, in combination with a

predisposition towards schizophrenia, may have pushed him over the edge. There is a persuasive correlation between increases in drug abuse in the late 1960s and increases in psychotic and mood disorder admissions to mental hospitals three to five years later.[3] More recently, researchers have demonstrated another statistically significant correlation specifically between marijuana use and an increased risk of psychosis later in life.[4]

Complicating such studies, those suffering from mental illness are more likely to use mind-altering drugs, including alcohol, as a way of dealing with their mental problems. This is commonly called "self-medicating." Because of this, several studies have attempted to distinguish "mental illness causes marijuana use" from "marijuana use causes mental illness" by looking for evidence of mental illness symptoms and personality characteristics before the subjects started use of marijuana. One study found a doubling of the risk of schizophreniform disorders (those illnesses that have the symptoms of schizophrenia) among those who were casual users of marijuana, even controlling for these pre-existing characteristics and symptoms. Other longitudinal studies have found these correlations hold true even when adjusted for signs of mental illness before starting marijuana use.[5]

Ron had used LSD as well when he was in the Army — and here the connection to schizophrenia seems a bit more obvious. The apparent similarity of the LSD trip to the symptoms of schizophrenia is one reason that scientists experimented with LSD into the 1960s. Some studies conclude that LSD does not just mimic schizophrenia, but can cause it.[6] While the parallels were intriguing, it soon became apparent that LSD was not a path to a cure.[7] While most scientists recognized the dangers of LSD, many young people did not, and began to engage in their own very uncontrolled "experiments" with it.

The year was 1973, and I was in my senior year of high school. I was the youngest of five children. I was born late in life for both of my parents, and my older siblings had all flown the nest by the time I was in junior high. We rented a modest house in a lower middle class section of Santa Monica, California, which was a much more working class community than it is today. My father's health declined while I was in high school, and he retired on a disability pension. When it came time to apply for financial aid for college, I was somewhat amused to find out that we were just barely below the poverty line. I knew that we weren't rich, but I had no idea that we could be called poor. Poor we might have been, but it was a family in love with learning and thinking.

Here's a picture from one of those of last happy moments before everything fell apart for Ron, taken in August of 1973, just as I was entering twelfth grade and starting classes at UCLA.

AUGUST 1973: RON, CAROLYN, SUSAN, MARILYN, AND ME

My brother's spiral downward began when I was starting my senior year of high school. After his enlistment expired, Ron worked at a number of jobs in the growing electronics industry of Southern California. At one point in 1972, he made the decision to save up his money, take advantage of the GI Bill, and complete college. Ron was taking classes at UCLA, and doing very well in them: honors calculus, honors physics, honors chemistry, and a remedial English composition class. The first trimester went well for him. Suddenly, during his second trimester, he withdrew from classes.

Over perhaps six weeks, his behavior became increasingly difficult to understand. During this brief period, he stood with one foot in the world of the sane and another foot in the realm of the psychotic. He told my parents that he was seeing patches of color appearing on walls. He was disturbed by it, and so were my parents, but no one knew what it meant. One evening, he invited my parents and me over to his apartment in Mar Vista to show off a new stereo. For some reason, he kept changing the station every few seconds, and gave very strange explanations for why he did so.

His behavior towards my sisters, whom he regarded as having married men unsuitable to them, became increasingly odd. One night he visited my sister Marilyn, and kept missing the hint from Marilyn and her husband that it was bedtime, and he should be getting on his way. To express his disapproval of the choices my sisters had made, he suddenly started dating a black woman (which in the early 1970s, was still rather a daring act). My parents were disturbed by how transparently this was done to shock and offend them. Stracey seemed like a nice young lady; my parents were concerned about Ron's use of Stracey for this purpose, not Stracey's color.

Perhaps seeking answers for what he was experiencing, my brother became involved with various unusual religious groups of the time, one of which was Nichiren Shoshu. The pursuit of spiritual knowledge came to nothing, and soon, he no longer seemed concerned about things that he did not understand. As his problems became more severe, he moved back in with my parents, because he either could not, or would not, hold a job.

Up to this point, I was not aware of the extent of my brother's mental difficulties. My parents saw no reason to let me know that Ron was having problems, and for the most part, other than his apparent lack of interest in school or work, he seemed much like the older brother up to whom I had always looked.

Then, one afternoon, the brother that I *thought* that I knew became someone else. My father, my brother, and I went to the local Safeway for some shopping. While my father was in the store, my brother suddenly leaped out of the car, grabbed an old man sitting on a bench, and yelled at him, "What did you say?"

The old man, in terror, responded, "Nothing, nothing!"

My brother yelled, "Well, you better not say it again!" When he returned to the car, Ron was grinning as wide as the Cheshire cat. "I sure showed him!" I was not yet afraid of my brother, but I was worried. What would he do next?

All of this had been odd, disturbing, and unfortunate. The moment that the world shattered down around our family came one evening when Ron decided that there *was* something wrong with him. It is a night etched in pain for me, even now. On his own, he called the mental health outpatient clinic near where we lived, and then walked there, a mile or so away. My mother drove down to the clinic, with me in tow.

After a brief conversation with the staff, the full extent of Ron's problem became apparent, and the psychiatrist decided that Ron needed to be hospitalized — immediately. Ron was starting to have second thoughts, and left. The staff asked the police to find Ron. About the time that my mother and I arrived, the police had returned Ron to the clinic.

An ambulance arrived. For their own safety, the attendants wanted to restrain him on the way to the locked, psychiatric ward of St. John's Hospital. My brother did not want that — and began yelling and cursing his disapproval. (This was a long time ago, when adults did not use language like that in front of children.)

My mother, already fearful of what was wrong with Ron, tried to persuade the attendants to dispense with the straps. Her well-meaning intervention was not making anything easier on the doctor or the ambulance attendants, and the doctor told my mother to stay out of this situation, or he would send Ron home with her instead. Eventually, Ron was forcibly restrained, and hospitalized. My mother was emotionally overwhelmed by this scene, as you might expect, and so was I. My mother spent what seemed like an eternity screaming herself to sleep, loud enough that I am sure that many of our neighbors could hear — and we lived in a house, not an apartment. I cried myself to sleep that night.

What had happened to Ron? Would he ever be well again?

2.   WHAT IS MENTAL ILLNESS?

If you have never been close to someone suffering from it, and you have never studied the subject, you are probably wondering, "What is mental illness?" I am astonished at how many well-educated people do not understand the various types of mental illness.

Broadly speaking, psychiatrists divide mental illness into psychotic disorders and mood disorders (roughly replacing the older terms psychosis and neurosis, respectively). Mood disorders consist of a wide range of mental difficulties from mild to severe, including depression or bipolar disorder. Depression's symptoms can be so mild that it may not be recognized, or so severe that the sufferer spends twelve or more hours per day asleep — and yet still has no energy or interest in life when awake. Depression sometimes leads to suicide — and in spite of what you might think, antidepressants may increase the risk of suicide: they give a severely depressed person enough energy to plan and carry out their own death.[1]

Mood disorders can also be relatively mild — such as the narcissistic, trivial emotional problems that Woody Allen's movies used to satirize, and that the messy details of Woody Allen's 1990s affair with his stepdaughter seem to exemplify. While a person with a mood disorder may have quite serious problems that require professional attention, he knows what is real, and what is not.

By comparison, psychotic disorders such as schizophrenia can impair a patient's grasp on reality, which unsurprisingly, makes it difficult for the patient to work and socially interact with others. Untreated psychotics have trouble holding onto jobs, except for the least demanding work, and even when they can hold a job, they tend not to do so. This may be because the work is boring, or because the difference in pay between these low-end jobs and disability payments is so small.

The dividing line between psychosis and mood disorder is a bit fuzzy. Bipolar disorder is a mood disorder — but occasionally, people with severe bipolar disorder develop psychotic symptoms, such as hallucinations that break their connection to reality. Similarly, some mild forms of schizophrenia do not impair the sufferer's ability to understand that what he is seeing or hearing is a hallucination.

This book focuses heavily on psychotic disorders, not because mood disorders are unimportant, but because the psychoses appears to be disproportionately involved in the tragedies that are most visible on the streets of our cities — and because of my brother. In the early 1980s, there were about two million chronically mentally ill people in the United States, with 93 percent living outside mental hospitals. The largest diagnosis for the chronically mentally ill is schizophrenia, which afflicts about 1 percent of the population, or about 1.5 percent of adult Americans.[2]

Because an enormous number of sufferers are not consistently treated, schizophrenia is a very costly illness. A 1991 estimate was that it costs the United States about $65 billion in direct and indirect costs,[3] declining to $62.5 billion by 2002.[4] In spite of the enormous number of patients who are not actively treated, schizophrenia treatment consumes about 2.5 percent of *all* U.S. health care expenditures, or about $50 billion a year. Schizophrenia is also responsible for more than 10 percent of *all* disabilities — not just mental disabilities. Government disability payments to schizophrenics in 2005 totaled more than $8 billion.[5]

The $19 billion in direct costs includes the criminal justice system dealing with a few spectacular and terrifying crimes, and a myriad of infractions, arrests, and short periods of observation.[6] A 1999 study found that 16.2 percent of state prison inmates, 7.4 percent of federal prison inmates, and 16.3 percent of jail inmates, were mentally ill.[7] As of 2002, about 26,000 inmates in state prisons across the United States who were convicted of murder were also mentally ill. A detailed examination of Indiana prison inmates convicted of murder found that 18 percent were diagnosed with "schizophrenia or other psychotic disorder, major depression, mania, or bipolar disorder."[8]

We know something of what schizophrenics experience

because about 30 percent recover spontaneously, and are able to tell us what life is like in a world that seems like a *Twilight Zone* episode. Schizophrenia has both positive and negative symptoms (sometimes called "Type I" and "Type II" symptoms). Positive symptoms include "delusions, hallucinations, thought disorder" and seem to be especially responsive to neuroleptic drugs (the antipsychotic medications that have a calming effect).

Negative symptoms include what psychiatrists call "flat affect" — the apparent lack of any strong emotions, or inappropriate emotions for the circumstances, and "poverty of speech."[9] The negative symptoms do not respond as well to pharmaceutical treatment.[10] Because the side effects of antipsychotic medications often produce behaviors similar to the negative symptoms, and the positive symptoms are more typical of the early stages of schizophrenia, it is unclear if the negative symptoms are part of the disease, or a result of the medications. (And as with most illnesses, not everyone with schizophrenia suffers the same mixture of symptoms.)[11]

Schizophrenia may not be one illness, but a collection (or "constellation," as mental health professionals prefer) of symptoms that have something in common[12] — and most importantly, there is some evidence of a biochemical, inherited trait.[13] Even more interesting, the most recent research suggests a common genetic cause for schizophrenia and bipolar disorder, with environmental factors perhaps determining both *if* an individual carrying these genes will become ill, and *which* disease will appear.[14] Unfortunately, the common genetic cause appears to involve a staggeringly large number of mutations that individually contribute to both illnesses.[15] This means that there will likely be no simple path to developing a cure.

Contrary to what used to be commonly accepted within the psychiatric profession, we now know that family and social factors do *not* play a large role in causing schizophrenia, if they play any role at all. One recent study grew neurons from stem cells using genetic material from schizophrenics. These lab-grown neurons had the same distinctive responses as the schizophrenic cells, and the same distinctive reactions to the common antipsychotic medicines. These neurons clearly could not blame bad parenting for their problems.[16]

At the same time, while genes may set some people up for schizophrenia, genetics alone is not enough. The environmental factors that *may* play a role could be delayed consequences of in utero or delivery complications, or perhaps viral infections.[17] The most recent research attempting to identify the genetic factors at play suggest that at least some of the problem may be associated with the major histocompatibility complex (MHC) region on chromosome six. This is an area that has long been associated with genetic predispositions towards infection and autoimmune diseases.[18]

There is also some suspicion that a particular endogenous retrovirus, HERV-W, already present in much of the human population, when activated by infection and with the appropriate mutations, causes schizophrenia, bipolar disorder, or multiple sclerosis. This explains why schizophrenics are disproportionately born in the winter and early spring months; infections are more common in winter, and may activate this virus.[19] (Endogenous retroviruses are believed to be ancient viral infections that have integrated themselves into the human genetic code.)[20]

In the popular consciousness, hallucinations are the symptom that is most strongly associated with psychosis. Hallucinations are sensory inputs that "exist in the absence of external stimulation. The most common are auditory hallucinations in which voices are heard from outside one's head." The fictional portrayal of crazy people "hearing voices" is based on truth: some schizophrenics hear sounds that are not there — and those sounds are just as real to a schizophrenic as when you or I turn on a radio. Like the person who takes LSD, and sees things that are not there — indeed, cannot be there — a schizophrenic's visual senses may show him things that are not there. These sensory distortions can affect vision, hearing, smell, and touch.[21]

Sometimes hallucinations may not be a completely imagined sensory input. A schizophrenic's sense of smell or of hearing may actually be more acute than normal; sometimes his senses are distorted. For example, my brother went through a phase where he took long showers several times a day. This is not an uncommon schizophrenic behavior; they are convinced that they smell strongly, perhaps because their sense of smell is exaggerating or distorting actual sensations. A person with schizophrenia may find that his senses have betrayed him; he may believe that his body is on fire, or that there are bugs crawling under the skin. It does no good to tell a schizophrenic that this is a hallucination — the feeling is just as real as if there really are bugs there.

Another common set of symptoms are delusions: "a faulty interpretation of reality that cannot be shaken despite clear evidence to the contrary."[22] Paranoia, the belief that someone is out to get you, is a very common such delusion. Delusions of grandeur are the belief that the sufferer is far more important than he really is. These can combine together to cause a schizophrenic to believe that the CIA or FBI is out to get him. These delusions can develop as a result of those untrustworthy sensory inputs. Try to magine how strange your thinking and behavior would become if you saw and heard things that weren't actually present. "The most common types of delusions in schizophrenia include thought broadcasting, or the belief that one's thoughts are broadcast to the outside world so that other people can hear them." Some forms of schizophrenia can also include catatonia, with the person apparently unable to move,[23] or an agitated state of "extreme psychomotor excitement, talking and shouting almost continuously."[24]

This makes it sound as though schizophrenia, like other serious mental illnesses, has a simple and clear cut diagnosis Sometimes yes; sometimes no. Many people seem to suffer from some of the symptoms, but not all, and those symptoms may change over time. Hobson and Leonard argue that because the causes are the sum of several brain characteristics that can vary over large ranges, "many normal and abnormal states appear continuous with one another." This explains the person who is schizophrenic for several years and then recovers, or fails to fit into a single diagnostic category.[25] I have a relative whose diagnosis changed several times from his teens to his early 30s, sometimes diagnosed with schizophrenia, and sometimes with bipolar disorder.

Schizophrenia often strikes during the teen years or early adulthood.[26] Informed speculation suggests that the reason may be related to how the frontal lobes of the brain develop. The frontal lobes continue to develop into one's mid-twenties. Because the brain engages in "pruning," or removal of unneeded neurons, there may be an interaction between the ending of development and the pruning process that causes the failure.[27] In light of the apparent connections between alcohol and marijuana use and the development of schizophrenia, the old joke about drinking "killing brain cells" might be closer to the truth than anyone realized.

Because schizophrenia has such a low cure rate — *perhaps* aggravated by failure to treat the illness early enough[28] or consistently enough[29] — and because most schizophrenics, when first afflicted, have fifty years of life left, this produces extraordinary social costs. Until deinstitutionalization, it was common for almost half of *all* hospital beds (not just mental hospital beds) to be occupied by the mentally ill.[30] Many of these institutionalized mentally ill were schizophrenics. Once sick, most schizophrenics never recovered, living decades in institutional settings. Today, many of them live somewhat shorter lives under bridges, in park benches, and on steam grates. Some die when their delusions lead them to acts of violence against the wrong person. A frighteningly large number end up in prison.

Schizophrenia would be a tragedy if it hit people of completely normal intelligence. But there are curious connections between schizophrenia and creativity that make the tragedy especially destructive on our society. It has long been noticed that insanity and creativity are linked — but why? Studies of creative people find that their brains are less likely to filter out incoming stimuli. A process called "latent inhibition" allows the brains of most people to ignore information that they have learned from long experience is not necessary.

It appears that latent inhibition is less present among creative people. This allows creative types to sense things that normal people no longer can. Creative sorts are thus able to take a fresh look at problems or ideas that less creative sorts cannot. Creative people still have *some* latent inhibition protecting their senses from being overrun with too much information. Latent inhibition disappears at the start of schizophrenia — perhaps leading to delusions and hallucinations as the brain is overwhelmed with more stimuli than it can handle.[31]

An interesting speculation is that the normal brain uses latent inhibition to protect itself from too much information because it lacks the processing power to handle the full bandwidth available to it.[32] Intelligent people may have less latent inhibition because they have the capability to handle the extra information, but even intelligent people have limits on how much information their brains can handle. Exceeding those limits may be like a computer that cannot stop the flow of incoming data long enough to respond to the user's commands. This may explain why apparently destructive defects such as schizophrenia and bipolar disorder can survive in the gene pool. For those who carry the gene but do not develop the disease, this creativity and intelligence may provide a powerful advantage over those who do not.

Mental illness is a tremendously costly problem, destructive to individuals, and destructive to the larger society. The problem has been recognized throughout human history, and different societies have dealt with it in different ways. Throughout American history, those who have seen themselves as concerned about the suffering and afflicted have worked to provide treatment or assistance to the mentally ill. What is remarkable about recent history is how the traditional advocates of the downtrodden played a major, although unwitting role, in putting the mentally ill into conditions that would have shocked previous generations of Americans.

3.   RON WAS NOT ALONE

I saw Ron's spiral down into mental illness. Because he is my brother, I've seen the tragedy — sometimes close at hand, sometimes from a distance — for decades. Over the years, I've had greater and lesser opportunities to see the damage done in the lives of others.

I had a girlfriend in the late 1970s who I will call Joan. We went to high school together, but seemingly never met until after we had graduated. (Our graduating class had a thousand students.) I met Joan as a result of what I call a double blind date: a blind woman that was a mutual friend set us up, sight unseen by all parties! Joan was a sweet and intelligent person, and most of the time, you would not think that she was disabled. Joan had simple schizophrenia, which meant that while she had hallucinations, she was still sufficiently in touch with reality to know that they *were* hallucinations.

Joan lived in a tiny studio apartment, a block from the beach, yet her parents lived in a very nice home in one of the best neighborhoods in Santa Monica less than two miles away. Why? Joan's mother worked for the Social Security Administration, and knew the ins and outs of the disability process. (Joan's mother didn't pull any strings — she just understood how to navigate the system for Joan.) As a result, Joan received a disability check sufficient to maintain a tiny apartment of her own. Had she lived at home, her parents' assets and income would have reduced the size of the government's checks. Joan did not work, nor did she go to college — and in retrospect, I wonder how much of this was because of the amotivational symptom of schizophrenia (which reduce interest in doing much of anything), and how much was that the disability check took away a reason to work or advance.

Joan's mental problems were certainly aggravated by some traumatic experiences and substance abuse. She was still under the legal drinking age, but drank to excess, in spite of the efforts of me and her other friends to persuade her otherwise. On one occasion, Joan and a girlfriend spent the night drinking one of the over the counter cough syrups, to the point where both were exhausted, but both claimed that they were physically unable to close their eyes. On another occasion, I saw her snort cocaine (or what, more realistically, was probably baby powder with a few dozen cocaine molecules scattered here and there). This substance abuse would have been a bad idea for someone who wasn't fighting with schizophrenia; I'm sure that it aggravated her problems.

At one point in 1977, Joan had spent two days unable to sleep, because the voices in her head were screaming, "Kill yourself." Contrary to the widely held belief that the mentally ill were wandering the streets because of budget cuts, when Joan went to the same mental health clinic in Santa Monica where Ron had gone on that painful night, she was immediately sent to Camarillo State Hospital, about fifty miles away from Santa Monica. What was the difference? She checked herself into the mental hospital; there was no need to persuade a judge that she was a threat to herself or others.

Because she was a voluntary admission, Joan was also free to check herself out. She called me two days after she arrived, and begged me to come and get her. The mental hospital was not sex-segregated, and one of the male patients, whom she described as big and strong, was demanding that she submit sexually to him. Her choice was simple: submit, or he would take what he wanted by force. Joan had no confidence that the staff would protect her, and she was tiny: 5'2" and slight of build.

As appalling as this sounds — consider the situation of the staff. You have a person in your hospital who admitted herself because of hallucinations — and now you have to decide which of two mentally disturbed people is telling the truth, or even knows what the truth is. Under the best of conditions, a mental hospital is a sad place for those inside it, and for family members visiting. I can remember visiting Ron with my parents in the locked ward of St. John's Hospital, a private and very well maintained facility. The people who worked there seemed to be genuinely concerned with improving the condition of their patients. Still, other patients would approach us, just to have someone with whom to talk. They gave us the impression that there was no one coming to see them.

I had already seen more of mental hospitals by twenty than most of my peers. One of my sisters had spent three and a half months in a private mental hospital in Los Angeles after a suicide attempt, and it was, as near as I could tell, exactly what a mental hospital should be: a place of hope and care. (Fortunately, there was no question if she was a danger to herself; her suicide attempt at age 16 had been quite serious. More importantly, she was a minor, and it was 1967. There was as yet no question about whether she could be hospitalized on the say-so of her parents and a psychiatrist.)

As I drove out to rescue Joan, I had considerable apprehension. Camarillo State Hospital had a fearsomely bad reputation in the mid-1960s. I can remember reading incredibly depressing accounts of the conditions there, and at other state mental hospitals — accounts that were deeply disturbing to me, even at age ten: severely retarded adults left for hours or even days in soiled diapers; peeling paint (a real problem for retarded patients prone to eating whatever they found); inadequate numbers of staff to supervise patients who were often a hazard to each other, or to themselves.

I expected, when I went to pick up Joan, that things would be much better at Camarillo a decade after these horrifying exposés. I was depressed to find that while conditions were not quite as bad as those mid-1960s newspaper accounts, I could see that money was not being spent on maintenance. There were a shocking number of broken windows. The paint was peeling. The interior of the ward in which Joan resided was astonishingly dark — conditions that might have depressed a healthy person confined there. Had I not been picking up Joan to take her back to her apartment, I might well have started to cry.

I still have a bittersweet memory of our last date, to see Jackson Browne in concert at the Universal Amphitheater. Joan was an enormous fan of Jackson Browne's often depressing music (which both conformed to, and perhaps amplified her own feelings), and I had bought tickets as soon as they went on sale. The night of the concert, she mixed beer and prescription medicines until she passed out in her seat, just as Jackson Browne came on stage. She came to as Browne walked off stage, but the combination of alcohol and drugs caused her to fall forward into the next row of seats. Once she was again vertical, she fell backward in the seats behind us. Along the way, she vomited on my shoes.

I was frustrated by that evening. I felt sorry for Joan, who was a sweet person, and quite a bit of fun — when she wasn't self-medicating, or suffering from hallucinations. But I also knew that I couldn't help her, and it became increasingly clear that whatever her path was in life, it wasn't the same as the road that I was taking.

Over the next several years, Joan moved to Santa Cruz; I stayed where I was in Los Angeles, and so our relationship declined. When I last visited her in Santa Cruz, she was again a voluntary inmate of a mental hospital — and again, there was no problem finding a bed for her, because she was well enough to realize that she was *not* well.

By the late 1970s, where I lived in Santa Monica was awash in mentally ill people living on the streets. Santa Monica was an especially good place for homeless people in the Los Angeles basin; being on the ocean meant that the climate was temperate. Crime rates were lower than a lot of regions further inland, where you did not need to be paranoid to be concerned about your safety when sleeping out of doors. In the area of Santa Monica where I lived, near the post office and Lincoln Park, there were perhaps a dozen "regulars" who I would see sleeping in any spot that would not attract police attention. Most of them were men — scruffy, and sometimes quite scary, especially when they were begging. I sometimes tried to open conversations with them, while bringing them sandwiches or giving them money, but it was difficult to get anything more than "Thanks" from most of them.

Rarer than homeless men, at least then and there, were homeless women. One woman in her late 20s specialized in graffiti that mixed Bible verses with vaguely apocalyptic concerns. It made very little sense, and having become a Christian at about that time, I tried very hard to see where her writing was taking her. Her thinking was so disordered, and her paranoia was so high, that it was impossible to have a conversation with her.

There was another homeless woman that I remember from those years who was not so paranoid, who called herself Rosie. Until we knew her name, the woman who became my wife (and who joined me on some of my late night sandwich deliveries to the homeless) called her "The Rouge Lady." Like many homeless people, bathing was a difficult situation, and both her skin and her clothes were dirty — but she somehow always had money for some makeup.   She wore bright pink rouge on her cheeks, and continuously walked on tiptoe.

For a long time, Rosie slept in the lobby of the main post office in Santa Monica, which was open all night. I first started to talk to her when I would walk the few blocks from my home to mail letters at night. Usually by about 8:30 in the evening, Rosie was camped out there. She knew that she had a mental problem, but when I would press her about seeking help at the mental health clinic, she became uncomfortable. She was not defiant or angry — but there was some reason that she was reluctant to seek that help.

For a few months, Rosie disappeared. In truth, I did not even notice that she was gone. Then she was back. Someone, whom she did not make clear, had helped her to get off the street, and get an apartment of her own. But, "I couldn't keep it together," and she was again out on the street.

Eventually, the post office made it clear that she was not to loiter in the lobby. Up to this point, the post office lobby had been open all hours in Santa Monica. Now the doors were locked in the late evening. Rosie no longer had a warm place to sleep at night. She continued to sleep outdoors around the post office, but eventually, she disappeared.

It was apparent to me, even then, that the homeless of Santa Monica overwhelmingly had mental problems. My brother Ron was, at times, homeless, and his mental illness was part of it. Yet I never drew a causal connection between their mental illness and their homelessness, perhaps because I was still a little too self-absorbed at the time.

This change in Santa Monica — and as it turned out, across America — happened while I watched. In a period of about ten years, Santa Monica went from a place with no visible homelessness to a permanent population of dirty, sometimes scary people, some of whom were not above armed robbery. The faces changed. Some, like Rosie, would talk. Others would accept what aid you offered them, but clearly had no interest in communicating. It seemed as though there was nothing that any of us could do for them besides provide the most fleeting of assistance.

Why were these mentally ill people living on the streets? Where were they ten years before? As with most tragedies, there is a bit of history that goes into it. Understanding how we reached this point requires us to know where we started.

4. COLONIAL AMERICA (1607-1775)

Considering the English origins of the American colonies, it is unsurprising that American laws for treating the mentally ill inspired followed the English model.[1] English law at least as early as 1690 recognized that if "one that is *Non compos mentis* or an Ideot kill a Man; this is no Felony, for they have not knowledge of good and evil, nor can have Felonious intent, nor a will or mind to do harm."[2] Even before the American Revolution, English law distinguished between mental illness and mental retardation with respect to both criminal liability, and competence to manage one's affairs.[3]

Similarly, English law before the Revolution defined legal insanity as requiring that the patient had a "belief of facts which no rational person would have believed, and in the inability to be reasoned out of such belief..." Yet the law recognized that religious beliefs, no matter how peculiar, were not sufficient to qualify as legal insanity; a belief "entirely within the domain of opinion or faith" was not sufficient reason for the law to define someone as insane.[4]

While the legal structure was taken over without changes from England, there was one quite dramatic difference: Unlike England, which had insane asylums as early as the fourteenth century, there appears to have been little need for institutionalization of the mentally ill until the last few years before the American Revolution. The reasons are both curious and startlingly humane.

In New England, where historians have done the most thorough research, mentally ill colonists seldom appear to be a matter of legal action. The law did occasionally lock up a mentally ill person who committed a serious crime for the safety of the community.

The few examples from the records are somewhat startling for their compassionate, family-based approach. One example is Connecticut, which tried one Roger Humphry, who "while a soldier in the army in the year 1757, become delirious and distracted and in his distraction killed his mother...." At trial in Hartford, he "was found not guilty altogether on the account of his distraction...."[5] Roger was at first confined to the jail in Hartford, but upon the request of Roger's father Benajah Humphry, the legislature granted permission for Benajah to take his son home to Symsbury. Benajah was "hereby directed and ordered to take and safely keep said Roger and provide for him." The legislature also instructed the Symsbury town government to supervise the securing of Roger. Benajah was to pay for keeping his son secure — but the legislature granted him £40 to help, a sizeable grant, equivalent to roughly a year's wages.

This must have been a very painful situation — Benajah's wife was dead; his son was insane; and he had taken it upon himself (with help from the colonial government) to maintain, effectively, an insane asylum for one.[6] We have similar examples of public funds to build family-operated individual insane asylums in Amesland, Pennsylvania in 1676[7] and in Braintree, Massachusetts in 1689 and in 1699.[8]

Another example of the limited nature of institutionalization from the Colonial period is Connecticut's orders concerning Mary Hall, whose behavior had become worrisome as she wandered "from town to town and place to place, to the great disquiet of many people where she goes by reason of her ill behaviour." In 1758, the legislature directed that if she was found outside her hometown of Wallingford, she was to be arrested and returned home — and Wallingford would be charged the costs.[9] There's no detail on exactly what Mary Hall did as she wandered, but it seems likely that her behavior was more than just strange or boorish.

There are doubtless many more instances of persons whose mental illness, while serious, did not prevent them from being cared for at home. John Howard, born in 1733, came from a comfortable family in Maine and showed great promise. But during the French & Indian War, while on an expedition to Canada, he

> fired on one occasion when in the woods at what he supposed to
> be a bear; it proved to be one of the party, and that he had

unfortunately taken his life. No blame was imputed to Howard, but the occurrence so affected him that he sank into hopeless insanity. "He lived long at the fort, gentle and inoffensive, but possessed of immense imaginary wealth."[10]

In a few cases, we find evidence that the courts committed persons if they were perceived as mentally ill — but the nature of these accounts suggests that they were more than just eccentric in their behavior. A Jonathan Wyat was brought before Judge Joshua Hempstead in New London, Connecticut, in December of 1739 by the town and found to be "Disorderly Idle Distracted or worse & Sentenced him to the work-house." Another account from Hempstead's diary, while less detailed, reports that he spent part of March 22, 1731 "Examining a Distracted woman & Committing her." [11] In Massachusetts, 1676 and 1694 statutes directed town governments and overseers of the poor to care for "Idiots and Distracted Persons" with concern that the mentally ill might otherwise "damnify [injure] others."[12]

New Englanders were often extremely tolerant of non-aggressive mentally ill members of the society. Samuel Coolidge, schoolmaster of Watertown, Massachusetts, was known for appearing in public half-dressed or not dressed at all. While he was dragged out of commencement at his alma mater of Harvard some years after his graduation for disrupting the event, there was no apparent interest in locking him up — and he kept his job as schoolmaster.[13] He was, however, "warned out" of Boston in 1742 and 1744 for being "in a Distracted Condition & very likely to be a Town Charge."[14] A more detailed biographical sketch suggests that by his late 20s, he was showing some indications of odd and inappropriate behavior — but that his problems were recognized not as immorality, but mental disturbance.[15]

This tolerance for odd behavior included a quite astonishing willingness to pay salaries to people whose job performance, from the contemporary accounts, would seem deficient. After 1738, Rev. Joseph Moody of York, Massachusetts would only appear in public with a handkerchief over his mouth — and soon he could not bear to even face his congregation while preaching. It took three years for his congregants to replace him.[16] Exactly in what way Moody was mentally ill, as opposed to eccentric, is debatable. An 1891 account of Moody's behavior indicated that he had accidentally killed a close friend in his youth, but showed no indications of eccentricity until he was 38 years old.

> He had been the cause of his young friend's death; it made his
> blood run cold; he hid his countenance, and as a token of his
> grief, he determined to wear a veil during the rest of his life.
> Accordingly, he wore, ever after, a silk handkerchief drawn over
> his face, and was called "Handkerchief Moody" till his death.[17]

Another example was the Rev. Samuel Checkley, who was at
first "unable to speak without weeping" — but then progressed to
preaching in gibberish. Even then, his congregation, rather than
fire him, hired an "assistant" to help him. Even actions that were
clearly blasphemous, such as carrying a sign that claimed, "I am
God," when performed by someone who was clearly mentally ill,
seem not to have led to incarceration.[18]

For the mentally ill who were not dangerous to others, the law
concerned itself primarily with matters of finance: Who would take
care of a mentally ill person if he lacked the means to care for
himself? There were two different categories of people, the
indigent mentally ill and those with property. While only the
indigent were a direct financial concern to the community, if the
government took no steps to preserve the assets of members of the
propertied class, even the wealthy might easily end up dependent
on the community.

As a result, while there are a few surviving examples of
Colonial governments ordering confinement of particular mentally
ill people, much of the legislative activity in this area concerned
guardianship. Colonial legislatures passed laws to protect the
property of the mentally ill, directing town government to manage
the mentally ill person's property so that it would provide for the
owner's needs. For the indigent resident, near relatives were
required to provide at least some support.

In contrast, towns would often "warn out" mentally ill non-
residents to prevent them from becoming a financial burden on the
town, in the same way that the poor laws required non-resident
poor in both America and England to return to their place of birth
to seek relief.[19] However, those "warned out" might be able to
avoid removal if they or someone else posted a bond protecting the
town from financial obligation to support such a person.[20]
Depending on the colony, a person had to be "warned out" within
some specified period of time, either three months or twelve

months (in the case of Massachusetts Bay Colony) or the town was obligated to provide for such a person under the poor laws.[21]

Still, we should not exaggerate the economic calculation of these concerns.   Distracted persons were also friends and neighbors, and we have examples such as Providence Colony's response to "a distracted person" named Mrs. Weston in 1650. The Colony was to take charge of "what is left of hers" and provide her with the necessities of life.[22]   They also provided both money and labor to assist Mr. Pike in caring for his "distracted" wife in 1655, and this was not the first time that the government provided such help.[23]

Still, the system did not lock up those who were not perceived as a threat to others, even when the consequences might be severe. Margaret Goodwin in January of 1651 was "given into the keeping of six reputable citizens of the town" who were to care for her and her estate "during the period of her distraction."[24]   She left the house during a thunderstorm shortly thereafter.   A coroner's inquest in March of 1651 concluded that she died of "either the terribleness of the crack of thunder... or the coldness of the night, being she was naked."[25]

The compassion and understanding of colonial governments is sometimes quite surprising. Even such blasphemous and shocking behavior as Charles Leonard cutting in half and burning a Bible in Taunton, Massachusetts, did not prevent the town from supporting him.[26] Colonial newspapers occasionally mention the actions of "lunaticks" who committed "outrages" but seemed to recognize the limited responsibility that the insane bore for their actions,[27] or identified a suicide as "lunatick."[28] Ads also seek the return of wandering mentally ill family members.[29]

In the middle of the eighteenth century, a few of the larger cities built institutions that housed the insane — but these were not mental hospitals or insane asylums in any modern sense.   In Boston, the workhouse confined together paupers, retarded, insane, and in some cases, those with contagious diseases.[30] Philadelphia's first publicly funded almshouse, established in 1732, confined the physically sick and the insane together for the same purpose.[31] This was not a good situation for the sick, the poor, or the insane.

Philadelphia's first public hospital, organized in 1751 with a combination of private and public funds — and the active involvement of Benjamin Franklin — still housed both the physically and mentally ill within one building. The cells for the insane "were damp and unhealthy, and a number of patients died of pulmonary disease."[32]

While the hospital was clearly intended to care for both physical and mental illnesses, the concern about the mentally ill seems to have been strongest selling point — at least as judged by the petition requesting governmental assistance. The petition to the Pennsylvania Assembly showed concern for both the well-being of the mentally ill, and the dangers to the community as a whole:

> That with the numbers of people the number of lunaticks, or persons distempered in mind, and deprived of their rational faculties, hath greatly increased in this province.

> That some of them going at large, are a terrour to their neighbours, who are daily apprehensive of the violences they may commit; and others are continually wasting their substance, to the great injury of themselves and families, ill disposed persons wickedly taking advantage of their unhappy condition, and drawing them into unreasonable bargains, &c.[33]

A sign of the potential for cure — and why involuntary commitment was necessary — is that the petition also observed that:

> That few or none of them are so sensible of their condition as to submit voluntarily to the treatment their respective cases require, and therefore continue in the same deplorable state during their lives; whereas it has been found, by the experience of many years, that above two thirds of the mad people received into Bethlehem Hospital, and there treated properly, have been perfectly cured.[34]

Franklin also observed something that promoters of deinstitutionalization two centuries later missed — that the mentally ill often had homes "yet were therein but badly accommodated in sickness, and could be not so well and so easily taken care of in their separate habitations, as they might be in one convenient house, under one inspection, and in the hands of skilful practitioners...."[35]

While Colonial Americans did not consider mental illness a permanent condition for *every* sufferer, most of those who wrote on the subject knew that at least for many, once it took hold, mental illness was a lifelong problem.[36] As a consequence, while the Pennsylvania Hospital admitted only those physically ill who were deemed "curable," this was not required for the mentally ill.[37] The first two years of operation for the hospital shows a total of eighteen admitted with a diagnosis of "Lunacy," of whom two were released as "Cured," three "Relieved," four as "Incurable," six taken away by their friends, and three still remained. A note explains that most of the "lunaticks taken in had been many years disordered" and were not considered likely to be cured. Those taken away by their friends were removed before an opportunity had been given for a cure — and therefore, the hospital had decided that it would no longer accept mental patients unless they would be hospitalized at least twelve months, or until cured.[38]

What did Colonial Americans think mental illness was? Some historians have emphasized the overlap between witchcraft, sin, and mental illness, a position that was certainly widespread as late as the nineteenth century among German doctors.[39] Most Colonial Americans seem to have understood that at least some forms of mental illness were physical in nature. The eminent Puritan minister Cotton Mather wrote in 1702 that madness was a result of Satan's temptations. Yet by 1724, his unpublished *The Angel of Bethesda* recognized that mania and melancholia had physical causes as well, for which a medicine such as St. John's Wort (a plant whose value for treating depression is now making a comeback), was the appropriate cure. Nor was Mather alone in this; throughout the eighteenth century, Enlightenment thinking was moving the causes of mental illness from the supernatural to the natural.[40]

That Colonial Americans by the eighteenth century regarded mental illness as analogous to physical ailments can be inferred from how they treated those who were temporarily afflicted with madness. Upon recovery — and sometimes even while still insane — politicians such as James Otis, Jr. and ministers such as Daniel Kirtland and Joseph Moody were able to hold offices and acquire new ones.[41] What evidence exists suggests that the mentally ill were primarily looked after, since there was no particular treatment in the medical toolbox for mental illness.[42]

Complicating our understanding of Colonial treatment policies is the confusing variety of terms used. "Idiot" in many of the laws refers to the mentally retarded. "Maniac" suggests the extreme mania phase of bipolar disorder today. More than a few colonists were "distracted," which suggests severe depression, perhaps hebephrenic schizophrenia (characterized by "incoherence, wild excitement alternating with tearfulness and depression")[43], or conceivably Alzheimer's. "Lunatic" appears frequently in the Colonial laws in a sense that implies a break from reality.

Civil commitment — that is, locking up persons against their will because of mental illness — was a fairly informal procedure under Colonial law, based on both English common law and statutes. The "furiously insane" could be arrested by anyone,[44] and perhaps because of the low rate of psychosis in the Colonial period (to be discussed later), there is no evidence of complaints of abuse of this process. The low rates of psychosis may also be why so few murders seem to have been committed by the mentally ill. Marietta and Rowe's detailed examination of Pennsylvania murders in the years 1682-1800 lists surprisingly few cases of clear insanity: there are only five murderers whose actions were driven by depression or delusions — out of 513 surviving accusations. (The first Pennsylvania verdict of not guilty by reason of insanity involved Terrence Rogers' murder of Edward Swainey in 1743.)[45]

By the close of the Colonial period, some governments had created institutions specifically to house the mentally ill. Virginia opened the first American institution for the mentally ill in 1773 — and designated it as a hospital, not an asylum. This was an important distinction; the goal of a hospital was to cure the patient, not simply hold him for his own safety.[46] Still, the rules governing what patients would be accepted demonstrate that public safety was very much at the forefront of the colony's concerns: nonviolent, chronically ill patients were not to be admitted. Unlike the rather informal commitment procedures that were still in effect elsewhere, the act creating the hospital required several magistrates to agree that a person properly should be committed to the hospital. The goal was to deal with acute mental illness — effect a cure — and then release the patient back into society.[47]

Much of what drove this development of specifically mental hospitals was that a few of America's larger towns became cities. In a small town, everyone knew everyone else, and if Mr. Jones or Mrs. Smith occasionally acted oddly, it was not a surprise. Everyone in town knew Mr. Jones or Mrs. Smith well enough to know what they might do — and would probably keep deadly implements away from someone regarded as dangerous. A mentally ill person who was violent or suicidal might be locked up; those whose behavior was abnormal but peaceful would create no fear.

In cities, where tens of thousands of people lived cheek-by-jowl, the chances were high that you knew only some of your neighbors. A stranger acting oddly might well cause concern or fear — what might he do next? Another area of difference between cities and small towns was that in cities "an extraordinarily high rate of geographic mobility tended to limit social cohesion and the efficacy of informal and traditional means of dealing with distress." The less you knew your neighbors, the easier it was to regard Mrs. Smith's difficulties as not your problem.[48]

Urbanization may not simply have been a factor in making Americans more wary of their mentally ill neighbors; it may have increased mental illness rates as well. While we do not know if this was true in the eighteenth century, some recent studies suggest that being born or growing up in an urban area increases one's risk of developing schizophrenia and other psychoses.[49] In the twentieth century, comparison of insanity rates revealed that urban areas had much higher rates of mental hospital admissions for schizophrenia and bipolar disorder — almost twice as high for New York City compared to the rest of New York State. State by state comparisons in the nineteenth and twentieth centuries also revealed that more urban states, such as California and the northeastern states, had much higher rates of mental illness.[50]

Older statistical examinations of mental hospital admissions argue that at least in the period from 1840 to 1940, while mental hospital admissions increased (because of increased availability), there was no large and obvious increase in insanity.[51] A more recent study of mental illness data shows, much more persuasively, that psychosis rates rose quite dramatically between 1807 and 1961 in the United States, England & Wales, Ireland, and the Canadian Atlantic provinces. A study of Buckinghamshire, England shows more than a ten-fold increase in psychosis rates from the beginning of the seventeenth century to 1986.[52] In 1764, Thomas Hancock left £600 to the city of Boston to build a mental hospital for the inhabitants of Massachusetts. The city declined to accept this gift, on the grounds that there were not enough insane persons to justify building such a facility.[53] Massachusetts had a population between 188,000 and 235,000 in 1764; if the population of the time suffered the same schizophrenia rates as today, that would mean that there

were about 2000 schizophrenics in the province.[54]   Even
accounting for the greater tolerance of small town life for the
mentally ill, this lends credence to Torrey and Miller's claim of
rising psychosis rates. Urban life today is not the same as urban
life then, and even the scale of what constitutes "urban" is
dramatically different — but it is an intriguing possibility that the
increased rates of mental illness at the close of the Colonial period
were the result of urbanization.

Irish immigration may also have played a role in the increasing
development of mental hospitals in America. It was widely
believed in the 1830s that Irish immigrants were disproportionately
present among the insane. More recent analysis shows that
throughout the nineteenth and twentieth centuries, Ireland's rates of
insanity were twice or more than that of the United States, England,
and Wales. Irish immigrants were also overrepresented in insane
asylums in the United States, England, Australia, and Canada at the
close of the nineteenth century.[55]

There is something gloriously idyllic about Colonial America
and its treatment of the mentally ill. It was a place where mental
illness appears to have been rare, and small town life tolerated all
but the "furiously mad" to live in the community. There might be
little prospect of effective treatment, but for those who recovered
— and even for those who were still struggling with mental illness
— the community was patient and accepting. America was about
to change.

5. THE STATE MENTAL HOSPITAL (1775-1900)

From the Revolution onward, American doctors saw mental illness as a manifestation of what was fundamentally a physical problem, but where Colonial doctors seemed unsure of how to cure mental illness, the Revolutionary spirit and confidence (some would say arrogance) associated with Enlightenment thinking took a more aggressive approach. Revolutionary Benjamin Rush, the pre-eminent American physician of his time, a signer of the Declaration of Independence and the U.S. Constitution, treated mental illness with bleeding, chairs that sought to cure mania by restraining the patient, cold showers, cold baths, even the threat of death, and other methods that seem brutal today[1] — and that we can say with some confidence, worked no better than a placebo.

Rush's methods, as brutal as they sound, did not actually kill the patient. Others were not so gentle. Part of what motivated Anna Marsh of New Hampshire to will $2000 towards creation of a Vermont Asylum for the Insane was the death in 1806 of Richard Whitney. Whitney's doctors attempted to cure insanity first with three to four minutes of total immersion, then a dose of opium, seeking "stupefaction of the life forces," that were believed at the heart of Mr. Whitney's mental problems. Whitney's doctors certainly accomplished that "stupefaction of the life forces" but a bit more vigorously and permanently than they intended.[2]

Adding to the Enlightenment confidence that mental illness could be cured was the religious movement we now call the Second Great Awakening. Previously, Calvinist Protestant thought was dominant in much of America. It had emphasized the depravity of human nature and that each of us was predestined to certain ends. The Second Great Awakening emphasized free will and the duty of individuals to make a more perfect society. Along with abolishing slavery and helping the poor came a desire to not simply care for the mentally ill, but to cure them.[3]

As part of this movement came the rise of what became known as "moral treatment." Originally, "moral treatment" referred to the attempts to address the psychological condition of the mental patient, as distinguished from any physical illness that might be the source of his mental illness. The patient might be *physically* treated with baths, or medications intended to alleviate depression or mania. The "moral treatment" was "that which is addressed to the patient's mind."[4]   Advocates of moral treatment, such Dr. Alexander Morison's *Cases of Mental Disease* (1828) distinguished between the older "Restraint System" and the newer "Non-restraint System" introduced by Pinel at the start of the nineteenth century that used restraints only as a last resort.[5]

Over time, "moral treatment" became identified exclusively with the "Non-restraint System," and focused on humane treatment of the mentally ill, occupational therapy, and a precursor of modern psychological methods.[6] As we learn more about the biochemical and genetic components of bipolar disorder, schizophrenia, and depression, it is easy to see the loss of the medical model of mental illness as an error. As barbarous and ineffective as the methods of Dr. Rush and others were, they at least recognized the fundamentally physical nature of psychosis.[7]

At the same time that "moral treatment" was replacing what was often intentionally a form of torture, or at least discomfort, reformers restructured the institutions. At least for a few decades after the Revolution, in some cities, the mentally ill were still locked up in the same facilities (and sometimes in the same wards) as the physically sick, paupers, and criminals. The reformers created insane asylums as freestanding institutions, often purposefully built as mental hospitals. Those states that had previously avoided creating institutions of any sort for care of the mentally ill, now did so on the newer model.[8]

New York City opened its first public hospital in 1791, and added a separate mental ward in 1808. In 1821, New York City opened the Bloomingdale Hospital — originally built to provide a more conducive environment for the "moral treatment" approach to mental illness. Furthermore, the New York legislature prohibited confining the mentally ill to prisons or jails starting in 1827.[9] Connecticut opened its first freestanding mental hospital in

Hartford in 1824.[10]   McLean Asylum opened in Somerville, Massachusetts in 1818,[11] as did mental hospitals in Lexington, Kentucky in 1824, in Columbia, South Carolina in 1827, in Staunton, Virginia (1828), Worcester, Massachusetts (1832), Brattleboro, Vermont (1836), Columbus, Ohio (1838), Boston (1839), Augusta, Maine and Nashville, Tennessee (1840). From then on, the list of state mental hospitals opening becomes a steady stream.[12]

In some mental hospitals, the goal was to cure. In others, especially in those states where hospital space was limited to dangerous mental patients, the goal was confinement for the protection of the society. Because in many states the costs for each patient were allocated to the local communities from which a mentally ill person came, there was a reluctance to send anyone to the state hospital who could not pay his own way.[13]

The creation of separate wards or buildings for the mentally ill did not always mean treatment. Especially in the South, such institutions were often strictly custodial in nature. Even this was often more humane than incarceration in prisons where mental patients might spend years confined to a single cell.[14] Such strictly custodial mental hospitals were often based on the assumption that a longstanding mental illness was incurable, and resources should not be wasted on attempting a cure.

Patients who had recently lapsed into madness were often regarded as candidates for a cure. By comparison, those who had been ill for a long time were considered chronic and incurable, and often segregated in the strictly custodial wards. As an example, in 1782, Peter Lesher was found not guilty of murder by reason of insanity in Bucks County. The judges who heard his case wrote to the managers of the Pennsylvania Hospital, "As his insanity still continues, and he is not yet eighteen years of age, and has frequent lucid intervals, we are of the opinion that he may be restored to his reason by proper management."[15]

Not all psychiatrists or judges agreed with the discouraging assumption that the long-term mentally ill were incurable, and should be abandoned to the custodial wards. Prominent pioneering psychiatrists such as Thomas S. Kirkbride argued against such segregation based on duration of illness:

When the chronic are in the same institution as the recent cases, there is little danger of their being neglected; but when once

consigned to receptacles specially provided for them, all
experience leads us to believe that but little time will elapse
before they will be found gradually sinking, mentally and
physically, their care entrusted to persons actuated only by
selfish motives — the grand object being to ascertain at how
little cost per week soul and body can be kept together — and,
sooner or later, cruelty, neglect, and suffering are pretty sure to
be the results of every such experiment.[16]

Similarly, where the earlier institutions had made little attempt
to distinguish between differing forms of mental illness, the moral
treatment movement made the first attempts at classifying patients.
This effort at the Quakers' private Frankford Asylum in
Pennsylvania was described as, "It is obviously disadvantageous to
mingle the furious and the melancholy, the imperious and the
fearful, the vociferous and the peaceful, the villainous and the
religious, the clean and the unclean, the curable, convalescent, and
incurable, together."[17] At the same time, at least some states, such
as Kentucky, made a point of excluding those who were simply
mentally deficient, reserving space for "maniacs, or persons who
are dangerous" and continuing a Colonial practice of boarding
"such as are quiet and peaceable" with families prepared to accept
them. This was another attempt at classifying patients, although for
a very pragmatic purpose.

With all this institutional change, there seems to have been
little change in the commitment laws. While some states by the
early nineteenth century prohibited confining the mentally ill in
prisons or jails, others were not so careful. Just like today, some
criminal defendants probably qualified as mentally ill, and either
through lack of counsel, or because their illness was not apparent or
clear-cut, nevertheless went to prison or jail.[18]

At least in this period, most families committed relatives only
after they had exhausted all alternative strategies. Often, threats of
violence or suicide would be the precipitating event. Sometimes
the threats were not enough; one woman in Utica, New York, was
committed after drowning two of her children, and attempting
suicide.[19] Many of these incidents are depressingly similar to the
problems that families with a mentally ill member experience
today.

Statutes of the period show that family members were expected
to be the primary mover of such efforts. Ohio's 1824 law is one of

the early examples of the change from informal commitment that shows this intent. It provided for "the safe keeping of Idiots, Lunatics, Insane persons, [and] the protection of their property," authorizing justices of the peace to accept applications by relatives or any overseer of the poor for commitment, with an inquest of seven jurors to return a verdict.[20]

Whatever the flaws of the Colonial system, where families were the primary caretakers of the mentally ill, at least the bonds of family acted as a restraint (or so one would hope). The rise of state mental hospitals meant that large numbers of people were now under the control of people with no family or community connections. Abuses within the hospitals, and the informality of the processes by which the mentally ill were hospitalized in most states, soon led to lawsuits and legislative formalization.[21] In at least some asylums, the state saved money by using prison inmates as asylum staff — and not surprisingly, abuse was a continuing problem.[22]

This desire to save money almost certainly reflected the public will. Victorian England was going through a parallel struggle over mental hospital funding. Until 1874, the building of English asylums was entirely the responsibility of local governments, and in many counties, attempts of public officials to obtain taxpayer approval for these building projects met with substantial opposition. As in America, the insane were sometimes housed in workhouses with the poor and the disabled, because workhouses cost anywhere from one-eighth to one-half of an asylum. As long as possible, counties avoided building asylums, and even when built, transferred only the most violent insane to the asylums.[23]

Until the 1840s, the legal questions related to civil commitment in America attracted almost no attention from experts. There were complaints of improper commitment or inhumane treatment, such as Robert Fuller's criticism of the McLean Asylum, published in 1833, but these complaints had little impact on the question of whether the informal procedures then in effect needed to be changed.[24]

Even Dr. Isaac Ray's *A Treatise on the Medical Jurisprudence of Insanity* (1838) focused on the questions of criminal liability by the insane and financial accountability.[25] Ray's discussion emphasized that:

To incapacitate a person from making contracts, bequeathing

property, and performing other civil acts, who has lost his natural
power of discerning and judging, who mistakes one thing for
another, and misapprehends his relations to those around him, is
the greatest mercy he could receive, instead of being an arbitrary
restriction of his rights.[26]

Ray did acknowledge that just a *few* delusions, even ones that
today we might characterize as psychotic, were not enough to
justify deprivation of one's liberty.[27]   Only briefly does Ray
discuss the question of civil commitment: "In confining the insane,
we have in view one or more of the following objects; first, their
own restoration to health; secondly, their comfort and well-being
merely, with little expectation of their cure; thirdly, the security of
society."

Ray acknowledged that there was a very real problem with
depriving a person of his liberty, and that doing so was a danger
that must be balanced against the good that hospitalization might
provide. In accordance with the widely held belief of the time that
the recently mentally ill were most likely to be curable:

It is in that large class of patients whose disorder is of too long
standing to admit of any rational expectations of cure that
restraint is most in danger of being abused..... The idea of
depriving a person of his liberty, merely because certain other
persons who would be benefitted by such a step say that he is
mad, is of so monstrous a nature, that one finds it difficult to
believe that it has ever been actually carried into practice.[28]

Yet in the years after Ray's book, there are a small number of
suits that make exactly that claim. One such suit involved a Josiah
Oakes, who was committed to a public mental hospital in 1845.
The circumstances that led to his commitment at first glance appear
improper — he was 67 years old, and intent on marrying a *far*
younger woman, to the discomfort of his children. The decision of
the Massachusetts Supreme Judicial Court, however, suggests that
Oakes' children may have been right — that perhaps Alzheimer's
was beginning to impair his reason. It was not just Oakes' decision
to marry a woman of scandalous character a few days after the
death of his wife, but a series of statements and letters, as well as
actions leading up to his wife's death, that suggested that something
was not right.

The decision, while rejecting Oakes's request to be released, set limits on the circumstances under which a person could be committed against his will:

> The right to restrain an insane person of his liberty, is found in that great law of humanity, which makes it necessary to confine those whose going at large would be dangerous to themselves or others. In the delirium of a fever, or in the case of a person seized with a fit, unless this were the law, no one could be restrained against his will. And the necessity which creates the law, creates the limitation of the law....

> The question must then arise, in each particular case, whether a person's own safety or that of others requires that he should be restrained for a certain time, and whether restraint is necessary for his restoration, or will be conducive thereto. The restraint can continue as long as the necessity continues. This is the limitation, and the proper limitation. The physician of the asylum can only exercise the same power of restraint which has been laid down as to be exercised by others in like cases.[29]

The right to exercise the "power of restraint" that persisted only as long as "necessary for his restoration" became, in the 1960s, the path towards deinstitutionalization. This limitation on the power of restraint relied upon the assumption that the patient could be cured.

When Chief Justice Shaw wrote this decision in 1845, the emerging psychiatric profession was going through one of its periodic phases of wild and irrational enthusiasm about its ability to cure mental illness — what Albert Deutsch referred to as the "cult of curability." In the eighteenth century, doctors recognized that while mental illness sometimes corrected itself, this was more the exception than the norm. Certainly for most psychotics, the general opinion was that the fall into madness was likely to be permanent.[30] By the 1830s, a great pendulum swing was under way, with recognized experts such as Thomas Kirkbride claiming that "80-90 percent of recent cases" were curable.[31]

The cause of this dramatic change in professional opinion seems to be part wishful thinking, part bad statistical methods, and part public relations. Two English physicians claimed to have cured nine out of ten mental patients. Their claims received extraordinary attention because one of them was King George III's doctor during his periodic spells of madness.[32] Next, Captain Basil Hall, a Royal Navy officer touring America, visited the Retreat, a Hartford, Connecticut mental hospital, and reported that they had cured 91.3 percent of their recent admissions — but this was based on twenty-one recoveries out of twenty-three recent admissions.[33] When published, Hall's account soon gave the Retreat an enviable reputation — one that other mental hospitals now had to match.[34]

Statistics was still a field in its infancy, and many hospitals were counting the same patient who had been admitted and discharged several times over a period of several years as equivalent to several different people who had been admitted and discharged. Was the patient "cured"? Well enough to leave — for at least a little while. Perhaps the circumstances outside the hospital were too stressful, or perhaps the patient learned to play the game well enough to leave the constraints of hospital life, without being cured.

These statistics often counted only "recent admissions," because it was the experience of doctors then (as now), that chronic mental illness had much lower cure rates.[35] The criteria used for defining "cured" varied substantially as well. As the enthusiasm for moral treatment advanced in the early decades of the nineteenth century, it is not surprising that the cure rates (as measured by subjective definitions) also improved.[36]

If one hospital could cure the vast majority of its recently admitted patients — what was wrong with hospitals that could not? The temptation for hospital directors to play games with statistics was apparently too strong to resist. To be fair, those hospitals that were not simply custodial *were* curing a fair fraction of their patients. The small size of these early hospitals may have also contributed to high actual cure rates — although almost certainly not at the levels claimed. Patients whose illness was depression might well have benefitted from the nurturing, protective atmosphere that the emerging "moral treatment" hospitals provided, and even with no treatment at all, the most severe psychoses have some sizable fraction of spontaneous remission.

This "cult of curability" had a powerful effect on state legislatures. Legislators in many states had resisted spending the money required to build sufficient mental hospitals. At least part of the reason was that mental illness was perceived as largely incurable; patients were likely to be permanent burdens on the state government. But if most patients would be present for only a few months before discharge, then the long-term costs to the state would be less severe.

The psychiatrists who promoted this "cult of curability" in the 1830s and 1840s appear to have believed these high cure rates, but the dark side of the old system may also have motivated the belief. In many states, the mentally ill who were not considered dangerous were farmed out to families to be cared for in a form of reverse auction. Whoever bid the lowest amount to house and feed a mental patient received a yearly contract. In much the same way that sheriffs of the time would skimp and cut corners on food for inmates, this contracting out of care for the mentally ill was awash in abuses, both potential and actual. It was easy for psychiatrists and social reformers to persuade themselves that state mental hospitals would provide a much more humane system of care for those mental patients who were *not* curable.[37]

There were other lawsuits challenging commitment to asylums — and from the descriptions, those commitments were considerably less justified than that of Mr. Oakes. An 1849 Philadelphia suit filed by Morgan Hinchman "brought an action of conspiracy against every individual the least concerned in the measure — his mother, sister, cousins, the sheriff, a passing traveler, the physicians of the asylum and the physicians who signed the certificate and others...."[38] Family members were convinced that Hinchman was mentally ill, yet witnesses at trial testified otherwise. Hinchman's commitment *may* have been motivated by greed, or at least mistrust of Hinchman's financial responsibility. He was offered the opportunity to leave the asylum if he put his property in trust for the benefit of his wife and family — a rather curious notion of being cured.[39]

The jury found that Hinchman's commitment was improper, and also concluded that there was indeed a conspiracy to acquire Hinchman's property. Hinchman was awarded $10,000 in damages.[40] Deutsch argues that such lawsuits led to more formal procedures for commitment to protect mental health practitioners and officers of the law,[41] and played a part in creating the intellectual justification for today's strict due process requirements.

More recent examinations of Hinchman's case, the decision itself, and the 1851 revisions to Pennsylvania's civil commitment law, show that Deutsch misread the effects of the Hinchman trial. The Hinchman trial, while it awarded damages, recognized the

legitimacy of the relatively informal commitment procedures —
but Presiding Judge Krause's decision in the Hinchman case was
very clear that, "The suing out of a commission of lunacy is not
actionable, unless it be done maliciously and without probable
cause." While Krause held that a commission of lunacy should
provide notice to relatives of the person being examined, failure to
do so was not sufficient grounds to call into question the
commission's decision.[42] Appelbaum and Kemp argue that it was
1861 and 1863 revisions to the commitment law that started
Pennsylvania down the path to a stricter standard, defining that
only those who were "unsafe to be at large" and likely to be
"curable" could be confined against their will.[43]

The suit that *clearly* started Pennsylvania towards a stricter
standard was Richard Nyce's 1868 action against Dr. Thomas
Kirkbride of the Pennsylvania Hospital. The judge hearing that
case decided that the evidence on both sides — both for and against
Nyce's sanity — was strong. "Judge Brewster, hearing the case,
decided that the fault lay in the informal system of commitment. It
was wrong, he concluded, for a man's liberty to depend on the
decision of a single judge and, by implication, even worse for the
decision to be made solely by his family and physician." Much
like the decision in the *Oakes* case, the judge acknowledged that a
person might be confined to a mental hospital for the "preservation
of the patient, and the public peace and morals." Judge Brewster
held that there needed to be danger to one or the other to justify
hospitalization without the benefits of jury trial.[44] The existing
commission of lunacy process, defined by an 1836 Pennsylvania
law, Brewster thought might not be enough. (Shortly after release,
Nyce was given the advantage of Judge Brewster's more
demanding due process standards, declared lunatic, and spent the
rest of his life in the asylum.)

Later the same year, Judge Brewster even seems to have
backed down on the "public peace and morals" argument, arguing
that a man who was committed after threatening his family should
enjoy some more formal procedure, and ordered his release. The
following year, another case came before Judge Brewster,
involving a man named Draper who had been found lunatic under
the 1836 law. Brewster decided that the lunatic determination
procedure was insufficient, because the determination of insanity
did not come from a judge.[45]

In 1869, Pennsylvania wrote a new mental illness commitment

law that largely reflected the concerns and beliefs of the psychiatric community. It now required two doctors to sign the commitment, instead of one, and allowed judges to commit anyone "manifestly suffering from want of care or treatment." In spite of the text of this new statute largely overturning Judge Brewster's decisions involving Draper and Nyce, the lower courts interpreted it as requiring that a person be dangerous to himself or others, and not simply in need of treatment. A number of mental patients were released from the state hospitals as a result, who then committed suicide. Eventually, one of the habeas corpus suits concerning involuntary commitments reached the Pennsylvania Supreme Court, which ruled that dangerousness to self or others was *not* required for commitment.[46]

Nationally more prominent was Mrs. E.P.W. Packard, committed to an Illinois mental hospital by her husband, Rev. Theophilus Packard, in 1860. In 1863, she obtained her release, and soon embarked on a mission to reform commitment laws. As Deutsch points out, "It appears to be established that she suffered from certain delusions.... She expressed the belief at one time that she was the third person in the Holy Trinity and the mother of Jesus Christ."[47] She also appears to have taught in her husband's church that her husband was the red dragon of Revelations — certainly a *unique* point of view.[48]

In Massachusetts, Mrs. Packard unsuccessfully lobbied for a revision to the law prohibiting commitment of any person "simply for the expression of opinions, no matter how absurd these opinions may appear." In Illinois and Iowa she was successful in persuading the legislature to require a jury trial for commitment. While these two states were Mrs. Packard's only direct successes, her very popular account of her experiences contributed to a rising popular mistrust of mental hospitals. Her efforts also led to a short-lived organization, the National Association for the Protection of the Insane and Prevention of Insanity. Even though this organization evaporated within four years, it left a residue of popular concern about the potential for abuse of power. The psychiatric profession responded by promoting state commissions to supervise mental hospitals and commitment.[49]

Some of the changes provoked by Mrs. Packard's campaign, such as guaranteeing a right of mental patients to write letters without censorship by the hospital, would seem necessary to make sure that any abuses of patients would come to light in a timely manner.   Perhaps instructive of how the psychiatric profession viewed itself, Dr. Isaac Ray, one of the leading psychiatrists of the time, complained that such laws were "utterly indefensible" because there was no evidence that mental patients were subject to abuse.   Dr. Ray went so far as to introduce a resolution at the meeting of the psychiatrists association in 1875 denying that *any* sane persons were held against their will in mental hospitals — and the resolution passed with only two dissenting votes.[50]

Those outside of the profession seem not to have shared Dr. Ray's confidence in how well the system worked.   In 1884, George Leib Harrison, "Late President of the Board of Public Charities of Pennsylvania," whose responsibilities included supervision of public mental hospitals, published a compendium of state insanity laws.   In his preface, Harrison expressed his concern that persons who were not mentally ill were being improperly committed. Sometimes these commitments were because of financial motivations such as appears to have been at play in the Hinchman case, and sometimes because of failures to properly identify why a person's behavior was peculiar.

Perhaps because of the state of libel law at the time, Harrison's examples of such inappropriate commitments are impossible to verify.   He also gave no information that would allow the reader to determine if such incidents were common, rare, or extraordinary.   It appears that Harrison's desire was both for improved due process to protect the rights of those committed, but also to remove the unlimited authority of mental hospitals to control the ability of patients to communicate with the outside world.[51]

There is an extraordinarily rich collection of documentation of Massachusetts' changing laws on commitment in the nineteenth century.   By 1859, the law authorized a variety of different procedures, depending on a person's residence and the severity of the situation.   Those who were "furiously mad" so as to be a danger to public safety could be committed by a Probate Court, Superior Court, or even Supreme Court.   "Two Justices of the Peace" could commit a person without a permanent residence in the state to one of the state hospitals.   For those with a permanent home, the town's overseers of the poor could commit any pauper "whatever may be the form or degree of their insanity," provided that the trustees of the state hospital agreed that the pauper needed treatment.[52]

The ability of two justices of the peace to commit a person seems to have been especially defective.   The Massachusetts

Commission on Lunacy observed in 1854 that unlike the more formal court proceedings of the higher courts, justices of the peace were often committing persons who were not mentally ill. The good news was that the state mental hospitals quickly recognized such erroneous commitments, and released such patients within a week or two. But the Commission was concerned that some of the county facilities, intended for the less dangerous mentally ill, did not have sufficient medical staff, and were failing to recognize these faulty commitments. Even worse, many of these county facilities were actually county jails. Sheriffs complained to the Commission that mixing mental patients and criminals was bad for both. Nor was the situation of holding the mentally ill in poorhouses any better.[53]

It would appear that there was progress in the following quarter century. In 1885, Henry F. Buswell's *The Law of Insanity* observed that American law required due process. It was no longer enough for a doctor to conclude that a person was insane, and required confinement. The exact details varied from state to state, with some requiring a jury trial to make a determination of insanity. But even without jury trial, the laws required some formal legal process for determining that a person was insane, and should therefore be committed. An insane person *could* be rapidly hospitalized against his will, to prevent a crime from taking place, or until such time as the legal process determining a person's sanity could be brought to bear, but this was only on a temporary basis.[54]

The concerns about abuse of civil commitment — a process that often became a lifelong arrangement — reflected not just the desire of the eccentric and disturbed to escape the confines of a mental hospital. Increasingly, by the middle of the nineteenth century, having won the battle to create state mental hospitals, the focus of those running these institutions had become custodial. The psychiatrists running state mental hospitals seem to have lost interest in the "moral treatment" ideals. Albert Deutsch — generally friendly to the profession — observes that

[T]he main emphasis in treating the insane during this period was placed on the mechanics of institutional arrangement. The problems of organization, administration and methods of therapy were, as a rule, considered to be of relatively small consequence in mental hospitals; the important thing was to build them. It didn't matter that some of the special hospitals and asylums were hardly better than the almshouses and jails where the insane had formerly been confined....[55]

At least partly this was because there was no effective treatment for the psychoses that usually caused a patient's commitment. Cruel treatment had been replaced with kind treatment, but insane asylums were more like permanent boarding houses than hospitals.[56] The concern that both inmates and the general public expressed about commitment may have been in reaction to this increasing focus on building and filling asylums, instead of curing patients.

On the other hand, there are reports that suggest that filling asylums was an improvement over the continued keeping of mentally ill patients in county poorhouses. The New York State Board of Charities made regular visits to county poorhouses, looking for evidence of mistreatment or inappropriate treatment, since some counties had been exempted from the requirement to send their mentally ill to state hospitals. The objective of the state law was to allow counties to maintain "custody and care of only quiet and harmless insane." The report suggests that there was no great problem *filling* the state mental hospitals — the problem was keeping them from becoming crowded.

The Board of Charities' visits found some clear violations of the requirement that counties keep only the "quiet and harmless insane." The Warren County poorhouse included "five insane, one man and four women." Most of these inmates were "confined most of the time in a strong room, being violent, homicidal, filthy and noisy." They were not being treated, and the keeper of the poorhouse "was necessarily largely engrossed by other constant and pressing duties, in the cultivation of the farm, and in the nursing and care of the over fifty pauper inmates, most of whom are aged, helpless and infirm." After considerable struggle with the county government (which was probably concerned about bearing the costs of state hospital treatment of these five inmates), the Board of Charities ordered these mental patients transferred to the state hospital.[57]

As so often happens with public services, the more that the states created mental hospitals to care for the insane at public charge, the more willing families were to institutionalize a member. There was both an increasing demand for beds in mental hospitals as the states created such institutions, and a higher utilization of mental hospitals by residents in the immediately adjacent counties. The mentally ill who could have been cared for at home, or otherwise within a community setting, increasingly became charges of the state.   While this benefited family members who would otherwise have shouldered the burden of care, it was perhaps not in the best interests of the patient, especially when such institutions were primarily custodial, not therapeutic.[58]

Just because institutionalization was increasingly driven by the needs of the patient's family did not mean that families were selfish. Grob argues that the stresses of dealing with a mentally ill family member meant that, "relatives began the process of institutionalization as a last resort and with a vague understanding that it was the lesser of two evils."[59]

After the development of the state mental hospital system and into the beginning of the twentieth century, families continued to be the majority of those initiating civil commitment. For the years 1846 and 1847 at New York's Utica State Lunatic Asylum, families started 75 percent of commitments, with 20.6 percent started by public authorities. Four decades later, families still started 57.9 percent of commitments, and public authorities initiated 38.6 percent. Early twentieth century San Francisco had similar ratios: 57 percent by relatives, 21 percent by physicians, and 8 percent by police.[60]

Unsurprisingly, civil commitment procedures varied from state to state, although as with so many other laws, states often adapted the laws of other states to their own needs. In 1892, for example, five states gave commitment authority to justices of the peace, eighteen required a judge to do so, five used a jury made up of ordinary citizens, and three others required "at least one member of the jury to be a physician." In three states a commission appointed by a court made the decision; two used "an asylum board" to make the same decision; nine states required only that a physician certify the patient's insanity. It would appear that whatever the legal requirements, families seeking civil commitment did not find the task particularly difficult.[61]

One might assume that this relative ease of commitment by family members was because the legal system did not protect the rights of mental patients. An alternative explanation is that family members were reluctant to commit a loved one to a mental hospital if there was any alternative available. By the time family sought commitment, it was likely that the circumstances were so severe that there was no serious question about the need for it.

At the end of the Colonial period, America was just beginning to create the first mental hospitals, and these were bold and creative experiments. By the end of the nineteenth century, the United States had mental hospitals that sought to cure those mental patients that it could, and as humanely as possible, warehouse those that it could not. In spite of the mid-century concerns about abuses of the commitment process, the fundamental assumption of the law was that institutionalization was done for the benefit both of the society and of the individual. Some of the mentally ill were clearly dangerous to others; others were a danger to themselves; and at least some of those who were hospitalized had a chance of recovering because of treatment. It was not a perfect system, but at its core, it made the assumption that an individual's liberty could be limited if there was good reason presented to competent authorities to do so.

6.   TWENTIETH CENTURY COMMITMENT UNTIL WORLD WAR II

By the opening decades of the twentieth century, the elderly were an increasing fraction of those committed to mental hospitals. The increased mobility of a more urban population meant that extended families were less available to help senile relatives. Improvements in public health (such as clean water and sewer systems) and medical care also meant that a larger fraction of the population was living to an age where senility became a problem. The absence of pensions (either private or public) probably aggravated the problem.

While the problems of a growing senile population meant that there probably was a need for *some* custodial facility, the traditional poorhouse might have been the better choice. By this point in history, however, the poorhouse as an institution was already in decline, leaving the mental hospital as the default institution. As with so many of the changes affecting the mental hospital system in American history, the decline of the poorhouse as an institution was an unintentional consequence of efforts to centralize financial responsibility for mental hospitals with the states, instead of counties.[1]

An 1898 New York State report complained about "Improper Commitments" of "cases that by virtue of advanced age have the imperfect use of their mental faculties and are bodily decrepit. They are in no sense insane within the meaning of the laws, as far as commitment to a State hospital is concerned, although they may be mentally defective." The report argued that some families were dumping such persons onto the state mental hospitals to avoid the frustrations of caring for such persons at home. County poor officers were doing likewise to move the costs of care from the county to the state.[2]

Along with the increase in senile inmates, there was also an increase of admissions of the syphilitic insane. Like the elderly, there was no hope of recovery; those suffering from tertiary stage syphilis (where the disease attacks the brain and nervous system) were certain to die from the illness, with increasing behavioral problems leading up to paralysis and death. A 1914 report, while careful not to overstate the connection between syphilis and insanity, observed that in some hospitals, 5-6 percent of the patients were syphilitic, while in others, as much as 22 percent of the patients tested positively for syphilis.[3] In the period 1911-20, twenty per cent of all admissions to New York State mental hospitals were "paretic admissions" — those suffering from tertiary syphilis. In the period 1916 to 1925, 13.1 per cent of first admissions to Warren State Hospital in Pennsylvania were syphilitic insanity. The behavioral problems and the risk of infecting others argued for confinement, as opposed to a less restrictive custodial situation.[4]

This problem of syphilitic insanity appears to have grown worse from the early nineteenth century into the twentieth — at least as measured by admissions. Massachusetts' records show continuing growth in the percentage of such admissions from the earliest records in the nineteenth century: 3.5 per cent in 1859; 5.9 per cent in the period 1880-85; 6.1 per cent in 1940.[5]

This change in the population of mental hospitals altered assumptions and goals. When mental hospitals were largely filled with patients who had some *hope* of recovery (even if most would not), both public officials and staff could see the institution as primarily therapeutic. As senility and syphilitic paresis increasingly dominated the patient population, it reinforced the late nineteenth century's existing custodial focus.[6] The senile and syphilitic patients were incurable; the hospital prevented the senile from accidental injury, and the syphilitic from infecting or injuring others.

The dramatic expansion of mental hospitals appears also to have played a part in the increasing importance of the custodial model. Thomas Kirkbride, one of the nationally prominent psychiatrists of the time, believed that no mental hospital should exceed 250 beds. By the end of the nineteenth century, so many public mental hospitals exceeded this level that a more custodial model was perhaps inevitable.[7]

In parallel with the growth of psychotherapy ("The Talking Cure," as Freud's methods were soon called), and partly in response to the rising rate of severe mental illness in Britain, Ireland, Canada, and the United States, psychiatrists adopted a variety of radical physical treatments for depression and psychosis. In retrospect, these "treatments" seem more like something that a twentieth century witch doctor might do. Some were utterly wrong, and did not persist. One of these was a procedure developed by "Henry Cotton, who removed teeth, tonsils, and parts of the intestine from hundreds of patients at the Trenton State Hospital in New Jersey. Cotton claimed that there were foci of infections in these organs that were causing the insanity and that removal of the infections would produce clinical improvement."[8]

Other techniques, as bizarre as they sound, actually seemed to work — at least well enough for doctors to adopt them. Dr. Julius Wagner-Jauregg of Austria promoted the use of "fever therapy," in which psychotics were purposely infected with malaria.[9] This was a mainstream practice; Wagner-Jauregg received the 1927 Nobel Prize in Medicine for this treatment. The evidence for its efficacy was not strong, yet the practice soon became widespread.[10]

Another Austrian physician, Manfred Sakel, introduced insulin shock as a treatment for psychosis, especially schizophrenia, after discovering that it seemed to cure opiate addiction — and in one schizophrenic patient, it seemed as though it also improved his mental condition as well. The patient was injected with insulin to put him into a diabetic coma, and then given sugar to bring him back out. The evidence of its effectiveness remained weak, but the mortality rate for those so treated varied from one to five percent. Perhaps indicative of the desperation of the medical profession to find a cure, this dangerous procedure was widely accepted.[11] The Hungarian physician Ladilas von Meduna believed that "epileptics rarely became schizophrenic," and so he decided that inducing convulsions by administering metrazol would cure schizophrenia. Again, the evidence for its effectiveness was weak, and while somewhat lower risk than insulin shock therapy, it was not risk-free.[12]

Derived from these previous techniques was electroconvulsive therapy (ECT), developed by Italian physicians using human guinea pigs in an experiment that would simply not be allowed today.[13] ECT was less risky than either insulin shock or metrazol convulsions, and even though its mechanism remains uncertain,[14] and its image to the general public is horrific, ECT remains in use today for severe depression. It even made something of a comeback in the 1980s, as its superiority over medication for bipolar disorder, severe depression, and schizophrenia became more apparent.[15] Even those psychiatrists in the 1930s and 1940s who were disturbed that no one knew *how* it worked, recognized that it helped many patients to recover from depression and schizophrenia.[16] Accounts of how ECT, even in its earliest days, achieved dramatic cures for those suffering severe depression, catatonia, and schizophrenia, are profoundly startling. But like many new treatments, it was misused and overused into the 1960s, sometimes with destructive results.[17]

All of these techniques sound like modern witch doctoring, but reviewing the literature of the time gives the reader an appreciation of the efforts to find a scientific explanation for the observed improvements. For example, one 1940 journal article described how the experimenter performed microscopic examination of nerve cell changes associated with use of metrazol.[18]

Another technique that gives some idea of the desperation of the profession was lobotomy — the surgical severing of nerve fibers in the front lobes of the brain. The Portuguese doctor Egas Moniz developed lobotomy in 1935. It spread to the United States almost immediately, because of its effectiveness in making violent patients manageable — an important issue in largely custodial institutions.

For some patients (as much as one-third in some studies), lobotomies made it possible for patients to live at home. Other patients, even if they did not recover enough to leave an institutional setting, became more easily controlled. This meant that the hospital no longer needed to use physical restraints, isolation, or sedation; this was better not just for the staff, but arguably better for the patient as well. For other patients, the consequences were less encouraging, with some left in a vegetative state for life.[19] By 1960, antipsychotic drugs had rendered such a coarse surgical procedure unnecessary, and mental hospitals no longer allowed the procedure.

In the mid-1960s, however, for a relatively small number of severely mentally ill persons, a new, more refined procedure, limbic system surgery, came into use. In spite of a well-organized campaign by anti-psychiatric activists to see it prohibited by

Congress, two separate studies of the procedure concluded that for some specific illnesses, such as severe chronic anxiety and some obsessive compulsive behaviors, the procedures were highly effective, and without serious side effects.   Nonetheless, the combination of effective pressure by anti-psychiatric activists and threats of violence against neurosurgeons performing it, effectively ended the procedure by the 1980s.[20]

While long-term institutionalization was the norm, some states did experiment with other approaches before World War II. Massachusetts and nine other states provided for boarding out "harmless and chronic insane patients in households," a practice that was common in the latter half of the nineteenth century in Britain.   The primary motivation would seem to have been economic, since boarded out patients were much less expensive to the state than those cared for in custodial institutions.[21]   How well such arrangements worked for the patients would have depended much on the homes in which they were boarded, and the nature of the public hospitals that would otherwise have housed them. It was a sufficiently common process that mental illness journals described a specific class of social worker to supervise assignment and maintenance of such patients by the "boarding-out department" of the state hospital. Considering the nature of the patients who were *not* suitable for "boarding out," and the increasingly custodial nature of pre-World War II mental hospitals, it seems likely that such practices were generally beneficial to those sent to live in private homes.[22]

Public mental hospitals varied substantially from state to state in funding, physical facilities, and the quality of care. Studies completed after World War II found that states with low rates of hospitalization of the mentally ill tended to have low expenditures per patient as well.[23]   This suggests that as the percentage of mentally ill persons in a state's population increased, the legislature's generosity in funding facilities increased. This is not surprising; as the number of mental patients increased, the number of families concerned about the welfare of their hospitalized relatives also increased, creating public sentiment to which legislators responded.

By the 1940s, the informal commitment procedures of the past were long gone, although different states used rather different methods of achieving due process, at least to the extent that the legal system required it.   There were several categories of commitment. Emergency commitment was supposed to provide a way for hospitalizing a person who was an imminent threat to himself or others. Such commitments were supposed to be short-term, limited in most states to a few days while waiting for a hearing. Because emergency commitment was so easy, in a number of states this became the standard method of commitment. The justification for allowing hospitalization based only on a determination made by a doctor or police officer was that the risk of leaving such a person unrestrained exceeded the loss of the patient's liberty, especially because this emergency commitment was supposed to be short term. But some state laws provided for extensions without due process, and a few, such as Maine, had no time limit for such an emergency commitment.[24]

There was almost certainly some room for improvement in how mental hospitals were run, and in the procedures used for commitment. This was a time when Americans generally did not question the competence or authority of doctors, police, or the government. The accepted medical practices for treating mental illness are horrifying to read today, but they were not badly intentioned; they were simply in error. The entire set of assumptions about mental illness and its treatment, however, were about to severely questioned, then demolished.

7. DEINSTITUTIONALIZATION AS A THEORY

It is often said that the road to hell is paved with good intentions, and nowhere is this more apparent than the path that led to deinstitutionalization of the mentally ill in the 1960s. As convenient as it might be to have a Snidely Whiplash villain to blame, there is none to be found. Supreme Court Justice Louis D. Brandeis's well-known observation with respect to liberty might well be applied to the situation of the mentally ill: "The greatest dangers to liberty lurk in insidious encroachment by men of zeal, well-meaning but without understanding."[1] Neither zeal nor good intentions were in short supply.

After World War II, the existing system of state mental hospitals fell into disfavor with mental health activists. One reason was how poorly it seemed to perform, compared to the military's World War II mental health first aid system. Almost two-thirds of soldiers suffering from combat fatigue were returned to duty within a week, and nearly all the rest were returned to non-combat duties after more prolonged treatment.[2] The military's success in treating soldiers suffering from psychological problems suggested that the same approach could work in civilian life, with community-based mental health care as a more humane and more effective strategy.[3] (Similar experiences led to a belief in the superiority of the "therapeutic community" and deinstitutionalization in Britain.)[4]

But this was an apples and oranges comparison. The psychiatric problems of soldiers were the products of the stresses and barbarism of warfare. The most obviously mentally ill were supposedly screened out during induction (and indeed, almost 1.9 million young men were rejected for military service during World War II because of psychiatric disability).[5] Furthermore, "The vast majority of psychiatric cases in the military would never have been considered for hospitalization in civilian life...." The performance requirements of combat — and that a soldier with mental problems might became a danger to himself or others in his unit — meant that the rate of casualties, and how well they responded to treatment, were not equivalent to civilian life.[6] The mental problems of civilian life were unlikely to respond so well to sympathetic treatment and rest.[7]

Another factor driving deinstitutionalization was the rise of "dynamic psychiatry." Before the war, most psychiatrists worked in public mental hospitals, caring for the severely mentally ill. Most psychiatrists before World War II saw mental illness in terms of "normal" behavior as distinguished from severe deviations from that norm. Dynamic psychiatry, which became dominant in the profession after World War II, saw mental health as a continuum from well-adjusted to severely ill, with no clear dividing line. Where traditional psychiatry had talked of mental illness, dynamic psychiatry thought in terms of mental health. The difference was that many persons might not be insane, or even deeply disturbed, but still not completely happy and well-adjusted — and thus in need of treatment and assistance.[8] One of the results of this were several studies in the late 1950s and early 1960s that concluded that less than 20 percent of the population was mentally healthy.[9] Most dangerously, this emerging approach refused to see neuroses and psychoses as qualitatively different. It saw psychotics confined to mental hospitals as differing from those with emotional problems "only in degree rather in kind."[10]

Dynamic psychiatry emphasized environmental causes of mental illness, not biochemical or genetic origins. World War II and combat fatigue seemed to support this largely environmental source of mental illness. Psychiatry was confident that screening had removed those most prone to mental problems — and yet the rate of neuropsychiatric casualties in combat divisions after D-Day was 250 per 1,000 soldiers. There seemed to be no particular pattern that explained which soldiers would be stricken — except for combat, and the length of that combat without a break.

If war caused mental illness, it was not a particularly strange idea that environmental stresses in civilian life might also cause mental illness — which fit well into Freudian theories about family structure and conflict. Physicians assigned to psychiatric care while in uniform during World War II took the dynamic psychiatric perspective, which worked so well with soldiers suffering from combat fatigue, and returned to civilian life as converts to the new philosophy.[11] Many of the dynamic psychiatrists who formed the Group for the Advancement of Psychiatry (GAP) that promoted community mental health treatment were World War II military psychiatrists.[12]

This transformation of the psychiatric profession also reflected political and ethnic factionalism. The dynamic psychiatrists were politically progressive and disproportionately Jewish, at least in part because Freud's movement in Europe had been primarily centered in a Jewish, cosmopolitan culture. Many of its proponents fled to the United States with the rise of Hitler, where they influenced psychiatric teaching. They saw the role of psychiatry as broader than just care for mentally ill individuals, but treatment for nearly everyone. William Menninger, for example, saw psychiatry's responsibilities as including such problems as, "Can the culture of a race, the Germans for instance, be changed?" Psychiatry's proper field of involvement included improving child rearing, economics, racism, and, it seemed, almost everything that made up society.

By comparison, the traditional psychiatric establishment was more likely to be Protestant, and looked at mental illness as primarily a biological problem (either biochemical or neurological in nature). They were reluctant to involve psychiatry in larger political causes, and believed that psychiatry's field of activity was the severely mentally ill.[13] (Sadly, Freud himself sought a connection between psychology and brain structure,[14] but the state of science was not advanced enough in those days to pursue that line of thought, and Freud's later followers seemed to have lost interest in the biology of mental illness. Freud also had the good sense to be "skeptical" of the "effectiveness of analysis for the therapy of psychoses.")[15]

Another part of this expansion of dynamic psychiatry was the post-World War II expansion of psychotherapy to "a middle-class clientele able to pay for and eager to use psychological services...." Jerome D. Frank of Johns Hopkins observed that, "the ablest, most experienced psychiatrists spend most of their time with patients who need them least." Psychotherapy was of very limited value for the psychotic; no matter, the money was to be made treating the neurotic and wealthy.[16]

Dynamic psychiatry also fostered a belief that preventative

individual mental health treatment promoted *community* mental health. The Freudian idea that psychosis was a reaction to family relationships was then very popular among psychiatrists; some dynamic psychiatrists believed that a more aggressive effort at preventing psychosis would pay off in reduced mental hospital admissions. Unfortunately, this belief was just that: "articles of faith rather than hypotheses to be investigated. Rhetoric proved so persuasive and powerful that it literally overwhelmed meaningful evaluations of programs and policies." At least until the 1960s, this faith in community mental health was not an argument for emptying public mental hospitals, but an argument for providing community mental health services to complement the institutions.[17]

Another aspect of the faith in preventative mental health was how it intertwined with radical politics. By the 1960s, the great social problems of the era, such as racism and urban riots, had become yet another area where preventative psychiatry planned to solve problems before they came up — and increasingly, community mental health advocates became opponents of public mental hospitals. If social injustice caused mental illness, it was easy to believe that mental hospitals were only a palliative that discouraged correcting the root social problems. If alleviating poverty reduced mental illness, it would also benefit other social problems, too. Similarly, if research demonstrated that mental illness was genetic in nature, then the eugenics movement that the Holocaust discredited might suddenly find itself revived.

Members of Group for the Advancement of Psychiatry, the dynamic psychiatric faction of the profession, dominated the National Institute of Mental Health (NIMH) established by Congress in 1946. Unsurprisingly, they strongly influenced NIMH's direction for many years thereafter. NIMH did, it is true, fund basic physiological and neurological research on mental illness. But NIMH also put great emphasis on community mental health, with the dynamic psychiatric emphasis on the continuum model, and relatively little on the severely mentally ill. States received funding assistance for community mental facilities, but not for the crowded and underfunded public mental hospitals.[18]

Consistent with the environmental model so popular with GAP, NIMH's research emphasized behavioral sciences, sociology, and anthropology. While reflective of the dynamic psychiatric model for mental illness, this was also driven by the primitive state of neuroscience at the time. The tools and knowledge base needed to do biochemical and brain structure research was simply not yet available.[19]

NIMH also provided training grants to increase the number of professionals with training in psychiatry, neurology, and related fields. Perhaps because of this increase in funding — or perhaps because of the prestige that GAP provided to psychoanalysis — new psychiatrists increasingly went not into public mental hospitals, their traditional location, but into private practice.[20] Dynamic psychiatric views increasingly replaced organic ideas of the origins of mental illness in medical schools and psychiatric training after World War II.[21]

Other factors also encouraged the movement away from institutionalization in state mental hospitals. Psychiatry's new emphasis on group therapy, which worked with non-psychotics, fit well into the notion of community-based mental health treatment. The new neuroleptic drugs,[22] such as chlorpromazine, approved by the FDA in 1954, seemed like the psychiatric equivalent of penicillin in the scope of the miraculous cures it produced among some psychotics.[23] Even for those psychotics who were not cured, the neuroleptic drugs calmed patients who might otherwise have required physical restraints.[24] These drugs made it possible to put many patients in unlocked wards, reducing bizarre, frightening, and sometimes violent behavior. It was increasingly easy to believe that many severely mentally ill patients could be returned to family or community settings.

Unfortunately, the severe side effects of these first generation antipsychotic drugs were not recognized early enough, or widely enough.[25] One such side effect was tardive dyskinesia, which caused the loss of control over some voluntary muscles, leading to tics — and it could persist for many months after the patient stopped taking it.[26]

Much like the cult of curability in the 1830s, the initial semi-miraculous results of these drugs caused the psychiatric profession to believe in its ability to cure the mentally ill that substantially exceeded reality. During Congressional hearings in 1963 concerning revisions to the District of Columbia's mental health commitment laws, Doctor Zigmond M. Lebensohn, representing the American Psychiatric Association, expressed confidence that "our new treatment techniques" — probably referring to the then new use of psychotropic drugs — restored a level of sanity so quickly that many patients involuntarily committed would, within a "a few days to a week" be sufficiently lucid to become voluntary patients.[27]   Professor Henry Weihofen of George Washington University similarly explained that "modern, intensive kinds of treatments, such as drug therapy" allowed ninety per cent of patients to be home "within less than a year. And many of them can be restored within such a period as 90 or even 30 days."[28]

The introduction of these wonder drugs gave psychiatrists hope that many of the traditional strategies for dealing with mental illness were no longer necessary — and many psychiatrists were glad for the chance at a new approach.   Louis Linn's 1968 *American Journal of Psychiatry* article optimistically argued that community psychiatry, as "the fourth psychiatric revolution" was made possible by the new drugs for "effective symptom control.... The most important consequence of effective symptom control was that it became possible for the first time to treat the major mental illnesses in the patient's own community, or the district in which he lived."[29]   It seemed as though the days of the incurable mental patient, and especially long-term hospitalization, were coming to an end.

There   were   also   non-medical   motivations   for deinstitutionalization.   Along with public officials and staff, the public's perception of the mental hospital seems to have been damaged by the increasingly hopeless nature of those being treated. The nineteenth century public perceived mental hospitals as places of hope, in spite of the occasional exposes of patient abuse. After all, the average patient in the nineteenth century stayed for less than a year (although he might return again and again). By the end of World War II, the public perception of the mental hospital was mired in despair. The increasing dominance of the elderly senile and the syphilitic insane in mental hospitals meant that average stays were measured in years — and for many patients, it was a life sentence. Under such circumstances, the public was extraordinarily open to alternative strategies for caring for the mentally ill.[30]

State mental hospitals until the 1950s were filled not only with psychotics — many of whom psychiatry had only limited success in curing — but also with those who were utterly incurable: the severely retarded, the senile elderly, and the syphilitic insane. Of necessity, such institutions were primarily custodial. Inmates were often cut off from the outside world, and usually lacked advocates with sufficient political influence to see that state legislatures funded these institutions adequately to provide a humane level of treatment. Unsurprisingly, there was enough genuine neglect and abuse of the patients to create a widespread perception that state mental hospitals were a shame to civilized society. Some writers compared these institutions to Nazi concentration camps.[31] To advocates of community mental health treatment, they were trying to overturn "a decrepit, overcrowded, public hospital system" that they saw as "anti-therapeutic."[32]

Another factor driving public perceptions of mental hospitals were popular novels and movies. Some, such as the Oscar-winning *The Snake Pit* (1948) presented mental hospitals as a mix of both brutal and uncaring attendants and well meaning doctors. Others, such as *Harvey* (1950), portrayed mental illness as a form of harmless eccentricity.

Another motivation for deinstitutionalization was the belief that prolonged time in such a setting was harmful. In the 1961 Joint Commission on Mental Illness and Health report, Dr. Robert C. Hunt, the superintendent of the Hudson River State Hospital, argued that state mental hospitals caused "Much of the unnecessary crippling of the mentally ill," both because of the degrading nature of being involuntarily committed, and the prison-like nature of the confinement once hospitalized.[33] As Pennsylvania State Senator W. Louis Coppersmith echoed several years later, "if a person is kept in a mental institution for more than two years, the chances of being able to live outside the institution for one year are six out of 100. The difficulties caused by prolonged commitment in a mental institution are frequently worse than those that caused the original admission."[34] Coppersmith's numbers on the inability of those institutionalized for more than two years might well be correct — but the question he should have asked was whether the prolonged commitment *caused* the inability to live outside the institution, or whether the severe mental illness that kept a patient hospitalized prevented him from operating outside the institution.

In any democracy, conflict between democracy and experts is inevitable. Throughout the twentieth century, psychiatrists and legislators had been at odds. Legislators were accountable to the voters for how taxes were spent; psychiatrists believed that their professional obligation to patients of state mental hospitals required them to be insulated from the demands of taxpayers.[35] This conflict would not necessarily have led to pressure for deinstitutionalization, except that radical hostility to governmental authority from the 1960s antiwar movement rapidly expanded to a wide range of social institutions. Adding to this movement was an existing, less radical hostility towards institutions "that idealized individuals as caring while condemning arbitrary bureaucratic organizations as controlling."[36]

As the 1960s opened, the movement towards deinstitutionalization had a certain inevitability. The existing public mental hospital system was seen as old-fashioned, ineffective, and primitive. Community mental health treatment, by comparison, was seen as compassionate, forward thinking, and sophisticated. When the movement collided with the revolutionary 1960s, it destroyed the public mental health system.

8.   "The Judge Will Almost Certainly Release Him"

The next few months after that night the ambulance took Ron to St. John's Hospital, strapped to a gurney, were chaos and confusion. My brother was first held for 72 hours observation, then for another fourteen days. From all that I could see and understand, the doctors and staff at the hospital were concerned and caring people, doing a very difficult job.

Unsurprisingly, there was a bit of gallows humor to all of it. My brother was in the locked ward of the hospital. During one of my visits to my brother, I approached one of the staff and explained that I was ready to leave, "You can't do that!" he explained.

"But I'm just a visitor here."

"That doesn't matter."

He was just kidding, and promptly unlocked the door. As I write these words, it sounds cold and heartless, to make a joke about something like this — but when I think of the working conditions and the tragedies that the staff confronted, I can't criticize their attempt at finding what humor they could in a bad situation.

The hospital pumped Ron full of the wonder drugs of the time, including, I think, chlorpromazine (Thorazine). Ron certainly calmed down. But this calming effect was a mixed blessing — and for a reason that is the core of this book. As one of the psychiatric technicians explained to my parents, "After fourteen days of Thorazine, very few people appear dangerous, and the judge will almost certainly release him." This turned out to be prophetic.

The psychiatrist at St. John's gave Ron a prescription for antipsychotic medications, and some appointments to see another psychiatrist in an outpatient setting, but he was convinced that family structure was the cause of schizophrenia. With what we now about schizophrenia's biochemical origins, this was not just wrong, but a tremendously painful accusation to throw at my parents. Especially tragic is that my father's twin brother had a daughter who was *also* suffering from schizophrenia — but like many families of the time, they kept this a family secret, made somewhat easier because they were located in the Panama Canal Zone, far removed from us. Had my parents known about my cousin's problems, they might have pushed back a bit harder, and asked if there might be a genetic factor.

Because the psychiatrist thought that Ron's family made him crazy, he wanted Ron to move into a halfway house for the mentally ill — but insisted that Ron do this himself. This was absurd; Ron just wasn't well enough to handle even this level of planning and follow through. Very briefly, Ron stayed with his cousin Michael, but soon he was back at home. At least temporarily, Ron knew that something wasn't right. He asked my mother, "Why am I so bad?"

There is a jumble of painful incidents in my memories from this period, and I have no hope of ever sorting them out as to month and year. Like many painful memories, the sequence matters less than the grief connected to the events. Over the next several years, the chaos and suffering of Ron's confused mind led to increasingly frightening behavior — not just to complete strangers, but to family members as well. Ron lived with us for a while — taking as many as six long showers a day. Along with increased costs for hot water, this was a problem because there was only one bathroom in our house.

Over the next few months, Ron's frequent showers became the least of the problems of having him there. One day, he took a brick, and smashed in the windows of his car. Why? We could not get a sensible answer out of him. Ron's car sat for what seemed like a very long time in our driveway (although my mother remembers that Ron had the windows replaced relatively quickly), and he soon took to walking.

Ron began to sport a grin that was somewhere between mischievous and malevolent — one that scared us all. My sister Carolyn remembers that same grin when Ron was young — but Ron's bizarre and frightening behavior made that same grin quite worrisome. One night, he stayed up late, tapping a spoon on the armrest of a wooden chair. By morning, the spoon was badly bent, and the armrest was heavily cut up — both objects were painful material reminders for many years of this frightening period. One night Ron smashed a wooden bookshelf that we had inherited from our grandmother. Increasingly this worried my parents, because there was no apparent reason for this violence, and attempting to talk to Ron was becoming increasingly difficult.

Many schizophrenics become obsessed with some concept, issue, or person. For some, it is religion. For some, it is an important historical figure — hence the Ruth Gikow painting "Psychosis--Two Napoleons and a Josephine" portraying what used to be a common problem in large mental hospitals — when two patients were *both* Napoleon.

Ron's obsession seemed to be mathematics, with regular and incomprehensible discussion of "5s" and "7s" or "nickels." (Many years later, we found out that he was talking about E-5 and E-7 — U.S. Army ranks of sergeant and sergeant first class.) Ron listened to the Grateful Dead album *Workingman's Dead* again and again, all day and all night. I'm not sure that I would ever have been a fan of the Grateful Dead, but the memories of those few months mean that hearing songs from that album still provokes a wistful melancholy.

Eventually, Ron's increasingly frightening and sometimes violent behavior caused my parents to ask him to leave. This was very hard on my parents, but they were beginning to see the destructive effects that it was having on me. It was also aggravating our father's heart condition — and it was apparent that giving Ron a place to live was not helping him. By this point, Ron had persuaded himself that there was nothing wrong with him — that there was something terribly wrong with his family. I remember the night that my parents told Ron that he had to move out, and put his suitcases on the front lawn. In his frustration and rage, Ron kicked one of the suitcases. In retrospect, it flew what seems an astonishing distance — and it was a reminder that Ron's years in the Army had made him potentially a very dangerous person.

And yet in all the chaos and confusion, Ron had not completely lost touch with us as a family. For Christmas, he knew that he was *supposed* to get me a gift — but he was unemployed and broke. He tried to give me his microscope. I kept trying to refuse it, because I knew that it was important to him — he had worked very hard to buy it when he was in high school. I was heartbroken to see my brother reduced to this state, and I do not think that I have ever accepted a Christmas gift with more sorrow.

I remember my mother's birthday in November of 1973. This was a very low-key event: a cake, some ice cream, a couple of gifts, my cousin Michael, and my parents. My brother was no longer living with us, but had come over to borrow an alarm clock. My parents had rather purposefully not mentioned my mother's birthday, in the hopes of avoiding an ugly scene. By now, Ron was incapable of being part of any social activity without acting frighteningly crazy.

Ron left on foot, since he had smashed in the windows of his car some weeks earlier. A few minutes later, my parents pulled out the cake and the ice cream, and made a very serious effort to have a normal family activity. Ron apparently had forgotten something, and returned to the house as we were getting ready to light the candles on the cake. Ron looked in on a scene of normality — and it seems to have enraged him, perhaps because he had not been invited. He smashed in the front window of the house with a chair from the front porch. By this point, we had no idea what to expect from Ron, and my parents immediately called the police. Ron stood out on the street in front of the house, with an indignant look on his face, apparently waiting for the police to arrive. It was a long time before the police showed up: perhaps thirty minutes, and by then, Ron had walked away. They made no effort to find Ron.

A smoldering anger at my father *perhaps* played some part in Ron's rage, and it was now coming to the surface. There was a lot of subterranean hurt as Ron and I were growing up. My parents built a house during World War II in Alderwood, a rural area north of Seattle, in Sonohomish County. Unlike many other men his age, my father was not in the armed forces. He was 31 — of draft age — at the start of the war. As he told me the story, part way through the induction process, shortly after someone decided because of his size that he was going into the Marines, a doctor came running up with my father's lung X-rays. There were what looked like tuberculosis scars visible — and so my father was classified 4-F, unfit for military service. For years afterwards, my father had regular checkups to make sure that these tuberculosis scars weren't about to become an active disease. (At autopsy, 35 years later, it turned out the lung scars were from San Joaquin Valley fever, a fungal infection — not tuberculosis.)

My father worked as a welder in shipyards throughout the war, and in spite of the material shortages brought on by the war, my parents built a house. Ron was born in 1944; I was born in 1956. I don't remember the house; we moved away when I was less than two years old. I visited the neighborhood in the 1980s and I can see why my older siblings felt sorrow about having to leave. Even in June, I could see a 170-degree panorama of snow-capped mountains.

We moved away in 1958, a recession year, at least in that part of Washington State. Hard as it may be to believe for those who only know the Seattle/Redmond/Everett area in the Microsoft era, there was a time when unemployment was a cyclic problem there. My father's job was one of those subject to this cycle, and my parents were struggling to pay the bills.

Credit cards were still fairly unusual items at the time; it was not until the mid-1960s that middle class Americans commonly carried them. (Those of my generation and a little older may still remember the MasterCharge television ads promoting this relatively new concept. The ad had bankers marching down the street, singing, "One hundred banks behind it, one hundred thousand places you can use it — MasterCharge.")

A common practice in this pre-credit card era, at least in that area, was to write a check to the grocery store or a repair shop, and have them hold it is as a form of enforceable I.O.U. My parents would bring in $5 or $10 in cash, and hand it to the merchant, who would keep track of the outstanding balance. When the amount of the check had been completely paid off, the merchant would return the uncashed check. Strictly speaking, this was illegal — writing a check when you knew that you didn't have sufficient funds in your checking account to cover it. But it was, in those pre-credit card days, a practice that many merchants accepted.

As near as I can tell, merchants only made an issue of these non-sufficient funds checks if you failed to make an effort to pay down the balance. As with many small towns, everyone knew everyone else, and there was some acceptance of the necessity for this informal procedure. At some point, the Snohomish County Sheriff decided to crack down on this practice, and started prosecutions. (Why my father? My mother tells me that the sheriff and my father were part of a Thursday night poker game — and my father had been winning, and the sheriff had been losing.) Worse, the bank closed my father's checking account without informing him — making those checks not simply NSF, but technically, forgery, because there was no bank account on the day that my father wrote a check. Perhaps adding to the reason to pursue my father, he had apparently been convicted of joyriding as a teenager, putting him at increased risk that a criminal conviction for what was essentially a bounced check might send him to prison.

About the time the district attorney decided to file charges against a number of people in our situation, my father had taken a bus to California to look for work — ironically, because he wanted to have enough money coming in to pay down these checks and support his family. My mother's explanation of why he was out of state didn't persuade the district attorney. Instead, my father was now wanted not only for writing bad checks, but also for interstate flight to avoid prosecution — a federal charge.

My parents sold the house in Alderwood in 1958. The realtor claimed that he couldn't get more than $2000 for it (which covered the mortgage) — but my parents later found out that the buyer was the realtor's brother-in-law — who shortly thereafter resold it for $10,000. This was one of many financial problems that plagued our family as Ron and I were growing up, greatly aggravated by the difficulty of my father applying for jobs that might have required a background check.

We moved around a lot for the next few years. We lived in Santa Barbara for a while, next to a stagnant body of water with mosquitoes. Some of my siblings ended up with boils — and Ron ended up in the hospital with osteomyelitis. He spent two months at home in a hospital bed, and limped for a year. Next we moved to a rough section of San Francisco south of Market Street. From the relative paradise of Alderwood, my older sisters now attended a junior high where boys attacked each other with knives, and girls went after each other with broken bottles.

For the rest of my father's life, he lived in varying degrees of fear that he was going to be arrested and sent to prison. As a result, he did not register to vote, for fear of being found and arrested. For many years, he worked away from home — and with good reason. In the early 1960s, my father worked at a shipyard in the Los Angeles area, while we lived near San Diego. The police would come into our apartment in the middle of the night searching for my father, threatening to take us kids away from our mother. I must have slept through these wrenching events, but my older siblings did not, and it was emotionally scarring. We always had an unlisted phone number as I was growing up, and I was taught, for reasons that were never explained to me, to regard with suspicion anyone that called up asking questions.

I won't claim that our father being on the run from the law caused Ron's mental illness, but if there are any environmental factors that interact with genetic components, there was plenty of stress and problems available to blame. Once Ron started to spiral downward in 1973, his hurt about how his life changed after we left Alderwood expressed itself in a very ugly way. I remember one night when he threatened to call the FBI, and turn in our father. In ten minutes my father was packed, out of the house, and gone. Up to that point, I did not even know that he was wanted. These were bad times.

9.   ACID TRIPS & ANTI-PSYCHIATRY (1960-1980)

The post-World War II period may someday be described as the Hallucinogenic Era. Among intellectuals, hallucinogenic drugs created a new perception of mental illness. Psychiatrists found strong parallels between the LSD "trip" and schizophrenia: "hallucinations, intense anxiety, paranoia, unusual color perceptions, and feelings of depersonalization — where the boundaries between the self and beyond dissolved."[1] Some researchers felt that there might be some hope of developing a cure for schizophrenia by understanding how hallucinogenic drugs mimicked the disease.

Unfortunately, while most psychiatrists recognized hallucinogenic drugs as dangerous, a few members of the profession, and a few people outside the profession, came to a very different conclusion. Rather than recognize that hallucinogens were distorting reality, intellectuals such as Aldous Huxley decided that there was a great "Mind at Large" whose knowledge was only visible while taking hallucinogens. Huxley's argument was that the human brain screened out the vast quantity of information that was available to use, and that these drugs were taking away the screen.

If hallucinogens were opening people up to a larger and more important reality — and the results were superficially similar to schizophrenia — perhaps the schizophrenic was not really insane. He might simply have the advantage of lacking the "screen" that blocked ordinary people from accessing the "Mind at Large." Huxley's *The Doors of Perception*, promoting this point of view, was powerfully influential among intellectuals. There is an obvious parallel between the loss of latent inhibition among schizophrenics that we have previously discussed, and this "Mind at Large" concept. Perhaps Huxley's great "Mind at Large" is a bit more than mere humans can handle.

LSD contributed to deinstitutionalization in another way as well. Ken Kesey's 1962 book *One Flew Over the Cuckoo's Nest*, and then the 1975 film version, created a widespread perception that mental hospitals were run by sadists, and that mentally ill people were just free spirits in need of some love and friendship. Kesey had taken LSD as a volunteer in a study at Stanford. While working as a night attendant at a mental hospital, Kesey again took LSD. Those confined no longer seemed insane to Kesey, and he wrote the novel that poisoned a whole generation's understanding of mental illness and hospitals.[2] (As I have talked to people who work in the mental health profession over the years, this one film was high on their list of why judges refused to commit patients.)

Merging with this LSD-induced delusion was the emerging leftist assault on middle-class rationality. The radical politics of the 1960s increasingly regarded the subordination of emotion to reason as a mistake. The rejection of middle-class American values about property, capitalism, and sexual morality soon included a rejection of the definition of sanity. The insane might simply be more "authentic" than uptight Establishment squares who went to work every day, lived in the suburbs, and paid their taxes. Involuntary commitment only further strengthened the leftist identification of the mentally ill as victims of an oppressive system.[3]

Faris and Dunham's *Mental Disorders in Urban Areas* (1939), although published before World War II, certainly strongly encouraged this view that mental illness was one of the consequences of an oppressive system. Faris and Dunham plotted public and private mental hospital admissions for Chicago by last residence, then used a number of measures of wealth, "social disorganization," education, national origin, and race, in an attempt to determine if poverty, ethnicity, or social dysfunction was correlated with various psychoses.

Faris and Dunham succeeded admirably in their effort: schizophrenia, alcohol-related psychoses, and drug addiction were strongly correlated with the poorest and least educated sections of town.[4] Bipolar disorder was somewhat randomly scattered — although slightly more likely to be associated with sections of Chicago with higher income and higher education levels.[5] Syphilitic insanity was strongly correlated with those poor sections of Chicago where "many forms of prostitution flourish."[6]

Reading *Mental Disorders in Urban Areas* today reminds us of how strongly the dominant worldview can override critical thinking. Faris and Dunham argued that the strong correlation of poverty and lower education levels with schizophrenia demonstrated the power of environment, and largely discounted that there could be an organic cause. Yet the preface by University of Chicago sociology professor Ernest W. Burgess acknowledges that schizophrenia rates were very high among the homeless, and that this doubtless played some role in why the homeless lived on Chicago's Skid Row. (The book consistently and colorfully refers to this area as "hobohemia.")

> Hobohemia, the area where homeless men concentrate, has a disproportionately large number of cases of paranoid schizophrenia…. It is highly probable that they are persons who have failed to adjust to conditions of life in other communities and so have drifted downward and collected in Hobohemia.[7]

Faris and Dunham, by using the last known address before hospitalization, failed to account for the possibility that schizophrenics ended up in the poorest sections of town because their mental illness made it impossible for them to work and afford more affluent housing. Oddly, the authors discussed this as a possibility, but dismissed it both because bipolar disorder was randomly distributed, and also argued that it was "a question whether this drift process… is anything more than an insignificant factor in causing the concentration."[8]

With respect to syphilitic insanity, Faris and Dunham acknowledged the possibility that "persons with syphilis eventually lose their earning power, find it impossible to compete successfully with other members of their respective occupational groups, and consequently drift into the low-income groups."[9] Yet Faris and Dunham did not see that schizophrenics would be subject to this same problem!

By the 1960s, not only was the radical disapproval of psychiatric authority growing among laymen, but also among some psychiatrists. The American psychiatrist Thomas S. Szasz denied that mental illness even existed, except as a method by which the government suppressed nonconformism.[10] A few years later, Szasz wrote:

The facts are that, in the main, so-called madmen — the persons whom we now call schizophrenic and psychotic — are not so much disturbed as they are disturbing; it is not so much that they themselves suffer (although they may), but that they make others (especially members of their family) suffer. The consequences of these facts are that, in the main, so-called schizophrenics or psychotics do not regard or define themselves as ill and do not seek medical (or, often, any other kind of) help. Instead, other people — usually members of their family, sometimes their employers, the police, or other authorities — declare and define them as ill and seek and impose "help" on them.[11]

Szasz insisted that psychiatrists "invented" schizophrenia, in exactly the same way that John S. Pemberton "invented" Coca-Cola. If there were no psychiatrists, there would be no schizophrenia. Szasz argued that psychiatrists invented schizophrenia by analogy with syphilitic insanity (which Szasz at least admitted was a mental illness caused by syphilis) as a method of exerting social control over people who were not really sick. According to Szasz, the bizarre and disjointed statements of schizophrenics reflected not a mental illness, but that "often the only thing 'wrong' (as it were) with the so-called schizophrenic is that he speaks in metaphors unacceptable to his audience, in particular to his psychiatrist."[12]

You might wonder how a psychiatrist could believe that there was no such thing as insanity. Would not the exposure to psychotic patients during Szasz's training have shown him the error of his ideology? It turns out that Szasz may not have had *any* exposure to psychotics. In a 1997 interview, he describes how he consciously selected a psychiatric residency "that did not include work with involuntary patients." The chairman of the Psychiatry Department told him, "Tom, you have only one year left of your residency. I don't think it's right that you should finish without any experience with psychotic patients. I think you should do your third year at the Cook County Hospital." So Szasz quit, and went elsewhere to avoid that experience.

Szasz was drafted into the Navy after completing his training, and his experiences there almost certainly reinforced his already well-developed belief that mental illness did not exist. "The servicemen didn't want to be in the Navy and played the role of

mental patient. I didn't want to be in the Navy and played the role
of military psychiatrist: My job was to discharge the men from the
Service as 'neuropsychiatric casualties'."[13] Szasz had gone out of
his way to avoid seeing psychotic patients, and then took a job that
he describes as certifying that sane people pretending to be insane
were actually insane as a convenient fiction. Is there anything
surprising about Szasz's projection of this situation onto the entire
profession?

Even as the biochemical cause of schizophrenia became
increasingly clear in the 1980s, Szasz simply denied that it could be
real, because there were no identifiable brain structure problems
associated with it. In short, a mental illness that could not be
identified at autopsy as a neurological structure problem, by Szasz's
definition, could not be illness.[14] Szasz often used absurd and
inappropriate analogies — comparing psychiatric treatment of
schizophrenia with the maintenance of slavery before the Civil
War,[15] and comparing psychiatric treatment of psychosis to
religious ritual:

> When a priest blesses water, it turns into holy water — and thus
> becomes the carrier of the most beneficent powers. Similarly,
> when a psychiatrist curses a person, he turns into a schizophrenic
> — and thus becomes the carrier of the most maleficent powers.
> Like "divine" and "demonic," "schizophrenic" is a concept
> wonderfully vague in its content and terrifyingly awesome in its
> implications.

> In this book I shall try to show how schizophrenia has become
> the Christ on the cross that psychiatrists worship, and in whose
> name they march in the battle to reconquer reason from
> unreason, sanity from insanity; how reverence toward it has
> become the mark of psychiatric orthodoxy, and irreverence
> toward it the mark of psychiatric heresy; and how our
> understanding of both psychiatry and schizophrenia may be
> advanced by approaching this "diagnosis" as if it pointed to a
> religious symbol rather than to a medical disease.[16]

The best that could be said for Szasz's position is that it was
internally consistent with his libertarian ideology — but utterly
inconsistent with the evidence of the real world.

In Britain, R. D. Laing made a somewhat similar argument —

that what we call insanity was merely a rational reaction to an irrational world.[17] Why anyone took Laing seriously eludes me — but as J. Allan Hobson points out, Laing arrived at the right time, when the counterculture was rising.[18] Laing's 1960 book *The Divided Self* is a mixture of Freudian psychobabble and some fairly obviously incorrect assertions about the nature of schizophrenia:

> If, for instance, a man tells us he is 'an unreal man', and if he is not lying, or joking, or equivocating in some subtle way, there is no doubt that he will be regarded as deluded. But, existentially, what does this delusion mean? Indeed, he is not joking or pretending. On the contrary, he goes on to say that he has been pretending for years to have been a real person but can maintain the deception no longer....

> A good deal of schizophrenia is simply nonsense, red-herring speech, prolonged filibustering to throw dangerous people off the scent, to create boredom and futility in others. The schizophrenic is often making a fool of himself and the doctor. He is playing at being mad to avoid at all costs the possibility of being held *responsible* for a single coherent idea, or intention.[19]

Laing's claims evolved over time. At first he asserted that schizophrenia was a rational response to an unlivable family structure, and that by decoding the behavior and statements of schizophrenics, all of their seemingly insane actions and statements could be made rational. This was not a particularly radical position from a biochemical disorder perspective. The schizophrenic's senses *have* betrayed him, providing him with false information, around which a schizophrenic, with time, may construct a logical framework.

In the mid-1960s, British anti-nuclear activists gravitated to Laing's ideas, arguing that schizophrenia was more "properly human" in a world of hydrogen bombs than conventional definitions of sanity. By 1967, Laing had reached the point where he no longer believed that schizophrenia existed at all. It was only a label to describe a "political event." One of his fellow radicals argued that, "a person who is labeled insane is often the sanest member of his or her family."

Laing's ever evolving thinking next argued that schizophrenia was not a breakdown, but a breakthrough. By the 1970s, Laing took the position of Huxley's *The Doors of Perception*, that schizophrenia was a form of sanity, not insanity. Laing's position increasingly became a political attack on Western society, and then morphed once again, rejecting the idea of schizophrenia by declaring it as hypersanity.[20] Eventually, Laing's celebrity led him to India and to drug abuse, and he became a shell of his former self.[21]

Similarly, Michel Foucault in France promoted the idea of the asylum as a method of maintaining bourgeois social control.[22] Foucault argued that madness was merely opposition to the modern capitalist industrial society, and was equally valid with sanity. Foucault claimed that mental hospitals were part of the system of oppression, not a method for treating or protecting the mentally ill. American advocates for the homeless such as Mitch Snyder, who was reluctant to admit the role of insanity in causing homelessness, adopted this view: "A psychotic episode is a socio-political event and not a medical event."[23] It is not surprising that when Mitch Snyder found himself being audited for failure to pay income taxes, he committed suicide. As Jesse Jackson observed at Snyder's memorial service, "Mitch was a little eccentric, Mitch was a little off."[24]

In America, sociologists seeking a "value-free" method of understanding social deviance (including mental illness) became enchanted with the idea that deviance was primarily in the eye of the beholder — that society, by making rules, created deviance. Sociologists of the labeling school made the deviant — including those who were mentally ill — into victims, and the society into the bad guys. In a few cases, proponents of this model, such as Thomas Scheff, explicitly declared that the society had it backwards: what we call sanity is undesirable, and what we call insanity should really be the preferred condition.[25]

In later years, Scheff acknowledged that the case for his labeling theory of mental illness was weaker than when first published because of the biopsychiatric perspective. He acknowledged that his theory "had its highwater mark in the 1970s" and that by the early 1990s "it had been all but dismissed by the mainstream disciplines" — but he was still prepared to argue that it was at least "one of many partial points of view" that needed to be integrated with other perspectives.[26]

The intersection of this radical political interpretation of mental illness and the 1960s counterculture soon created movements with names such as Insane Liberation Front, Mental Patients Liberation Project, and Mental Patients Liberation Front. Soon, they had a journal, *Madness Network News*.[27] While organized primarily of those who had been hospitalized for mental problems, there were radical therapists involved as well — insistent that the *real* illness was capitalism.

Unsurprisingly, considering the level of political violence of the times, these ideas soon bore bloody fruit. By some accounts, the Baader-Meinhof terrorist group that assassinated German politicians and businessmen with guns and explosives from the 1970s through the 1990s came out of the Socialist Patients Collective, organized in Heidelberg in 1970.[28] Other accounts hold that the Socialist Patients Collective was a contemporary of the Baader-Meinhof group, which was formally organized at about the same time.[29] There does seem to be general agreement that the second generation of Baader-Meinhof included members of the Socialist Patients Collective, who had connections to Baader-Meinhof from the beginning.[30]

This Marxian view was not confined to the mentally ill. Along with Michel Foucault, writers such as David Rothman, Andrew Scull, and Roy Porter decided that the early nineteenth century expansion of insane asylums was not a response to increasing mental illness, or the complexities of the mentally ill living in increasingly anonymous big cities, but a method by which capitalism segregated those who were not suited to work in the new and more regimented system of urban factories.

Scull argued that psychiatrists enriched themselves by defining deviance as mental illness, so that they could profit from operating private mental hospitals. These Marxist models made for marvelous conspiracy theories, and might explain *private* insane asylums — but public institutions were a burden that impacted *all* taxpayers, especially the wealthy property owners who paid most of the taxes.[31] If the heartless capitalist class was simply looking out for its own economic interests, why not just leave the insane out in the streets to starve? Why create institutions that were substantially more expensive than the workhouses and poorhouses in which the mentally ill had formerly resided?

Blaming insanity on the struggles of competition in a capitalist society was not entirely a new idea. When, in the late 1940s, Goldhamer and Marshall first started examining statistical evidence concerning changing rates of psychosis over time, at least part of the reason was that many writers

> lean heavily on the presumption that these disorders are
> intimately related to characteristics of contemporary social
> existence, particularly those that are incident to the growth of
> "civilization.."... The psychiatrists of the 19th century also
> believed that mental disease was on the increase, and they, too,
> appealed to the competitive character of social existence and to
> increased personal responsibility and freedom as an
> explanation.[32]

As an example, Dr. Samuel B. Woodward in 1855 blamed the
fierce competition of America for mental illness. "But in the
contest, where so many strive, not a few break down. The results
on their minds may not, perhaps, be any less disastrous, whether
wealth and station are obtained or not. The true balance of the
mind is disturbed by prosperity as well as adversity."[33]

In 1960s America, anti-psychiatry's fusion with anti-capitalist
doctrine was less violent than in Europe, but the rhetoric seems no
less ludicrous today — such as including "mentalism" with racism
and sexism as evils of our society, because it gave sane people a
preferred status over a person who was mentally ill.[34] As absurd as
these claims were, they might be best understood as a reaction to
the way in which the dynamic psychiatric model had completely
undermined a biological basis for understanding mental illness.

In the 1960s, several studies attempted to measure the
effectiveness of psychoanalysis relative to the use of antipsychotic
medications. One such study took place at Massachusetts Mental
Health Center in Boston, led by two psychiatrists who believed that
psychoanalysis was effective in treating schizophrenia. Their goal
was a controlled experiment that would provide the statistical
evidence to support this belief. The most renowned psychoanalysts
in the Boston area were part of the experiment. When the results
were in, the conclusions were clear: the antipsychotic medications
clearly helped, but psychoanalysis made no measurable
improvement in the condition of the patients. Other studies came
to similar conclusions — and psychoanalysis as a treatment for the
most severely mentally ill went into decline.[35]

LSD and an emerging skepticism of the concept that there was
one reality encouraged a generation of intellectuals to regard
psychosis and its break from reality as only a social construct —

something that reflected only the biases and assumptions of the dominant culture.   The Soviet Union had blatantly misused psychiatric treatment to punish political dissidents; Western psychiatry had used the label of "mentally ill" to justify often cruel treatment of homosexuals and other deviants from the social norms of the time. These examples seemed to argue in favor of the social construct model.   The abuses of psychiatry cast doubt on its legitimate claims. As is often the case, the overreaching claims of dynamic psychiatry about only a small fraction of the population being mentally healthy damaged the credibility of the more modest claims of traditional psychiatry.

For these reasons, Szasz's and Laing's ideas for a while enjoyed some popularity, and contributed towards an increasing willingness to destroy the existing public mental hospital system worldwide. All of these radical critiques of psychiatry soon combined with dynamic psychiatry's enthusiasm for community mental health treatment as an alternative to the now discredited institutional mental health system.

10.   "SNAKEPITS" TO CHMCS (1945-1980)

Throughout the Depression and World War II, state governments were chronically short on funds. One result was that states allowed their public mental hospitals to deteriorate, with limited expansion and worsening staff to patient ratios. Insufficient building and staffing budgets led to severe overcrowding and a decline in the quality of care.[1] A ward for incontinent men held 300 patients — who were never given clothes, presumably, to reduce laundry requirements. A lack of rooms meant that patients slept in corridors.[2] While a few states recognized the severity of these problems, most did not — and even states that confronted the problem found themselves helpless to make changes during the war.[3]

A curious situation also assisted in exposing this decline in conditions. Conscientious objectors who refused military service during World War II were often given alternative national service as attendants in state mental hospitals. These C.O.s were not particularly concerned about keeping silent to keep their jobs — they weren't there by choice. They were also men with strongly held moral beliefs, and unsurprisingly, when they saw bad conditions, they were quite prepared to let journalists, legislators, and opinion makers know about it.[4]

Psychiatrists were generally accepting of the criticism, which focused on a lack of funds for staff and maintenance. The professional staffs were not the bad guys. Even those psychiatrists who were partial to community treatment recognized that in their wildest dreams, public mental hospitals would be necessary for a very long time, and improving funding and staffing enjoyed support across the profession.[5]

After World War II, when state governments again turned their attention to the existing mental hospital system, most were willing to spend money — and did so, building more hospitals and hiring more staff. Public funding of mental hospitals rose from $568 million in 1954 to $854 million in 1959 — more than a 50 percent gain in five years.[6] Most psychiatrists, many of whom now had limited contact with the public mental hospital system because of the boom in private practice for the affluent starting around 1920, still thought of these institutions as though it was 1940.[7]

Increased funding improved conditions within most public mental hospitals (more so in some states than others), but many remained "snake pits," to borrow the title of Mary Jane Ward's very popular 1946 novel about mental hospitals, *The Snake Pit*. The American Psychiatric Association created the Central Inspection Board in 1947 to evaluate existing mental hospitals in the United States and Canada. The results were not encouraging. By 1953, it had evaluated 45 hospitals, approved two, given ten a "contingent approval" and disapproved the rest.[8]

Yet, at the same time that many psychiatrists and the general public increasingly saw public mental hospitals as custodial institutions, places without hope — something very positive *was* happening. There *were* patients who entered public mental hospitals, and stayed there for life — the elderly suffering from senility, the syphilitic insane, and many schizophrenics. These were a large fraction of the population of public mental hospitals, and for patients in these categories, there was little that the system could do for them.

For many others, however, the public mental health system worked. A study of 15,000 patients admitted to Pennsylvania's Warren State Hospital between 1916 and 1950 found that 42 percent of first admissions in the period 1919-25 were released within a year. In the interval 1946-50, first admissions released within a year had increased to 62 percent. National studies by the Biometrics Branch of the National Institute of Mental Health for the period from 1940 to 1950 showed that first admission schizophrenics were recovering, and being discharged, in shorter intervals. The senile, the syphilitic, and the chronic schizophrenics, who were a large fraction of public mental hospital patients, created a false perception of public mental hospitals as hopeless institutions.[9]

Still, recovery of the mental health system after World War II was not uniform. In some ideal world, every psychiatric hospital would have been a cheery place filled with concerned people committed to curing the curable, and caring for those who could not get well. The reality was much more ugly than that. Even in mid-1960s California, flush with public funding, I can remember reading newspaper articles that reported conditions in California mental hospitals among the severely retarded that shocked the conscience.

The introduction of the first really effective antipsychotic medications, such as chlorpromazine and reserpine, certainly played some role in deinstitutionalization. New York State started widely using these drugs in 1955, making patients more manageable while institutionalized — and for at least some patients, more capable of being returned to their homes. Patients treated with the medicines had twice the discharge rate (20 percent) of those in the control group. Not only did these drugs reduce the need for physical restraints but staff found the patients more pleasant to manage and treat: "more like general hospital patients and less like prisoners." Perhaps most encouraging, the number of suicides fell.[10] That some state mental health officials felt a need to warn of the dangers of overoptimism[11] suggests that professionals and the public were in danger of repeating the mistakes of the nineteenth century's cult of curability.

The wartime experience of rapid psychotherapeutic treatment of soldiers, in combination with the perception of state mental hospitals as "snake pits," made a community mental health center (CMHC) approach seem all the more attractive. The National Mental Health Act of 1946 gave the National Institute of Mental Health discretionary funding authority that both launched CMHC research, and some limited creation of CMHCs.[12]

One objective of deinstitutionalization was to end the depersonalization that large institutions were believed to cause. When the Congressionally-funded Joint Commission on Mental Illness and Health issued its 1961 report, it argued that no more state mental hospitals exceeding 1000 beds should be built.[13] One of those involved in the Joint Commission later admitted that his "hidden agenda was to break the back of the state mental hospital," but the Joint Commission was not prepared to go quite that far — at first.[14] In 1963, Professor Henry Weihofen of George Washington University was doubtless speaking for many of his colleagues when he spoke of the advantages of treating the mentally ill outside of large institutions:

> Psychiatrists I think are pretty clear in feeling that where the person is has a tremendous effect on what happens to him. To ship [him] off to a state hospital where he stays far away, out of sight and out of mind, has a harmful effect on him and makes therapy a good deal more difficult. It he could live at home, in good surroundings, that would probably be best.

> Sometimes of course the home atmosphere is not good. But at least we can provide facilities within the community, outpatient facilities, clinics, nursing homes, and so forth. I think we are moving in that direction. [15]

Another motivation for moving mental health treatment into "Neighborhood Health Centers" was to destigmatize mental illness, and increase both availability and utilization of mental health services by having them available in the same building as primary care physicians. Community mental health advocates also hoped that because primary care physicians saw many patients with physical problems who also had mental problems, these local facilities would make it easier for physicians to provide referrals and coordinate care with psychiatrists. Perhaps most optimistic of all was the hope that, "The provision of mental health services within the NHC can increase the priority of and concern for mental health problems among community citizens."[16]

The first phase of deinstitutionalization was characterized as "opening the back doors" of the mental hospitals. This meant that those who had been recently admitted would be released as soon as possible after stabilization, and "higher functioning long-stay patients" would be moved into community care programs. A consequence of this policy was that many of these patients were readmitted when it became apparent that they could not handle a return to the community.[17]

By 1977, community mental health center advocates claimed that not only did existing large institutions need to close, but, "the very legality of constructing isolated institutions under present federal law is suspect." While acknowledging that there were persons with severe disabilities that still required "lifelong, 24-hour, institutional-type care" it was easy to believe that such situations would be by far the exception.[18]   As the Joint

Commission saw the future in 1961, community mental health centers and general hospital psychiatric units would provide treatment for those with "acute mental illness" and care for mental hospital patients after release. The goal was not to abolish state mental hospitals, but to catch mental illness in its earliest stages, and thus make hospitalization less necessary.

But along with reducing the size of state mental hospitals, the Joint Commission wanted them transformed from largely custodial institutions to treatment-intensive mental hospitals: institutions that would cure those who were considered curable.[19]   Unlike the radicals of the anti-psychiatry movement, the Joint Commission knew that mental illness was real, and had no illusions about being able to prevent it.[20]

The Kennedy Administration looked at the 1961 Joint Commission report, and decided to take action — but perhaps not quite the action the report recommended.   That report saw community mental health centers (CHMCs) as part of a system to reduce the load on state mental hospitals. With substantially fewer patients, state mental hospitals would have the resources to devote to treatment, not simply custodial care.[21] The Joint Commission was not opposed to public mental hospitals (although limited to 1000 beds each), but wanted to expand the list of options for treating the mentally ill.

Those psychiatrists who worked in the public mental hospitals — and who were the most knowledgeable about the conditions and challenges of dealing with the severely mentally ill — led the attack on a number of the Joint Commission's proposals, characterizing them as unproven and unrealistic. Perhaps most interesting of all, considering the popular perception of public mental hospitals as custodial, Newton Bigelow, the leading critic, objected to the Joint Commission's proposal to label some patients as "chronically mentally ill" who would be placed in "custodial, second-class hospital[s]" with the senile and the syphilitic insane. Bigelow found the concept "barbaric" because it meant giving up hope for patients who might still be cured, or at least might go into remission. In spite of the strong criticisms from those with the greatest expert knowledge, when Congress considered the bill, there were no legislative opponents to the community-centered approach, which treated large public mental hospitals as a relic of the past.[22]

The Kennedy Administration instead proposed, and Congress

passed the Community Mental Health Centers Act of 1963, with CHMCs essentially replacing state mental hospitals. CMHCs would both *prevent* mental illness and treat the chronically ill on an outpatient basis. There was simply no basis for believing that mental illness could be prevented, and President Kennedy's comforting claim that two-thirds of schizophrenics "could be treated and released within 6 months," based on the initial results of using chlorpromazine (Thorazine), turned out to be overly optimistic.

State mental hospitals were supposed to receive some federal funding as CMHCs replaced the function of the state mental hospital, because, as Kennedy again cheerily promised, "[I]t will be possible within a decade or two to reduce the number of patients now under custodial care by 50 percent or more."[23] The level of funding through the Hospital Improvement Program, however, turned out to be quite minor. Grants were limited to $100,000 per year. The objective was to make minor improvements to public mental hospitals as they withered away, to be largely replaced by CMHCs.[24] (Not all agree that the deinstitutionalization and CMHC connection was this strong. Brown argues that CMHCs and deinstitutionalization were competing policies, and that advocates of both who claimed to have a coherent national mental health policy were overselling what they were bringing to the table.)[25]

There were certainly patients treated in CHMCs who, in the 1950s, might otherwise have ended up in a state mental hospital. The extant evidence, however, suggests that CMHCs were treating those with the *least* serious mental disorders. Much as psychotherapy treated primarily those with money but relatively minor emotional problems, CMHCs predominately helped low-income women with "nonsevere psychological disorders," not the severely mentally ill. Even had those with severe mental illness showed up for help, it is unclear how much the CMHCs could have done, since psychiatrists were only a tiny part of the clinical staff.[26] In the years before passage of the federal Mental Retardation and Community Mental Health Centers Construction Act of 1963, the emphasis of activists was clearly on the non-disabling emotional problems and preventative mental health care, with insufficient attention to how, if at all, psychotics would benefit from CMHCs.[27]

There was also an ugly political motivation for the destruction of the state mental hospital system. When the Kennedy Administration proposed what became the Community Mental

Health Centers Act of 1963, the advocates for CMHCs had not spoken with one voice about federal assistance to state mental hospitals. Some CMHC advocates wanted federal funding to improve the conditions of state mental hospitals; others felt that it was best to encourage deinstitutionalization. John Kennedy's 1960 election was at least in part the result of winning large majorities of the urban poor. Federal funding of state mental hospitals would have been a general benefit to each state; the CMHC system would more directly pour federal money into inner cities. As James Cameron explains, "Directing the flow of federal funds to newly created community organizations and integrating community activists into program implementation would serve to generate community support for the new federal initiatives; moreover, it would foster strong political support among the poor and disfranchised for the Democratic party."[28]

Less ugly, but reflecting the changing political sentiments of the 1950s and 1960s, mental health activists saw the predominance of state governments in mental health issues as an outdated strategy. As with many other social issues of the time, the activists saw the state governments as "backward, parsimonious, and reactionary." The solution was to move public policy setting to the federal government, who could be counted upon to be progressive and generous for such an important cause.[29]

Governmental finance considerations played a role, but not the heartless "let them eat cake" attitude that homeless advocates of the 1980s imagined. Especially because such a large number of patients were not curable, the costs were staggering. In 1951, states were spending an average of eight percent of their total operating budgets on mental hospitals. There was again considerable variation, with some states spending as little as two percent, while New York State spent one-third of its budget on mental hospitals.[30]

A series of federal commissions, in both Canada and the United States, advocated the transfer of mental patients from centralized, usually custodial institutions to community mental health centers. By providing federal funds for local mental health centers, the 1963 Community Mental Health Centers Act encouraged states to return inmates of state mental hospitals to communities. The custodial mental hospitals were funded by the states; the community mental health centers by the federal government. With this economic incentive, the states implemented a policy that appeared to humane and caring Americans as a step forward.

11.   EMPTYING THE "SNAKEPITS" (1965 - 1980)

At the same time that CMHCs were replacing public mental hospitals, President Johnson's Great Society of the 1960s expanded assistance to the disabled, encouraging both physically and mentally disabled Americans to live outside of state institutions, which encouraged the disabled to live on their own.[1]

For the mentally disabled, CMHCs were to be part of the extrainstitutional support network. The federal government spent what would eventually become more than $3 billion setting up CMHCs, back when a billion dollars was a lot more than it is now. The regulations setting up the CMHCs, however, somewhat shortchanged the chronic mental patients who would soon be turned loose. At least one of the officials of the National Institute of Mental Health, the agency responsible for the regulations, later observed that, "CHMCs were originally intended more to serve new constituencies in their own communities than large numbers of a great under-constituency of patients discharged 'better but not well' from mental institutions into these communities."[2]

Nor does this appear to have been a later rationalization for the failure of CMHCs to help the severely mentally ill; the initial language defining their intended clientele explicitly included those who were not severely mentally ill.[3] One of the officials of the CMHC program later admitted that the CMHCs "were not equipped to deal" with the chronically mentally ill,[4] who were about to be released in large numbers, from state mental hospitals.

The belief that mental hospitals caused mental illness, or at least made the mentally ill worse off than they were before, combined with an idealized view of how caring communities would be for the severely mentally ill. The activists and bureaucrats who wrote the CMHC regulations were about to start the release of mental patients into caring communities that, for the most part, *did not exist*. As one of those involved later admitted: "We were federal bureaucrats on an NIMH campus talking about the community, but really from some conceptual level as opposed to hands-on experience."[5]

If CMHCs were not primarily serving the chronically mentally ill, then whom were they serving? Two especially notorious examples were Lincoln Hospital Mental Services in New York City and Temple University Community Mental Health Center in Philadelphia. In both cases, the belief that mental illness was somehow an expression of class struggle meant that broader social and political causes — such as landlord/tenant relations, poverty, and oppression — became significant activities of the staff. Racial and ethnic tensions within the staff destroyed both CMHCs, with threats of violence, sit-ins, Viet Cong flags, posters of Che Guevara and Malcolm X as symbols of the fight. What did this have to do with mental illness, except, perhaps, as an example of organizations that needed to heal themselves first?[6]

These two CMHCs were the most extreme examples, but at its core, the CMHC movement believed that preventing mental illness meant preventing the environment that caused mental illness. This meant going after capitalism, poverty, and racism, which many of the CMHC advocates and activists had persuaded themselves caused the disproportionate mental illness of the inner cities.[7] A 1971 article in the black magazine, *Jet,* quoted "Drs. Claudewell S. Thomas of the National Institute of Mental Health... and James P. Comer of the Yale Medical School, two Black psychiatrists" as arguing that therapists were needed that would help black patients accept that "the society can be wrong." Thomas and Comer praised the development of CMHCs as "a giant step forward" but that the mental health care system "must encompass some effort at changing the basic racist background."[8]

Along with the problems of radical politics, a 1967 survey of eight early CMHCs found serious non-political confusion about their objectives. In spite of Congressional intent that CMHCs should provide outpatient services to those who might otherwise end up in state mental hospitals, all eight sent patients to the state mental hospital if they believed that a person would require "long-term" treatment, which they defined as more than seven days. The National Institute of Mental Health (NIMH) asked proponents of the CMHC movement, and directors of the CMHCs, to explain what they were doing, especially with respect to chronic schizophrenics. The answers were astonishingly candid, acknowledging that "community treatment" for some of the patients that were then being released from state mental hospitals was neither better for the patients, nor for the communities to which they returned. As Isaac and Armat observed, "If the testimony at Congressional hearings a few years earlier had been so candid, it is doubtful the centers would ever have been funded."

Worse, it became apparent that now that the CMHCs were funded, and the mental hospitals were releasing psychotics to the streets, advocates of deinstitutionalization essentially said that the chronically mentally ill were not their problem, or at least not their only concern.[9] CMHCs did not replace mental hospitals, nor did they provide much in the way of care for the newly deinstitutionalized mental patients.[10] The CMHCs were there to help the neurotic, and those with "less persistent mental disorders." And of course, *preventing* mental illness, by engaging in social activism, was the real goal for many of the CMHC proponents.

By the latter part of the 1960s, CMHC funding increasingly provided substance abuse treatment for young, poor, nonwhite populations. While there are certainly mental illnesses that are induced or aggravated by substance abuse, CMHC funding for substance abuse was not specific to the mentally ill. CMHCs became another mechanism for providing social services with more and more tenuous connections to the severely mentally ill.[11]

When the American Psychiatric Association studied eleven of the new CMHCs in 1966 (and apparently ones not in the inner city), they found many of the same treatments used in public mental hospitals, including drugs and electroconvulsive therapy. But the primary focus was individual psychotherapy, "an intervention especially adapted to a middle-class educated clientele and congenial as well to professional staff." The APA was skeptical that individual psychotherapy was necessarily the best choice for the well-educated middle class patients with whom the psychotherapists had much in common. They were even more concerned about the appropriateness and effectiveness of such an approach with the poorly educated, culturally different racial minorities that CMHCs were *supposed* to help.[12]

In the 1970s, many CMHCs went further down the path of providing psychotherapy for people who did not have *serious* mental illness problems. Increasingly, CMHCs were not even focusing their energies on the racially and economically oppressed population that some thought the CMHCs were supposed to target. As one defender of CMHCs admitted, the staff at many of these facilities primarily did "dynamically oriented analytic psychotherapy. People who had interesting dreams."[13]

The percentage of CMHC patients who were schizophrenics, the most serious and chronic of mental illnesses, fell from 15 percent to 10 percent between 1970 and 1975. This was at a time when vast numbers of schizophrenics were being released from state mental hospitals. In some CMHCs, families of the severely mentally ill reported being forced to use separate waiting rooms, out of fear that they would scare off people who were there for counseling.[14]

Predictably, audits began to show that many CMHCs were improperly spending federal money. Federal construction funds were used to build swimming pools and tennis courts at several CMHCs. Orlando Regional Medical Center used grants intended to hire staff to hire a gardener, lifeguard, and swimming instructor. There *were* CHMCs that *exactly* fulfilled the original promise: provide after-hospitalization care for the mentally ill, and mental illness treatment early enough to substantially reduce admissions to state mental hospitals. But these were very much the exception.[15]

In 1965, the dramatic expansion of the elderly population, and increasing concern about the poor, encouraged Congress to create two new insurance programs that included psychiatric benefits: Medicare (for the elderly) and Medicaid (for the poor). Both programs provided for up to 190 days per lifetime for psychiatric treatment in freestanding mental hospitals, but with no limits in *general* hospitals (some of which had psychiatric wards) and nursing homes. Both programs essentially decided to encourage treatment of the mentally ill in the institutions least specific to mental illness.

Because Medicare would not reimburse states for caring for the senile elderly in state mental hospitals, but would pay private nursing homes for this care, the senile elderly became a federal responsibility; the states quickly moved such patients into private nursing facilities.[16] In California, for example, "the number of elderly housed in state and county mental hospitals declined by almost 95 per cent between 1955 and 1977."[17]

Nationally, the mental hospital institutionalization rate for those 65 years and older fell from 773 to 164 per 100,000 between 1965 and 1979. The vast majority of these were not deinstitutionalized, but transinstitutionalized — moved from the largely custodial back wards of public mental hospitals to (usually) for profit nursing homes.[18] By the late 1970s, nursing home surveys showed that many of the elderly patients who had moved from public mental hospitals to nursing homes were suffering from various psychiatric disorders — and nursing homes were often woefully deficient in psychiatric diagnosis and treatment.[19]

The custodial "back ward" of the public mental hospital had not gone away; it had simply moved from a centralized, easily observable non-profit public institution to a usually profit-making private institution that was less easy to check for competence and mistreatment of patients. While the public mental hospital might fail to care for its charges, it at least had no economic incentive to cut corners. The relocation of the elderly into private nursing homes "was often marked by increases in the death rate."[20] It is not difficult to see how aggressive cost-cutting could increase death rates among a population already mentally incompetent, and thus unlikely to bring attention to poor nursing care.

Changes in direct funding to the disabled also altered the equation. For the physically disabled, the expanding government program that provided them with disability checks doubtless increased individual dignity. For those suffering from mental illness, the interaction of disability checks, addiction, and self-medication, produced a generation living on steam grates, in cardboard boxes, and on park benches, with predictable effects on their physical health. The scale of movement was dramatic, with a 62 percent decline in mental hospital population between 1955 and 1974.

The number of mental hospital beds declined by 50 percent between 1970 and 1984 (from 524,878 to 262,673). Most of the decrease was in state and county mental hospitals (413,066 to 130,411). At the same time, there was an increase in private psychiatric hospital beds (14,295 to 21,474) and more than a doubling of the psychiatric ward beds in general hospitals (22,394 to 46,045). The total capacity of the system, including residential treatment schools (such as are often used for teenagers with serious mental illness problems) and Veterans Administration psychiatric hospitals, however, suffered a dramatic reduction.[21]

Large numbers of non-elderly mental patients were no longer

under direct, supervised care. There was considerable variation from state to state, with California being perhaps the most dramatic. There was a 67 percent decline in non-elderly mental hospital patients between 1955 and 1977, driven by a conscious decision to provide care in community-based mental health treatment facilities.[22] In the period 1955 to 1990, the number of public mental hospital patients fell from 559,000 to 110,000[23], at a time when the population of the United States rose from just under 166 million to more than 249 million[24]: a 50 per cent increase. (Of course, some of this decline was the movement of the senile elderly — an important point that some opponents of deinstitutionalization fail to adequately acknowledge.)

At least *part* of the decline in the number of mental hospital patients was because there was a decline in the average length of stay — and only some of this was because of deinstitutionalization. The increased use of psychotropic drugs certainly played a part in this decline, as it became faster to stabilize patients with both psychoses and suicidal depression.

Public and private mental hospitals both experienced a decline in the average duration of a patient's stay, but the differing rates of change suggest that deinstitutionalization was probably the more important reason for the decline. The average stay in *public* mental hospitals dropped from forty-one days in 1970 to twenty-three days in 1980, while the rapidly expanding *private* mental hospital system experienced a far less dramatic change, from an average stay of twenty days to nineteen days over the same interval. [25]

If the shortening length of stays in the public hospitals was a sign of how much more effectively they were treating patients, it is a little strange that the private hospitals were not making equal progress. The admissions rates for public mental hospitals during this period also show that these shorter stays were not just because they were curing patients so much more quickly in 1980 compared to 1970. Instead, the public mental hospitals operated a revolving door system, in which patients were stabilized enough to be pushed out the door — and then readmitted a few months to a few years later.

Another curious factor is the changing demographics of mental hospital admissions during this period. By 1980, racial minorities and males were becoming a larger part of public mental hospitals. Racial minorities were admitted at more than twice the rate of whites in 1980, while in private mental hospitals, admissions rates were nearly identical. Public mental hospitals also admitted a far larger proportion of schizophrenics and mental patients with alcohol-related mental problems than private hospitals.[26] This should be no surprise. Schizophrenia and alcohol-related mental illness often develops over a period of time, during which an employed (and therefore usually insured) person becomes unemployed and uninsured. Consequently, unless a family member with significant resources steps in, these two categories would be especially likely to end up in a public hospital.

While the number of patients in state mental hospitals fell dramatically, state funds that had been spent on the institutionalized did not follow those patients to the streets.[27] The net effect was to increase the funding per patient available to state mental hospitals. From 1970 onward, the beneficial effect for those who remained was measurable.[28] Unfortunately, as is often the case, the public's perception and even the psychiatric profession's perception of mental hospitals as hopeless "snake pits" persisted, even as the institutions improved in their ability to treat the most severe cases.

In 1972, Congress again expanded the safety network by creating the Supplemental Security Income for the Aged, the Disabled, and the Blind program (commonly called SSI). Because many of the mentally ill were disabled (*i.e.*, unable to work), they were eligible for SSI payments in addition to Social Security disability payments. The theory was that these payments would be sufficient for mentally ill persons to live in the community, instead of in a state mental hospital. In combination with the emerging civil libertarian pressure (to be discussed in a later chapter), this encouraged many states to release patients from state mental hospitals.[29]

As late as 1977, one could still find optimistic statements such as: "[T]he thrust toward deinstitutionalization will help the mentally ill to find treatment and support within their own communities and will allay the burden that institutionalization has often imposed upon them."[30] The same year, President Carter's Commission on Mental Health looked at the existing CMHC system, and again argued that the current objective on treating everyone with any mental problems, rather than narrowly focusing on the severely mentally ill, made sense.[31]

Many of the deinstitutionalized patients did successfully return to the community, and studies show that for some, this was an improvement over the regimented, often hopeless conditions of state mental hospitals.[32]   Several studies completed in the 1980s concluded that deinstitutionalized schizophrenics did as well — and sometimes better — in community treatment than in mental hospitals.   Still, the high numbers of schizophrenics among the homeless in the 1980s suggests that what might work well for the average was a disaster for a minority.[33]

Grob argues that the first wave of mental patients, those released in 1965 and immediately thereafter, did relatively well because they were older adults, and had spent many years dealing with the rules of institutions.[34]   One conjecture is that having learned to follow the disciplinary rules of a state mental hospital, they were prepared to discipline themselves on the outside. More recent studies of deinstitutionalization of long stay patients in Britain have found similarly positive outcomes.   But again, the average age of these patients was 54 years — and significantly, "There was considerable loss of data over the five-year follow-up due to deaths and refusals [to participate] by patients."[35]   Would the data be so encouraging with the missing data points included?

For a younger generation — those who had never been hospitalized, or whose stays were short — the results were not so good.[36]   After 1970, the mentally ill were increasingly Baby Boomers with either limited time in a state mental hospital, or who, because of the civil liberties revolution, had never been subject to long-term hospitalization.   Furthermore, these mentally ill Baby Boomers were younger than those deinstitutionalized in the period 1965 to 1970.   Perhaps because of age, or perhaps because of the countercultural movement of those years, they were more mobile, and less rooted to persons and community institutions that might have helped them.

Differing patterns of substance abuse might also explain some of the generational difference.   Just as substance abuse was more common among healthy Baby Boomers, the mentally ill part of this generation was also more likely to aggravate their problems through intoxication and psychoactive drugs.[37]   At least since 1963, psychiatrists have recognized that there is a complex relationship between drug abuse and mental illness, with mentally ill people using intoxicants as a form of self-medication — but that this drug abuse also aggravated existing mental illness.[38]

Yet the CMHC advocates continued to claim that the system was working well.   Much like the "cult of curability" in the nineteenth century, the Community Mental Health Centers

Amendments of 1975 bill claimed that this system was working well to coordinate "successful treatment of the mentally ill." In the late 1980s, James Cameron characterized this as "a procrustean determination to make the evidence fit the theory."[39]

Anyone living in an American big city at the time could see that while some mental patients were, indeed, returned to the community, many others had been returned to the streets. The combination of disability payments and SSI would have provided a meager existence for a person who was completely sane; because checks arrived monthly, budgeting was often a strain. But for persons who were delusional, using intoxicants as a form of self-medication, often living by themselves, this governmental assistance often meant two or three weeks in a urine-soaked hotel (like the places I sometimes had to enter to find my brother), and the remainder of the month was spent sleeping in doorways or alleys.

Deinstitutionalization was not limited to the United States. Canada followed a somewhat similar model, with Ontario provincial mental hospitals holding 19,507 patients in 1960, and 5,030 patients in 1976, a period in which the province's population rose 32.5 per cent.[40] As the studies referenced on previous pages show, Britain also seems to be headed down this same path, somewhat later than North America.

By the late 1970s, the changing mixture of interest groups, and the general rightward drift of American politics, caused a change in federal government policy. Many of the liberal social activists who had played a role in passage of the CMHC Act of 1963 were dead or retired. Unions who represented workers in public mental hospitals began to look out for the interests of their members, but also, the full consequences of deinstitutionalization were becoming apparent.[41] In response to this, and a General Accounting Office report critical of how CMHCs were dealing with the severely mentally ill, the Mental Health Systems Act of 1980 sought to change the focus of CMHCs to the chronically mentally ill.[42]

Another useful change was how funds were distributed. Up to this point, federal funding for mental illness, alcoholism, and drug abuse, had been in the form of "categorical grants," which funded specific programs. These grants involved substantial federal oversight, and were tied to specific locations. States had effectively no discretion in how to spend those funds, or to reallocate them in response to changing community needs. Starting in 1981, the Reagan Administration replaced the categorical grants with block grants to the states, to spend as each state saw fit.

The Reagan Administration had several objectives. The Reagan Administration was concerned that the federal government had encroached on powers and responsibilities that the Constitution gave to the states. More pragmatically, there was a belief that the states were better suited to making decisions about spending, because they were closer to the problem, and would be more efficient in the spending of federal money than the federal agencies and the local agencies that received categorical grants.

Another problem was that the existing CMHCs and categorical grant system had spent too little on the most severely mentally ill, and too much on those with relatively less severe problems. There was also a perception that the categorical grant system had failed to adequately coordinate programs at city and state levels, because the organizational model was by program, not by geography.

In many respects, the change in funding model achieved the desired results. Federal funding fell dramatically after block grants replaced categorical grants, from $625,100,000 in 1980, to $487,300,000 in 1988 (roughly a 24 percent drop, after adjusting for inflation). However, states made up, and sometimes more than made up the difference from their own budgets. Some of the hoped for efficiency improvements also seemed to happen, as states found themselves spending less on reporting to the federal agencies.

Perhaps most importantly, the tendency of CMHCs to focus on those with emotional problems alone, at the expense of the chronically and severely mentally ill, changed. State control over funds and the corresponding guideline changes meant that the severely mentally ill, those who were most desperately in need of CMHC help, were now getting it.[43] While the Reagan Administration generally reduced funding to programs aimed at the poor, programs aimed at helping the severely mentally ill were less impacted than many others.[44]

All of these well-intentioned reasons to deinstitutionalize the mentally ill had one great advantage, compared to the forces at work in a later chapter: they were legislatively mandated. The actions of a state legislature or of Congress could be reversed or adjusted by a subsequent legislative act, as different policies were tried and found wanting. As we will see in a later chapter, there were other forces that drove deinstitutionalization that were less easy to correct.

12.   "SHE WAS TALKIN' ABOUT HER NICKELS"

My senior year of high school was 1973-74. Somewhere in this painful year, Ron was arrested in downtown Santa Monica. He had approached a couple walking through the older outdoor mall, and kicked the man. "She was talkin' about all her nickels," was how Ron explained his actions. Not surprisingly, he was again arrested, and hospitalized at Camarillo State Hospital for observation. He was again released after fourteen days, and another trip to court, where a judge decided that there was not sufficient reason to commit him.

After his release, Ron ended up staying at Hirschhorn Manor, an apartment building in Santa Monica that was now a residential treatment center for the mentally ill. He started seeing a psychiatrist at the Veterans Administration in Westwood, who finally decided that Ron needed to be hospitalized again. Unfortunately, the psychiatrist said this within Ron's hearing, and he took off.

Somewhere during this time, my father decided to take no chances about my safety. My bedroom was separate from the rest of the house, above the garage, and therefore especially vulnerable. My father put two massive bolts into the studs on either side of the door. On one of the bolts he mounted a 4x4 piece of wood that latched down over the other bolt. It was all quite medieval — but it also meant that nothing short of a battering ram could force that door.

Ron's disability check was surprisingly large. It was not enough money to live a normal, middle class existence, but enough to pay his rent and keep him fed. Because Ron's mental illness came so soon after he had been working in highly paid jobs, my brother's disability check, after only a few years of working, was substantially higher than my father's Social Security disability check, and my father had worked for more than forty years as an encyclopedia salesman, bookkeeper, and welder.

Ron moved to an apartment in the Miracle Mile area of Los Angeles, a block or two south of Wilshire Boulevard, paying his rent with his Social Security disability check. Doubtless, the landlord must have noticed that there was something a bit odd about my brother, but it did not prevent Ron from renting a small, not terribly expensive apartment.

Within a few months of that move, Ron had decided that he was trapped by his possessions. He was going to hitchhike to the East Coast. He informed my parents that he didn't care what happened to his stuff. We were welcome to come and get it from his mid-Wilshire apartment; otherwise, it was the landlord's problem. We had only two or three days to box and move Ron's possessions, while Ron thumbed his way east on Interstate 10. My father told me that I was free to take anything that I wanted, for having salvaged it. More than thirty years later, I'm still using Ron's desk. It's old, and a bit battered, but it works — and it is a link to a time of pain, but also a time when I still hoped that Ron would get well and recover.

My parents could not continue to live in the Los Angeles area, as the cost of housing rose. They moved out of Santa Monica at the end of my first year of college. The chaos of Ron's situation certainly played a part in creating considerable tension between them. My mother was content to live in their camper and travel around the Western U.S.; my father wanted something a bit more spacious and permanent. (My father was 6'0"; my mother was 5'2" — it was easy to see why one of them felt a bit crowded in that camper, and the other did not!)

Eventually, they moved to Lenwood, a small town on the outskirts of Barstow, in California's Mojave Desert. The house wasn't pretty — it was actually condemned — but they were able to buy it for $5000 in 1975, and started to work on bringing it back to code while living in the camper. I moved into a series of apartments, sometimes with roommates, sometimes by myself. (I had dropped out of college after my first year, partly because of the economic stress of trying to support myself while going to school. Fortunately, I had taught myself software engineering in high school, and found a job at Jet Propulsion Labs, working on the

Voyager mission.)

Over the next several years, Ron would call from hospitals, usually to my parents, more rarely to me. Most of the time he was homeless, hitchhiking around, and living in homeless shelters in big cities. Sometimes he earned money playing pool, sometimes washing dishes in restaurants.

It's all a jumble in my memories now, but I recall that he was arrested in Oakland for throwing rocks at a railroad bridge. It wasn't that the action itself was unlawful, but that it showed that there was something not right with him. On another occasion, my sister Carolyn, who lived in Berkeley, called the police about Ron, but again, he was released, not hospitalized. Ron was in and out of jails and hospitals for observation several times between 1973, when he abandoned his apartment, and 1976, when our father died of a heart attack.

Like many mentally ill persons living on the street, Ron was sometimes victimized. When Ron lived in Seattle, one person he knew broke his arm, stole his car, and sent Ron's dog to the pound. But because of Ron's fear of the police, he was easily taken advantage of by such thugs.

By 1978, Ron was living in a downtown Los Angeles flophouse. His disability checks were much larger than many of the other mentally ill homeless, and so he did not seem to have as many problems as his peers with running out of money before the end of the month. Still, he could not follow through with the paperwork connected to his Social Security disability checks — and realistically, how many severely mentally ill people could?

I was living in an apartment near the ocean in Santa Monica. Ron would sometimes show up at my door to talk. I wasn't spectacularly afraid of him at that point — although I was wary, because I had seen his tendency towards violence — but I would not think of letting him spend the night. That seemed far too risky.

For a while, we would have long conversations that made absolutely no sense to me. Eventually, I began to see that these conversations didn't even make sense to Ron. As near as I could tell, he would come over just to waste my time (or perhaps to have some company). Perhaps he just wanted someone to talk to, and this was the best that he could do.

Some of the anti-psychotic medications he was prescribed seemed to help, but he stopped taking them within a few weeks of leaving the hospital. Each time, he quickly spiraled back into bizarre conversations about angles, nickels, and numbers.

At the time, I was upset that these hospitals didn't keep Ron locked up long enough for him to get well. The question of why mental hospitals operated on a revolving door model of treatment plagued me for many years. The answer turned out to be the intersection of deinstitutionalization theory and the ACLU's emphasis on due process.

13.   THE RIGHT TO TREATMENT (1960-1975)

Especially under the leadership of Chief Justice Earl Warren, the post-World War II U.S. Supreme Court took an increasingly expansive view of civil liberties. Often, the federal courts turned history on its head, or found remarkably broad protections hiding in the Constitution that had gone unnoticed by generations of Americans. In many cases, judges confused their personal public policy preferences with Constitutional mandates. The consequence was what some have characterized as "closing the front doors" of the mental hospital. Where "opening the back doors" sought to accelerate the return to the community of new admissions and long-stay patients, "closing the front doors" was an attempt to reduce the number of new commitments.[1]

There were several substantially different civil liberties issues that unintentionally reinforced each other. Some of these questions involved the rights of the mentally ill; others involved the rights of the mentally retarded. At first glance, these are two very different populations, and yet the judicial precedents for one would often be used to decide questions for the other.

One question was whether the involuntarily committed had a right to treatment: could a person be held in custody without being treated? A related set of questions: could a mental patient refuse treatment? Which forms of treatment could he refuse? What level of incompetence was necessary before a patient had the right to refuse treatment?

If a person accused of a crime was not sane enough to stand trial, could he be held indefinitely? Could he refuse treatment? What if, by refusing treatment, he would never been well enough to stand trial? If a mental patient had a right to treatment, but refused it, to avoid trial, did the state have the authority to continue holding him?

How dangerous did a person have to be to himself or to others before he could be involuntarily committed? What proof would the government need to justify involuntary commitment?

While outside the scope of this book, there is an astonishingly complex set of problems related to questions of insanity with respect to trial. The U.S. Supreme Court concluded in *Dusky* v. *U.S.* (1960) that the crucial question is whether a person has "sufficient present ability to consult with his lawyer with a reasonable degree of rational understanding — and whether he has a rational as well as factual understanding of the proceedings against him."[2]   Obviously, some defendants are so severely mentally ill (or at least, can seem that way) that they are incapable of understanding the charges against them, the seriousness of those charges, or of working with their attorney.

In other cases, a person might be found competent to stand trial, and yet be found not guilty by reason of insanity. Adding to the complexity of these questions was the need to distinguish between a defendant's mental state at the time of the crime, and at the time of trial. At least until civil libertarians had their way with the system (and to a lesser extent afterwards), defendants charged with relatively minor crimes would be examined for competency to stand trial. The results of that competency hearing could then be used to involuntarily commit a person who could not have been *civilly* committed as a danger to himself.[3]

The right to treatment appeared first. As is often the case, scholarly journals were the first to articulate it. Dr. Morton Birnbaum's "The Right to Treatment" appeared in the May 1960 *American Bar Association Journal*, arguing that since the state governments institutionalized mentally ill persons involuntarily, and often failed to provide anything more than custodial care, the courts should find that such patients had a right to treatment. Birnbaum's argument for such a right to treatment was not based on any recognizable Constitutional provision, but simply that if this "right to treatment were to be recognized and enforced, it will be shown that the standard of treatment in public mental institutions probably will be raised...."[4]

Birnbaum was making a pragmatic argument; the courts should recognize this right to treatment because of the beneficial effects that it would have on psychiatric care. He made no pretense that there was a legal basis for this claim, acknowledging that the courts were primarily interested in the questions of whether a patient's rights were sufficiently protected in commitment proceedings. Birnbaum openly stated that if the courts found such a right to treatment, it would force the states to improve care for the mentally ill, because the alternative was too worrisome — and that was release:

> To release a mentally ill person who requires further institutionalization, solely because he is not being given proper care and treatment, may endanger the health and welfare of many members of the community as well as the health and welfare of the sick person; however, it should always be remembered that the entire danger to, and from, the mentally ill that may occur by releasing them while they still require future hospitalization can be removed simply by our society treating these sick people properly. This is an important reason why the right to treatment is being advocated.[5]

Unsurprisingly, when the question came up of a right to treatment versus involuntary commitment, it was not difficult to find psychiatrists arguing for a right to treatment. The manner in which they advanced these arguments showed a genuine concern for improving care for the mentally ill. In the 1963 Congressional hearings, both Senators and witnesses referred to what Senator Sam Ervin called "a denial of due process" when the government deprived "a person of liberty on the basis that he is in need of treatment, without supplying the needed treatment...."[6] While the lawyers looked for reporting requirements that would protect the right to treatment, mental hospital administrators, such as Dr. Dale Cameron, pointed out that the real problem was not a lack of paperwork, but a lack of funds for staff. He agreed that some understaffed mental hospitals might occasionally forget about a patient, but:

> Requiring that badly understaffed institution to make a period report is not going to help a great deal as far as the treatment of that particular patient is concerned.... If people want to feel better about what goes on in mental hospitals, then they have to learn to provide through public funds the necessary staff to provide good treatment.

> The mere fact that you have someone peeking over an overworked physician's shoulder should not make anyone particularly glad. It would make him feel a lot better if he knew there were two physicians instead of one.[7]

The Joint Commission on Mental Illness and Health had made that same point two years earlier: that there were serious shortages of professional staff for mental hospitals, and regardless of what solution might be wished for, the government needed to create incentives for more doctors and nurses to go into psychiatric care.[8]

The first application of Birnbaum's right to treatment was *Rouse* v. *Cameron* (D.C.Cir. 1966). A man arrested in the District of Columbia on a weapons charge was found not guilty by reason of insanity, and hospitalized. After several years, he filed suit, arguing that he had a right to be treated, and not merely confined.

Judge David Bazelon, who wrote the *Rouse* decision, acknowledged three years later that his decision was controversial, and attempted to defend what more than a few psychiatrists evidently regarded as judicial overreach. His argument darted from side to side, at one point admitting that commitments "frequently have a dual justification: an individual is confined both because he needs help and because he is dangerous." Because the patient is being committed for his own good "there has long been a tendency to almost ignore... the requirement that he be dangerous; after all, he is going to a hospital, not to a prison, and we are helping him, not punishing him."[9]

But "for his own good" and "for the safety of the society" are two very different situations. If public safety played no part in the decision, Bazelon's concern about purely custodial care that provided no treatment would be completely appropriate, but if a patient was committed because he was a danger to others, then as repugnant as a purely custodial situation might be, it could be more easily justified than "for his own good."

Like Birnbaum, Judge Bazelon acknowledged that this right to treatment was a method of forcing the legislature to spend more on mental health:

> The fact that courts will release committed patients unless treatment can be provided for them seems to offer a compelling argument for a larger appropriation from the legislature. Of

course, it might be argued that legislatures may simply eliminate the promise of treatment and rely solely upon dangerousness to justify commitment. Such a development, however distressing, would at least eliminate much of the present hypocrisy. But a legislature wishing to take such a step would face the stiff constitutional requirements that hedge the criminal law.[10]

The movement to abolish involuntary commitment now allied itself with Birnbaum's campaign to recognize a right to treatment. The case that would do so, *Wyatt* v. *Stickney,* ended up imposing substantial costs on the state, but not necessarily for mental health treatment.

The *Wyatt* suit sought to force Alabama to dramatically improve the quality of care that it provided in state hospitals for the mentally retarded and mentally ill. Even critics of the *Wyatt* suit agree that Alabama's custodial care was worse than simply inadequate: one psychiatrist for 5000 patients; astonishingly low funding for clothing, food, and upkeep of the buildings.

On one side of the suit were organizations that wanted Alabama to dramatically upgrade the quality of care that state mental hospitals would provide, including the American Psychiatric Association. Allied with them was the ACLU — whose attorney, Ennis, later acknowledged that he was not initially interested in pursuing "right to treatment" cases, because his primary goal was abolition of mental illness commitment laws. At most, Ennis' *Prisoners of Psychiatry* (1972) acknowledged that to meet the new standards, "states would be forced to discharge vast numbers of inappropriately hospitalized patients." (Two years later, Ennis admitted that the goal was actually to make involuntary commitment almost impossible.)

The ACLU's goal with this suit was *not* to provide dramatically better care for Alabama's state mental hospital inmates, but to create a situation where Alabama would have no choice but to release patients. To Birnbaum, deinstitutionalization was a threat to force states to adequately fund mental hospitals, with "right to treatment" as a means to that end. By contrast, the ACLU saw deinstitutionalization as the goal; gold-plating the "right to treatment" would force the states to shut down most of their hospitals. It appears that the ACLU's fellow plaintiffs did not fully understand this divergence of interests at the start of the suit.

The final decision in *Wyatt* v. *Stickney* was remarkable not simply because it found that there was a Constitutional right to treatment, but how precisely the judge defined that right.   The decision included an appendix titled, "Minimum Constitutional Standards for Adequate Treatment of the Mentally Ill."   Many of the provisions would seem to have some Constitutional basis — for example, "an unrestricted right to send sealed mail" and to receive mail from attorneys, courts, and government officials.   But other parts of the appendix specify *exactly* how many employees in different job classifications the state mental hospital had to have for each 250 patients — right down to the number of Clerk Stenographer II positions (three), the number of Clerk Typist II positions (three), cooks, vehicle drivers, and similar support positions.   A Constitutional right to treatment could well exist; yet to declare that the right had this level of detail to it seems more like a judge substituting his judgment for that of the legislature, rather than deciding points of law.

Birnbaum, who had initially been part of the *Wyatt* suit, soon realized that the ACLU's suit was likely to lead to funding obligations for Alabama government that would achieve the ACLU's goal of deinstitutionalization, but not Birnbaum's goal of adequate treatment.   Consequently, Birnbaum filed *Legion* v. *Richardson,* in conjunction with various civil rights organizations, attempting to force the federal government to provide Medicaid funding for patients confined to state mental hospitals, and not just those patients who were being treated in private facilities. Birnbaum's argument was that state mental hospital inmates were disproportionately black compared to private hospitals; Medicaid's rules prohibiting reimbursement in state mental hospitals therefore had a disparate racial impact.

One might expect that such an argument would appeal to the ACLU, with its concern about racism, but the ACLU declined to join Birnbaum's effort, and Birnbaum lost *Legion.* The net effect of *Wyatt* (which the ACLU won), and *Legion* (which Birnbaum lost), was to encourage states to deinstitutionalize as rapidly as possible, for fear of being sued, and then losing.[11]

The doctrine from the *Rouse* decision that criminals found not guilty by reason of insanity had a right to receive treatment for their mental illness now evolved.   It soon became a right to a least restrictive approach to civil commitment, a strict application of the due process of law, and a right to *refuse* treatment.[12]   In *Lake* v. *Cameron,* decided in 1966, Judge Bazelon (again) heard an appeal from a senile woman who had been committed to St. Elizabeth's Hospital in 1962. Her psychiatrist agreed "she was not dangerous to others and would not intentionally harm herself," but she was confused, prone to wandering the streets, where she was sometimes the victim of minor injuries. The courts had committed Lake because she had no family that was able to provide supervision for her.

The federal law that governed commitment provided that a court could order hospitalization "for an indeterminate period... or order any other alternative course of treatment which the court believes will be in the best interests of the person or of the public." Judge Bazelon concluded that because the court *could* order an alternative course of treatment, that it *must* do so — thus creating a right to least restrictive treatment. Furthermore, Judge Bazelon concluded that the burden was not on the patient to find out if there was a less restrictive treatment option available, but rather on the court, as an alternative to commitment.

Bazelon's argument was not that this was simply a statutory right, but strongly implied that this was a Constitutional right. Bazelon, however, did not bother to identify exactly which clause of the Constitution was violated by this attempt to protect the health and safety of a senile woman living on her own: "Deprivations of liberty solely because of dangers to the ill persons themselves should not go beyond what is necessary for their protection."[13]

In spite of finding this right to least restrictive treatment, when Lake's case was again reheard by the District Court, it turned out that there was no less restrictive treatment option available within the District of Columbia. She had no money for "a properly supervised private nursing home" and the only public facilities within the District were not suited to a wandering senile patient.[14] While the *Lake* decision was cited in some of the "right to due process" cases, it seems to have had relatively little direct impact, although the idea of applying "least restrictive alternative" was soon in the legal water, so to speak. There are only two U.S. Supreme Court decisions that cite it, *In re Gault* (1967)[15] and *O'Connor* v. *Donaldson* (1975).[16]

The notion of a least restrictive alternative treatment produced a wide range of studies that claimed that residential care worked as well or better than hospitalization and at lower cost. These studies made this claim even for populations of the chronically mentally ill, those considered to be "moderate to high suicide risks" and those with previous histories of hospitalization. However, at least one such study involved only voluntary patients.[17]

The way that Dr. Birnbaum's desire to improve mental health care in state hospitals became a mechanism for turning mental patients out to the streets is a sobering reminder of how ideologues can hijack the best of intentions. Birnbaum's right to mental health treatment sought to force states to adequately fund state hospitals. Over a period of twelve years, it mutated into both a right to the least restrictive treatment and an obligation of the state to have a specified number of clerical staff employed in mental hospitals. When combined with due process requirements, the ACLU's lawyers were about to demolish long-term involuntary commitment for the vast majority of the mentally ill. For people like my brother, the consequences were severe.

14.   THE RIGHT TO DUE PROCESS (1960 – 1980)

Most Americans never think about due process, which is the right to a trial, or something like it, before the government takes away your liberty or property. Yet the federal courts have been worrying about it for more than a century, slowly imposing more and more exacting standards for what rules apply before the government locks someone up, denies them a license, or confiscates their property.

The systems of commitment at the end of World War II were as varied as other state laws. While the procedures were more formal than they had been a century earlier, the system was still built around what came to be called the medical model. If a person was mentally ill, and those responsible for the commitment decision believed that the patient would benefit from hospitalization, commitment was very likely. There was no need to establish that a mentally ill person was a danger to himself or others. The ideal was to provide treatment to bring the patient back to mental health. It was supposed to be primarily for the benefit of the patient. Commitment provided the patient with a custodial setting to protect him from injury or abuse. Due process concerns definitely took a back seat to protecting both the society and the individual.

Into the early 1970s, *at least* twenty-seven states provided for temporary or observational commitments for periods of a few days to as much as three months. Relatives, hospitals, doctors, and a few other professionals had the authority to request such observational commitments. (In most states, police officers had similar authority under emergency commitment procedures.)

The goal of these temporary or observational commitments was to allow psychiatrists to determine whether a patient was sufficiently mentally ill for long-term commitment. Especially once psychotropic drugs came into use in the late 1950s, treatment during these short stays allowed some patients to recognize that they were in need of help. Such patients would sometimes agree to voluntary hospitalization, or to return for outpatient treatment.[1]

This is really not surprising. It was often the case that when my brother was hospitalized for observation, a few days of antipsychotic medications would give him sufficient grasp on reality to recognize that he had a problem. Often, he would voluntarily take his medication, and return for follow-up visits, at least for a few weeks.

When most people think of "commitment," they are thinking about involuntary, long-term commitment. By the early 1970s, with the exception of Massachusetts, which required annual renewal of involuntary commitments, these commitments were indeterminate in length. Once committed, a patient was usually hospitalized until the psychiatrist in charge decided that he had recovered sufficiently to be released.[2]

A few states provided what lawyers would today recognize as modern standards of due process, but in most states, the patient did not have a right to be informed of the hearing, or to be present at it. In some states, patients were allowed to waive a right to a hearing. At least one study casts doubt as to whether patients were actually *signing* these waivers, much less understanding them. A number of states also had a commitment procedure for "nonprotesting" patients, those who had not voluntarily hospitalized themselves, but were not arguing against it, either.[3] At least two states required a jury trial before involuntary commitment, with another nineteen making a jury trial optional (presumably at the request of the person whose commitment was in question).[4]

Was a person who was involuntarily committed also *legally incompetent*? A person who was legally incompetent lost many rights: the right to make contracts, to vote, to drive, to manage their own financial affairs, to own a gun. This was no surprise. A mentally ill person might be taken advantage of in the making of a contract, and in management of his financial affairs. For at least the most severely mentally ill, it was and is common sense to suspect that operating or possessing dangerous machinery was a public safety hazard.

A few states on the eve of the deinstitutionalization, such as

Ohio and Colorado, made commitment and a declaration of legal incompetence a single action. If you were committed to a mental hospital, you automatically lost many of your other rights. More commonly, the states made commitment and legal incompetence into separate proceedings — although commitment created a presumption of legal incompetence. Only a few states distinctly held that commitment created no such presumption.[5] (The federal Gun Control Act of 1968, however, prohibited firearms possession by any person who had been adjudicated incompetent by federal or state courts because of retardation or mental illness — but not simply those who had been committed.)[6]

Due process questions with respect to mental illness started to be answered by the Warren Court in the 1950s. One representative case from the period was *Greenwood* v. *U.S.* (1956). The plaintiff was arrested for robbery of a post office and felonious assault on a postal employee. Psychiatrists determined Greenwood was insane. He was hospitalized first in a federal mental hospital, then a state mental hospital, because there seemed no likely prospect of his recovery. The Supreme Court upheld the federal law that allowed Greenwood to be held until he should recover sufficiently to stand trial.[7]

A strict reading of the text of the Sixth Amendment's guarantee of a right to speedy trial certainly seems to be contrary to holding someone indefinitely without trial. In 1963, these concerns were the subject of Congressional hearings that sought to resolve this discrepancy, along with questions of whether the procedures used conformed to the Fifth Amendment's guarantee that no one should "be deprived of life, liberty, or property, without due process of law."

The focus of these 1963 hearings was the District of Columbia's mental illness laws, which Congress was considering revising. Before 1938, no one could be involuntarily committed in the District without a competency hearing before a jury. (In the District, to be found incompetent was essentially identical to involuntary commitment.) One of the witnesses before the committee was federal district Judge Alexander Holtzoff, who explained why this requirement for jury trial had been abandoned, even for patients who were not challenging the commitment. The jury trial was logistically complex, because patients had to be present for these hearings in a courtroom. The public nature of such a trial was embarrassing for family members and traumatic for

the patient. (Shame about mental illness in the family was much
more widespread into the 1960s than it is now.) Some patients
were also too violent or too physically ill to be safely transported
across town.

Starting in 1938, to alleviate these problems, a Commission on
Mental Health, consisting of a lawyer and two psychiatrists,
traveled to each of the mental hospitals in the District each day,
holding competency hearings. In theory, they were public, but in
practice, they were not. In addition to the advantages for patient
and family, the Commission, acting as "special masters" (court
appointed experts who decide points of fact rather than of law)
were able to devote more time to the task of competency hearings
than a federal judge, who had many other responsibilities. Because
two members of the Commission were psychiatrists, there was an
assumption that professional expertise would make the
Commission's decision more accurate than a judge.

While this did not conform exactly to the jury trial guarantee of
the Sixth Amendment, patients were free to appeal to a federal
judge. According to Judge Holtzoff, "all he has to do is write a
letter to the court, and we treat that letter as a petition for a writ of
habeas corpus." Judges had some discretion on this; as Holtzoff
explained, "that doesn't means [sic] that a patient is entitled to file
a new petition every day and be heard every time he files a
petition."[8]

One area where there seemed to be no serious dispute was the
need to separate competency from commitment. As every witness
who addressed the subject in these 1963 hearings admitted,
declaring a person legally incompetent as part of involuntary
commitment greatly impaired the patient's reintegration into
society.

Once declared incompetent, a patient lost the ability to obtain a
driver's license, make contracts, draw up a will, or manage his
financial affairs. Regaining these rights, even once discharged by
the hospital, was sometimes a very complex task. A person once
involuntarily committed could not petition for a restoration of his
rights for six months after release. The superintendent of St.
Elizabeth's Hospital, Dr. Dale Cameron, pointed out that there
were mentally ill patients who should not be driving, but this was
not true for every patient, and separating competency and
commitment allowed for more appropriate distinctions.[9]

One of the other issues that the hearings raised was concern about improper commitments — or "railroading" a sane person, as several witnesses colorfully referred to it. But in spite of multiple witnesses who expressed concern that this *could* happen, and almost certainly, somewhere, *did* happen, there were no horror stories presented by any of the witnesses. Indeed, Judge Holtzoff admitted, "Such cases are rare...." Chief Judge of the D.C. District Court, Matthew H. McGuire went even further, and claimed that he was not aware of any cases where the existing D.C. law had led to such improper commitments. "We have had outstanding success here in the District of Columbia... and certainly the so-called railroading of an individual to a mental institution under its provisions is something that couldn't possibly happen." Many other witnesses, even those that one might expect to be concerned about this possibility, generally discounted that this had been a problem.[10]

Even the ACLU's representative at the hearings, Elyce H. Zenoff, was careful not to claim that there was an existing problem. Referring to St. Elizabeth's Hospital, "There are many dedicated men and women on its staff who, we know, are solicitous of the legal rights of patients. However, there is no way of knowing whether those who may join the staff in the future will be equally solicitous." If this problem had been widespread outside of the District, it is hard to imagine that Zenoff would have failed to give examples to buttress her concerns.[11]

There is one curious exchange between Senator Sam Ervin and Professor Henry Weihofen of George Washington University. Weihofen observed that "there are organizations throughout the country who think that hospitalization laws, and especially emergency procedures, are likely to be abused. They suspect that people's rights are being subverted." Senator Ervin agreed: "If I may go off the record to corroborate your observation — " and then the official record stops. Professor Weihofen's next remarks imply that such concerns might themselves be indicative of serious problems: "I think the kind of people who oppose this have a personality which makes them afraid that something is going to be done to them, that someone is going to commit them."[12]

The one witness who was prepared to admit that some inmates might be hospitalized somewhere improperly or for too long, was Dr. Cameron: "I question very seriously, and you have not suggested it, that many persons are 'railroaded' into mental hospitals. But I do agree that they can be forgotten or lost sight of in a badly understaffed institution."[13]

The ACLU's zealous concern about the fine details of due process — for example, their insistence that the normal rules of evidence should apply to competency hearings, requiring those who filed written reports appear in person to be cross-examined[14] — seems focused on a non-problem. No one at the hearings, even the ACLU, believed that this problem was present in D.C.'s mental hospitals. It was apparently so rare a problem elsewhere in the United States that even those worried about it were more inclined to see the fear as a sign of mental illness, rather than a sign of abuses of the commitment process.

One rather odd concern that the ACLU's representative raised at the 1963 hearings, and which is perhaps a foreshadowing of the ACLU's later efforts to destroy involuntary commitment, was their opposition to a New Jersey statute that provided for "nonprotesting" commitment. These were patients where family, friends, or doctors had sought hospitalization, and the patient either did not object to hospitalization, or was not sufficiently aware of the circumstances to object. This would describe many senile mental patients, and some severely depressed or catatonic patients. The ACLU's representative at the hearings, Elyce H. Zenoff insisted that such a person could not be considered a voluntary patient: "If they are so confused that they don't where this is or what the purpose is of being there, this is not a voluntary patient."[15]

Along the same lines, a number of witnesses had pointed out that there was no real advantage to requiring the patient to be seen by a judge as a condition of commitment. The time pressures and logistical problems of transporting mental patients to a courthouse meant that a judge would often see a patient for a very short period of time. Unlike the District's Mental Health Commissioners, a judge would lack the professional expertise to evaluate a patient's mental condition. Yet Zenoff insisted that this was necessary to avoid abuses, and pointed to the example of Chicago, where such a requirement was already in effect. Yet Zenoff admitted that many such hearings did not "take more than a minute..."[16] Like the regular reporting requirements that the ACLU wanted, the net effect was to increase legal paperwork and procedures, with a negligible benefit to the patient, although an increased demand for lawyers.

This curious concern about railroaded patients — without any evidence of anything but isolated incidents — continued to appear throughout the 1960s. M.F. Abramson's critical evaluation of California's 1969 Lanterman-Petris-Short Act, which substantially tightened the standards for commitment of the mentally ill, observed that while the legislature's action was driven by a fear "that patients were being 'railroaded' into state hospitals," the report itself is surprisingly short on examples of such improper commitments. Instead, Abramson notes that the bibliography points to the "voluminous writings of Thomas Szasz" and others whose ideology should have made them less than reliable sources.[17]

There were quite significant changes in the direction of more rigorous commitment procedures in the 1960s, but they suggest that bureaucratic failure was the big enemy, not malice. Among the early adopters was New York State, which revised its Mental Hygiene Law in 1964. Examination of the involuntary commitment procedure found that patients who were held for sixty days of observation were routinely committed by the state mental hospital, overwhelmingly without hearings, and without notice to either patient or family.

While the motivations of the doctors involved were almost certainly altruistic, the state legislature decided to require periodic judicial review of long-term commitments, and notices to the patient, nearest relative, and the state's Mental Health Information Service. The Mental Health Information Service existed to provide an independent agency reviewing the reasons for the commitment, so that it was not simply the opinion of the psychiatrists at the patient's mental hospital.[18]

The ACLU's concerns in the 1963 hearings were about making sure that all the right procedures were followed. Six years later, even this was not enough. In 1969, the New York Civil Liberties Union decided that involuntary hospitalization was "incompatible with the principles of a free society." Bruce J. Ennis was a young University of Chicago Law School graduate. By Ennis' own admission, he had no knowledge of mental illness (other than his reading of Szasz's anti-psychiatric claims). As a civil liberties matter, however, Ennis was convinced that the current system needed overturning.

While Ennis did not go so far as Szasz — Ennis acknowledged that mental illness did exist — he came to much the same conclusion. Ennis argued that, "You don't lock up people because they've got a heart problem. The fact a person has a mental illness

rather than a heart illness doesn't justify locking them up." The
analogy fails because heart disease does not prevent a patient from
understanding his need for treatment. Had Ennis and the other civil
liberties lawyers sought to replace the commitment procedures used
in many states with one a bit closer to the increasingly demanding
standards of due process used in criminal law, the consequences
might have been less destructive.

As some of the cases to be discussed later demonstrate, there
were *some* adults committed on the say-so of a single doctor that
seemed questionable, or where legitimate questions arise as to how
long a mentally deficient person charged with a crime could be
held. Furthermore, involuntary commitment could easily lead to
hospitalization for life. Because commitment hearings were only
civil matters, the standard of proof was lower than in a criminal
case. One need not be an ideologue to wonder if civil commitment
might be used as an end run around the exacting standards of
criminal law.

One chilling example of the dangers of this is a footnote from
history. Secret Service Agent Larry Newman, assigned to
President Kennedy's security detail, describes what happened when
the sheriff delivered two prostitutes to President Kennedy's suite in
1961. Kennedy's personal aide, Dave Powers, took the prostitutes
inside, but left the sheriff outside, who warned the prostitutes, "If
any word about this night gets out, I'll see that you both go to [the
western Washington State mental hospital at Steilacoom] and never
get out."[19]

Perhaps this was not a realistic threat – although making the
claim that the sheriff was the Panderer-in-Chief might have
sounded pretty crazy in 1961. Perhaps covering up criminal
behavior by the President of the United States should not be
considered typical of how things worked back then.

Bruce J. Ennis' *Prisoners of Psychiatry* (1972) claimed that
less than five percent of mental hospital patients "are dangerous to
themselves or to others" and that the rest were improperly locked
up "because they are useless, unproductive, 'odd,' or 'different.'"[20]
Yet the very first example Ennis provides in *Prisoners of
Psychiatry* of "people who have been labeled criminally insane" is
not a particularly persuasive example. Ennis told the story of
Quinton Roger Adams (although Ennis calls him Charlie
Youngblood in *Prisoners of Psychiatry*), who was charged with
making threats against government officials. The U.S. Attorney

sought to have Adams declared incompetent to stand trial by reason of insanity.

Ennis defended Adams' competence to stand trial, but described a person who, even by Ennis' own account, was prone to threats of violence, and paranoid. "I knew I could not persuade Judge Charles M. Metzner that Youngblood was entirely sane — even our own psychiatrists thought he was a paranoid schizophrenic — but I hoped to persuade him that a defendant can be severely ill in psychiatric terms and still be *legally* competent to stand trial."[21] The testimony of Dr. David Abrahamsen concerning his examination of Adams reveals a deeply paranoid person, often incoherent, who told Abrahamsen, "You are going to murder me for \$75."[22]

Ennis also describes his failure to get George P. Metesky released from a New York State mental hospital. Metesky "who allegedly planted sixty bombs in an effort to gain revenge against the Consolidated Edison Company" was found incompetent to stand trial in 1957, and involuntarily hospitalized. Ennis did not claim that Metesky wasn't the bomber: "there was little evidence against him other than what he himself had supplied."

Subsequent U.S. Supreme Court decisions had made the evidence Metesky had supplied to the prosecution inadmissible in court, and so Ennis thought it likely that demanding Metesky be given a chance at trial would lead to his release. Ennis was quite clear, "I do not know if he was guilty. I never asked, and he never told me." It would appear that the principle was more important to Ennis than public safety.

Ennis was unsuccessful at getting Metesky released. Ennis suspected that a bomb threat that caused evacuation of the federal courthouse a few weeks before the courts decided Metesky's suit might have been a factor.[23]

Ennis gives examples of cases that *seem* to show that people were at least sometimes hospitalized with little or no reason.[24] But other examples that Ennis uses are sufficiently incomplete (and utterly free of sources) as to call Ennis's accounts into question, and therefore, how widespread such cases were. Ennis' account of the Alfred Curt von Wolfersdorf case could be interpreted as an innocent man confined to a mental hospital without reason for twenty years.[25]

The district attorney, however, maintained into the 1970s that von Wolfersdorf had feigned insanity to prevent being tried and executed for kidnapping and murder of a 14-year-old boy. Joseph Louis Paonessa, the person who identified von Wolfersdorf as his conspirator in the kidnapping and murder, was found competent to stand trial, and was executed in 1953.[26] Von Wolfersdorf was not released.[27]

Ennis' *Prisoners of Psychiatry* (1972) is careful to suggest that his goal was to make sure that only those who were dangerous to themselves or others were involuntarily committed. But by 1974, Ennis' stated goal was "to abolish involuntary commitment or to set up so many procedural roadblocks and hurdles that it will be difficult, if not impossible, for the state to commit people against their will."[28]

There are examples that I have found of improper commitments, such as the one that led to the lawsuit *Maniaci* v. *Marquette University* (Wisc. 1971), in which officials of Marquette University committed Saralee Maniaci because they believed that she had "illogical" reasons for dropping out of school. Complicating the matter was that she was a minor, and the university was at least initially under the impression that she was doing so without parental permission. (Universities were still expected to operate *in loco parentis* for college students, and especially so for a minor.) While Maniaci was indeed locked up in a mental hospital against her will, she was released the next morning. At least as the Wisconsin Supreme Court decision described it, there was no danger that anyone believed that Maniaci belonged in a mental hospital.[29]

By contrast, in the vast majority of the cases fought out in courts related to the question of commitment, there is no serious reason to believe that sane persons were improperly committed. In *Baxstrom* v. *Herold* (1966), the Supreme Court struck down a New York State law that allowed a criminally insane convict to be civilly committed at the end of his sentence to a mental hospital. The Court did not completely rule out the possibility of such a civil commitment, but insisted that the patient had a right to the same due process rights as a non-criminal subject to civil commitment. New York law did not provide that opportunity.[30]

In *Lessard* v. *Schmidt* (1972), a three-judge panel struck down Wisconsin's involuntary commitment statute. The legal process was remarkably complicated for a decision that, in the end, was made at the federal district court level. The U.S. Supreme Court heard appeals, striking down the original decisions, and ordering the lower court to reconsider it twice, but without ever making a decision of its own.

That a patient would have challenged the Wisconsin involuntary commitment statute is not surprising. The Wisconsin law in effect in 1971 allowed for involuntary commitment for the benefit of the community, or of the patient. Without question, the statute was either broadly or vaguely worded, depending, I suppose, on how you regarded the authorities.

The plaintiff, Alberta Lessard, was arrested by Milwaukee police officers after threatening suicide, and running through her apartment complex "shouting that the communists were taking over the country that night." Other statements that she made were not even that rational. She was held for emergency observation for ten days. A psychiatrist diagnosed schizophrenia, and recommended commitment.

Lessard contacted Milwaukee Legal Services and asked for their assistance. Her lawyers, whose knowledge of mental illness was based on reading one of Thomas Szasz's books,[31] filed a class action lawsuit seeking the overturning of the Wisconsin commitment statute, with a substantial list of problems with the statute and the procedures followed by the police, hospital, and courts.

The final decision largely upheld Lessard's complaints about vagueness and due process violations. For example, Lessard received no notice that commitment proceedings had been commenced against her, and no opportunity to have a lawyer defend her in those proceedings. It would seem that if a person were genuinely mentally ill, having access to a lawyer would not substantially change the outcome of the proceedings. For someone who was not mentally ill, having a lawyer to represent her interests would certainly be a benefit.

Another of Lessard's complaints was that she had not been given the option of having an independent psychiatrist evaluate her mental state. However, when the judge who ordered Lessard's commitment asked her attorney if he wished to have an independent psychiatric evaluation, he refused. This suggests that the police officer accounts of Lessard's statements and behavior were correct, and her attorney knew better than to ask for another opinion.[32]

Some of the other complaints about violation of due process fit in with Ennis's approach of attempting to make involuntary commitment so difficult as to be impossible. Lessard demanded proof beyond a reasonable doubt as a requirement for commitment. The decision acknowledged that the reason why commitment laws did not require the criminal conviction standard of proof was because the motivation was different, at least in part. Commitment served two purposes: to help (not punish) the mental patient, and to protect the society. The judges disposed of the "protect the society" argument in a sentence and a half, pointing out that "[i]f a sociologist predicted that a person was eighty per cent likely to commit a felonious act, no law would permit his confinement...."33 The bulk of the decision was therefore whether helping the patient was sufficient reason for commitment.

The judges traced the development of commitment laws forward from the Colonial period, arguing that because of the absence of mental hospitals and limited knowledge of how to treat mental illness, "those confined were generally clearly deranged and violent." They blamed the Josiah Oakes decision of 1845 for the expansion of commitment authority to include those who were a threat to themselves — failing to recognize that the informal nature of commitment before then meant that many had been confined who were a danger only to themselves. Oddly, they admitted that English law from the thirteenth century onward allowed commitment for those who were a danger to themselves, but distinguished this from Wisconsin's law:

> During "lucid moments" the incompetent was permitted to manage his own property, and to generally exercise his civil rights. He was also entitled to an accounting from the King. There was thus a very real difference between the English practice, which could only be for the benefit and protection of the incompetent, and which was only effective during periods of insanity, and the American innovation, which resulted in total, and perhaps permanent, loss of liberty.[34]

The decision also argued that "many mental illnesses are untreatable" because the cure rate for paranoid schizophrenia (which was Lessard's diagnosis) was very low, and that long term hospitalization made mental patients worse, not better.[35] The judges claimed that because death rates in mental hospitals were roughly ten times higher than in the general population, commitment could not be justified based on concern for the patient.

While the judges acknowledged that this higher death rate might be related to the higher average age of mental patients,[36] they seemed unaware that mental hospitals into the 1960s had large numbers of senile and syphilitic insane patients, which might account for the much higher death rate.

The decision next argued that the loss of civil rights caused by involuntary commitment was worse than being a convicted criminal. Wisconsin law at the time prevented those who had been committed from voting, driving, making contracts, marrying, or serving on juries. The decision also claimed that for purposes of employment or finding housing, it was better to be a convicted felon than a person who had been committed to a mental hospital.[37] Not surprisingly, with consequences more severe than a criminal conviction, the judges decided to take a very strict view of the due process requirements for commitment.[38]

You can see something of the judges' inability to critically examine arguments from their approving citation of this claim by an ACLU representative in 1970 Congressional hearings about the rights of the mentally ill.

> Although 7 days may not appear to some to be a very long time, experience has indicated that any kind of forcible detention of a person in an alien environment may seriously affect him in the first few days of detention, leading to all sorts of acute traumatic and iatrogenic symptoms and troubles. By 'iatrogenic' I mean things that are caused by the very act of hospitalization which is supposed to be therapeutic; in other words, the hospitalization process itself causes the disturbance rather than the disturbance requiring hospitalization.[39]

This is an astonishing statement. Hospitalization could conceivably aggravate a patient's problems. Whether it did so, and how often, would be a legitimate question. Phrasing this claim as "the hospitalization process itself causes the disturbance rather than the disturbance requiring hospitalization" implies that a patient was not disturbed before being hospitalized, but only became that way after being committed. Lessard was hospitalized because of a suicide attempt. To suggest that hospitalization caused mental illness rather than mental illness causing hospitalization would mean that many people committed for observation were sane when taken into custody, but mentally ill by the time that they left.

Remarkable claims require remarkable evidence, not merely an opinion.

The *Lessard* decision not only forced Wisconsin to adopt a much stricter due process standard for commitment, but largely ended commitment unless the patient was an *imminent* danger to himself or others. The effect was that large numbers of mentally ill people in Wisconsin "died with their rights on," as Darold Treffert, a psychiatrist with the Wisconsin Mental Health Institute described it. To conform to the *Lessard* decision, many other states followed Wisconsin's example.[40]

In 1974, just as civil commitment became dramatically more difficult, Albert Brooks published a comprehensive compendium of legal issues associated with mental illness. He speculated that if civil commitment went away as a mechanism for dealing with mentally ill persons accused of everything from murder to public disorder problems, that something else would take its place. His prediction turned out to be remarkably accurate:

> It is assumed that if coercive commitment were abolished, most of the persons presently confined would not be confined, and would be either treated on an outpatient basis or simply left alone. It is more likely, however, that a probable consequence of abolishing civil commitment would be that persons who engage in undesirable behaviors now controlled by the civil process would become subject to our already overloaded criminal justice system, and would be treated as "criminals"....[41]

Two years earlier, M. F. Abramson, a psychiatrist who consulted "to a county jail system, county courts, and the adult division of a county probation department," described the effects of California's cutting edge Lanterman-Petris-Short Act (1969). While acknowledging that some of the effects were positive, Abramson also warned that, "There may be a limit to society's tolerance of mentally disordered behavior. ... [M]entally disordered persons are being increasingly subjected to arrest and criminal prosecution." Because so many of these deinstitutionalized or never-institutionalized mental patients were using illegal drugs, when they came to the attention of police, drug possession was likely the basis for processing them — but as criminals, not as persons in need of care. The state prison system was suddenly awash in mentally ill prisoners.[42]

Unsurprisingly, a J. Monahan responded to Abramson's concerns by arguing that forcing mentally ill people into the criminal justice system was actually a *good* thing:

> But the criminal justice system forces society to confront its tolerance level, to think out, evaluate, and agree upon exactly what behaviors are so deviant that their perpetrators should be incarcerated. By holding up for public debate in the courts and the legislature such issues as homosexuality, prostitution, abortion, and marijuana use — all of which have mental health aspects — the system forces society to come face to face with its norms and values.

Perhaps most disturbing is how Monahan's attempt to force society to confront deviance was couched not in terms of concern for the mentally ill offender — for Monahan admitted that "on a purely humane level mental hospitals may be preferable to jails in many jurisdictions" — but that the mental patients would bear the costs of confronting what Monahan clearly saw as a hypocritical and rigid society: "[T]he current paradigm clash between criminal justice and mental health may be a portent of true progress, a sign that revolutionary advances in our ways of conceptualizing and responding to antisocial behavior are in the offing."[43] Monahan was quite prepared to put the mentally ill in prison as a way of achieving his larger political goals. As 1930s apologists for the Soviet Union jocularly responded to concerns about mass murder, "You can't make an omelette without breaking some eggs."[44]

Another landmark commitment case was *O'Connor v Donaldson* (1975). Kenneth Donaldson had been involuntarily committed in 1957 to a Florida mental hospital for paranoid schizophrenia at the insistence of his father, after previous episodes of mental illness that had been cured by electroconvulsive therapy (ECT). Donaldson repeatedly claimed that he was not mentally ill. And even if he was mentally ill, why was he not being treated for it? But Donaldson had repeatedly *refused* treatment. The most effective treatments for schizophrenia were antipsychotic drugs and ECT — both of which Donaldson refused to allow — and which it appears that the state hospital did not force on Donaldson.[45]

Was Donaldson mentally ill? Ennis' account of the circumstances that led to Donaldson's commitment suggests that there was at least good reason to wonder about Donaldson's mental

health.   While visiting his parents in Pinellas County, Florida,
Donaldson complained of becoming drowsy, and "he mentioned to
his father that someone, perhaps one of the neighbors, might be
putting something in his food."   Donaldson claimed that some
years earlier, a diner in Lynnwood, California, had drugged his
food.[46] Donaldson's parents, unsurprisingly, were concerned about
this paranoia, especially in light of his previous mental illness
history. Donaldson was committed to the state mental hospital, but
refused any treatment.

J. B. O'Connor, the hospital's superintendent during most of
Donaldson's stay, perhaps because of ill health, seems to have been
unable to defend his reasons for either the initial commitment, or
holding Donaldson until 1971.   Much of Ennis' account of
Donaldson's continued confinement suggests that once the state
hospital staff realized that Donaldson no longer needed to be there
(assuming there had been a good reason at the beginning), the
director was reluctant to admit that hospital had erred in keeping
him.[47]   This may have been especially important because
Donaldson's lawsuits sought damages not simply from the State of
Florida, but from O'Connor as an individual.

The U.S. Supreme Court concluded that because there was no
evidence that Donaldson was a danger to others or to himself, and
because he was not being treated for mental illness, there was no
legitimate basis for the state to confine him against his will: "A
State cannot constitutionally confine... a non-dangerous individual
who is capable of surviving safely in freedom by himself or with
the help of willing and responsible family members or friends...."

The Supreme Court was very careful *not* to tackle the
considerably tougher question of involuntary commitment for those
who were a danger to themselves or others. They also avoided
directly answering the question about someone who was actually
being treated for mental illness. They did, however, imply that a
person who was no threat to himself or others might still be
legitimately hospitalized against his will, as long as he was
receiving treatment.[48] The Catch-22 situation in which Donaldson
had claimed that he had a right to either treatment or release — but
refused treatment, and so deserved to be released — seemed to
have eluded most of the justices on the Supreme Court.
Psychiatrists did get the message that they could be held *personally*
liable for holding someone against their will in a mental hospital,
creating   a   strong   incentive   to   err   on   the   side   of

deinstitutionalization.[49]

Chief Justice Burger, in a concurring opinion, agreed with the result for this particular case, but he also pointed to some serious flaws in the theories from which the majority derived those conclusions. While there was a strong Constitutional argument for protecting a patient's right to due process in the involuntary commitment process, the majority had gone far beyond that. They had just made a rather dramatic change in American law, abandoning the notion that the state police power might be legitimately used to confine mental patients who were not treatable.

Burger pointed out that:

> [T]he idea that States may not confine the mentally ill except for the purpose of providing them with treatment is of very recent origin, and there is no historical basis for imposing such a limitation on state power.... [I]n the exercise of its police power a State may confine individuals solely to protect society from the dangers of significant antisocial acts or communicable disease.... Additionally, the States are vested with the historic *parens patriae* power, including the duty to protect 'persons under legal disabilities to act for themselves.' ... The classic example of this role is when a State undertakes to act as "'the general guardian of all infants, idiots, and lunatics.'"

Burger was concerned that "it remains a stubborn fact that there are many forms of mental illness which are not understood, some which are untreatable in the sense that no effective therapy has yet been discovered for them, and that rates of 'cure' are generally low." Chief Justice Burger clearly saw where this would lead, pointing out that many mentally ill people are not sufficiently in touch with reality to recognize how badly they are in need of help. "It may be that some persons in either of these categories, and there may be others, are unable to function in society and will suffer real harm to themselves unless provided with care in a sheltered environment."[50]

Unfortunately, the rest of the Supreme Court did not heed Justice Burger's thoughtful warning. Instead, it continued down a path that applied almost as exacting a standard to involuntary commitment as a criminal conviction. Four years later, in *Addington* v. *Texas* (1979), the Supreme Court decided what standard of proof the state must provide to involuntarily commit a mentally ill person. Involuntary commitment was a civil process, not a criminal procedure, and ordinarily, a mere preponderance of evidence would be sufficient, as it is for other civil trials. The Supreme Court decided that because indefinite involuntary commitment was a substantial deprivation of one's liberty — and because of the stigma associated with such involuntary commitment — a preponderance of evidence was not enough. Instead, they decided that the state must provide "clear and convincing evidence" of mental illness.

The plaintiff in this case had been hospitalized for mental illness seven times between 1969 and 1975, and involuntarily committed on at least three occasions. As the Court's opinion explained:

> The State offered evidence that appellant suffered from serious delusions, that he often had threatened to injure both of his parents and others, that he had been involved in several assaultive episodes while hospitalized and that he had caused substantial property damage both at his own apartment and at his parents' home.

Two expert psychiatrists testified "that appellant suffered from psychotic schizophrenia and that he had paranoid tendencies. They also expressed medical opinions that appellant was probably dangerous both to himself and to others."[51]

Other decisions followed, such as *Vitek* v. *Jones* (1980), in which the U.S. Supreme Court overruled Nebraska's practice of transferring prisoners to a state mental hospital based on the opinion of a state physician or psychologist that the prisoner was mentally ill. The Court decided that such a transfer violated the due process requirement of the Fourteenth Amendment. The plaintiff Jones was already in prison; it is hard to see how his liberty was more restricted by a mental hospital than a prison, but the Court held that the stigmatizing effect of being declared mentally ill meant that even a felon confined to prison had a right to a hearing before such a transfer.[52] In response, a number of states altered their statutes and regulations to conform to the requirements of written notice of intended transfer, a hearing, "an independent decisionmaker," the right to call witnesses, and legal representation.[53]

Due process, by itself, should have not dramatically changed the equation. The most seriously mentally ill, even with the additional due process protections, would still have been found incompetent and hospitalized. At most, this change should have prevented only the commitment of a few people who were eccentric, or who were only marginally or arguably mentally ill. But as with many other changes that took place during this period, a robust due process requirement was not implemented in isolation.

15.   REFUSING TREATMENT (1969 – PRESENT)

A strong due process requirement by itself would not have prevented involuntary commitment. For patients like my brother, who had attacked complete strangers, proving that they were likely to be a danger to others would not have created an insurmountable obstacle. Even someone who was only a danger to himself because of repeatedly failing to obtain shelter, food, and clothing: this would not have been too high of a burden to meet. But due process was not the only factor in play.

By the 1970s, the legal academy was intent on proving that psychiatrists were unable to diagnose mental illness, were incompetent, sexist, and in general, insufficiently expert to testify as expert witnesses. If psychiatrists had no expertise as to whether a person was mentally ill, or was likely to be dangerous ("less accurate than the flip of a coin," in the words of one law review article), why should they be trusted to decide what treatment a patient was to receive? A 1974 *Yale Law Journal* article (rather astonishingly authored by an "anonymous state legislator") argued that mental illness was a "suspect classification," akin to race, because the definition of mental illness was because of "numerical domination of legislatures by persons not mentally ill." Majority will, in short, defined insanity, and the definition of insanity was therefore suspicious.[1]

Next, an existing legal concept "suspect classifications" combined with an emerging idea "strict scrutiny," to impose a new and more demanding legal standard for commitment. The courts held that certain "suspect classifications," such as race or national origin, are subject to "strict scrutiny" because they are especially prone to governmental discrimination. What makes a classification "suspect"? Members of the group are unable to change their membership in the group; they have a history of being discriminated against; they are politically powerless.

What is "strict scrutiny"? This is a judge-made requirement that a law that impacts on a constitutionally-protected right must meet three requirements. First, the law must serve a "compelling governmental interest": something necessary or critical to government's function, not simply something that would be nice to have.

Second, the law must be "narrowly tailored": the law must affect only those at whom it is aimed. If a law aimed at problem X punishes people who are not doing X, then the law is overinclusive. At the same time, the law must make a serious effort to deal with everyone doing X, or who is a member of group X. If a law aimed at problem X fails to include members of that class, then the law is underinclusive.

Thirdly, the law must use the "least restrictive means" to accomplish its legitimate goal. If a statute provides for a mentally ill person to be involuntarily committed to protect that person from harming himself or others, this requirement means that there can be no less restrictive means of preventing that person from harming themselves or others. If there is a less restrictive means available, then a more restrictive means is unconstitutional.[2]

Laws that are examined under strict scrutiny *usually* (but not always) fail to survive judicial review[3] — and then the legislature must draft a new law. Then lawyers challenge the new law. If the courts found that the old law was too broadly written as to whom it applied (overinclusive), the new law, in trying to be "narrowly tailored" may end up underinclusive. If the old law was too narrowly written as to whom it applied (underinclusive), the new law may end up overinclusive. In practice, it does not take too many times through the court system for legislators to give up on writing a law that meets such Goldilocks ("too hot, too cold") standards — especially if only a small fraction of the electorate is aware that there is a problem, or cares about that problem.

Unsurprisingly, legal advocates combined strict scrutiny with the due process requirement, skepticism of the expertise of psychiatrists, skepticism of the efficacy of mental illness treatments, and exaggeration of the dangers of those treatments, to create a new right: the right to refuse treatment. Even better, both state and federal governments were now paying the legal advocates. If the lawyers lost, their salaries were paid by agencies such as the federal Legal Services Corporation. If they won on an allegation of a civil rights violation, the loser (almost always a state or local government) had to pay the winning side's legal fees — often running into millions of dollars at a time when a million dollars was a lot more money than it is now.[4]

If a patient had a right to treatment as a condition of being involuntarily committed — and a right to refuse treatment — was there a right to hold a person against their will if they refused treatment? And what psychiatrist would waste bed space on a patient who refused treatment, especially when it might lead to a sizable judgment against the agency providing mental health care? *That* would be crazy.

While the push for deinstitutionalization preceded this expansion of the definition of civil rights, there was a synergy there, as the courts increasingly intervened against existing state laws that assumed that a loss of civil rights was sometimes, even often, in the best interests of the mentally ill.[5] False analogies also started to appear, with mental institutions compared to racial segregation of schools. "Is not segregative treatment of disabled individuals in large, custodial institutions an inherently unequal and therefore unconstitutional practice, just as separate schools for blacks was judged inherently unequal?"[6]

Similarly, lawyers attacked how state mental hospitals used the labor of patients, claiming that it was outlawed by the Thirteenth Amendment's prohibition on slavery, and demanding that patients no longer be required to perform any work. In the nineteenth century, psychiatrists considered patients working to be a form of therapy, as well as a way to keep the costs of the hospital low.

The demand that hospitals not be allowed to put their inmates to work sounds at first absurd, but as with many other issues raised by Ennis and others, there may have been at least occasional abuses that justified these concerns. Ennis' *Prisoners of Psychiatry* describes one case that he handled involving an Edna Long who was first hospitalized in 1951 for "psychosis due to alcohol." After several incidents of release and rehospitalization for public drunkenness, she was permanently hospitalized in 1952. As Ennis tells the tale, Long received no treatment during the next fifteen years, but was kept busy working at menial jobs in the hospital. After the death of her husband in 1960, the state hospital had her declared incompetent, and seized her assets to pay for her care.

Then, they put what assets remained under the management of an attorney, who made a bit of money from reducing the value of her estate by 86 per cent (according to Ennis, a common practice at the time in New York). Once Long had become too physically ill to continue working, the hospital suddenly found her "competent to manage her own affairs" and released her, to a life of elderly poverty. Most of the money that she and her husband had accumulated had been consumed by attorneys supposedly protecting her assets.[7]

Was Long's experience unique? Ennis would like us to believe that it was not. If Mrs. Long had been single, it is at least plausible that she had no family or friends on the outside who made efforts to get her released. If Mrs. Long's problem was simply that she drank until she saw pink elephants, it seems hard to believe that her husband would not have made an effort to get this injustice corrected in the eight years that she was locked up, and he was alive. Like many of the other stories that Ennis's book told, this tragedy was not impossible, but a careful reading, and the lack of independent corroboration, leads me to wonder if there was a bit more to the story. Regardless of whether Mrs. Long's experience was typical, rare, or misrepresented, the net effect of prohibiting mental hospitals from having patients perform any labor towards the operation of the facilities was that the lawyers managed to make "large state hospitals both uneconomic and unmanageable."[8]

The right to refuse treatment developed with astonishing speed. As late as 1969, state supreme courts in New York and Massachusetts were treating compulsory treatment as the norm, condemning state hospitals for failing to involuntarily medicate patients.[9] A 1968 decision in New York State granted damages to a patient because "he was confined without treatment" and the courts ruled that failure to treat him simply because he had refused the drugs was "illogical" and "unprofessional." There was no right to refuse treatment, and failure to treat against the patient's will would put the hospital at risk.[10]

Yet within ten years, the situation had reversed; the legal system now regarded involuntary treatment as, at best, questionable. One reason was that state legislatures started to separate the question of involuntary commitment from the question of competence. Formerly, a person committed against his or her will was presumed to be incompetent (as we examined with the *Lessard* decision), and lost many rights as a result.

By the mid-1970s, people who were involuntarily committed were no longer assumed to be incompetent. The analogy that increasingly took hold was that a person with a *physical* illness had the right to decide whether to go ahead with a medical procedure or not. The only significant exception involved minors whose parents refused to allow treatment on religious grounds. The courts usually overrode such decisions on the grounds that the state had a compelling governmental interest in protecting the child from his parents. If a patient were competent to refuse heart surgery, why would he not be competent to refuse treatment for mental illness?[1] That mental illness impairs the ability of a patient to make rational choices seems not to have occurred to the clever sorts who filed suits and handed down decisions from the bench.

As so often happens when the courts make decisions, a precedent from one category of case was applied to a different category of case with only a superficial similarity. The case involved a state hospital that withheld medical care from a mentally *retarded* person dying of leukemia. Through the magic of law, this became the basis for a right of mentally *ill* patients to refuse treatment. This was a different category of person, and where the first case involved a patient who could not express an opinion, the second involved someone who could. This was at least an apples and oranges comparison, if not apples and onions.

In the 1977 decision *Superintendent Of Belchertown State School* v. *Saikewicz*, the Massachusetts Supreme Judicial Court decided that a severely retarded man named Joseph Saikewicz who had been diagnosed with leukemia, should be allowed to die without treatment — even while acknowledging, as the trial court had found, "That the majority of persons suffering from leukemia who are faced with a choice of receiving or foregoing such chemotherapy, and who are able to make an informed judgment thereon, choose to receive treatment in spite of its toxic side effects and risks of failure." Saikewicz was incapable of communication except by "resorting to gestures and grunts to make his wishes known to others and responding only to gestures or physical contacts."

The courts decided that Saikewicz was unable to make a decision for himself, and so they decided to follow the advice of the hospital's physicians that he should be allowed to die. The decision includes a rather remarkable sentence which reads like what would happen if the Marx Brothers had made a movie about

Nazi Germany's T4 program for euthanizing the terminally ill, retarded, disabled, and deformed.   For some reason, I keep picturing Groucho Marx delivering this line, while raising his eyebrows and smirking. The Massachusetts high court explained how they decided that Saikewicz should be allowed to die:

> In short, the decision in cases such as this should be that which would be made by the incompetent person, if that person were competent, but taking into account the present and future incompetency of the individual as one of the factors which would necessarily enter into the decision-making process of the competent person.[12]

There was no chance that Saikewicz would ever get past his mental retardation.   He had few years left to live, whether leukemia, chemotherapy, or old age carried him off. But in 1981, the Massachusetts high court used this "substituted judgment" precedent in a *very* different context.   This time, it was not a severely mentally retarded person who could not express his opinion about a difficult end of life decision, but a mentally ill young man identified in the court documents as Richard Roe III.

Richard Roe III's decline into paranoid schizophrenia started at age 16, following illicit drug use. He was briefly hospitalized after his arrest for a number of crimes, including unarmed robbery, assault and battery, and receiving stolen property.   While hospitalized, he attacked other patients. A probate judge appointed his father as guardian.   At the request of Northampton State Hospital, Roe's father authorized them to involuntarily administer anti-psychotic medications to Roe if needed.

In much the same way that the judges decided what Saikewicz would have decided to do about chemotherapy, if he were competent, the judges decided to substitute their judgment for that of Roe's father:

> If the judge determines that the ward, if competent, would accept the medication, he is to order its administration. If the judge determines that the ward's substituted judgment would be to refuse treatment, we set forth ... those State interests which are capable of overwhelming the right to refuse antipsychotic medication.[13]

The Court set a very high standard for allowing Roe's father to authorize involuntary treatment:

> Absent an overwhelming State interest, a competent individual
> has the right to refuse such treatment. To deny this right to
> persons who are incapable of exercising it personally is to
> degrade those whose disabilities make them wholly reliant on
> other, more fortunate, individuals.[14]

What the Court seemed to have missed, however, is that
without treatment, Roe would likely *remain* incompetent to make
his own decisions. With treatment, there was at least a chance that
Roe would reach a point where he would be sufficiently sane to
make his own decisions.

> In order to accord proper respect to this basic right of all
> individuals, we feel that if an incompetent individual refuses
> antipsychotic drugs, those charged with his protection must seek
> a judicial determination of substituted judgment....   The
> determination of what the incompetent individual would do if
> competent will probe the incompetent individual's values and
> preferences, and such an inquiry, in a case involving
> antipsychotic drugs, is best made in courts of competent
> jurisdiction.[15]

The Court thus decided that judges were more competent to
assess Roe's "values and preferences" than Roe's father. If there
were some evidence presented that Roe's father was not concerned
with his son's welfare, there might be a strong question as to
whether Roe's father should be making this decision. But the
Court never identified any such reason to be concerned. At most,
they discussed some of the side effects of anti-psychotic
medications, compared their use to electroconvulsive therapy, and
pointed to the past abuse and misuse of psychiatric medications as
a reason why the father and psychiatrists at the state hospital should
not be trusted with such a decision.[16]

Instead, they decided that only an emergency medical decision
would justify allowing the father to authorize such treatment. The
psychiatrist who testified at trial pointed out that the longer Roe sat
untreated, the more likely it was that his condition would become
chronic.[17] This was not enough for the Court.

> We think that the possibility that the ward's schizophrenia might deteriorate into a chronic, irreversible condition at an uncertain but relatively distant date does not satisfy our definition of emergency, especially where, as here, the course of the illness is measured by years and no crisis has been precipitated.[18]

Because Roe's father had been given a guardianship over Roe, but no court had formally declared Roe to be incompetent, the Court refused to allow Roe's father to make a decision on Roe's behalf. While they acknowledged that Roe was insane (and even Roe's attorney did not dispute this), they concluded that the Court was right to override the father's decision because of their objectivity:

> Decisions such as the one the guardian wishes to make in this case pose exceedingly difficult problems for even the most capable, detached, and diligent decisionmaker. We intend no criticism of the guardian when we say that few parents could make this substituted judgment determination by its nature a self-centered determination in which the decisionmaker is called upon to ignore all but the implementation of the values and preferences of the ward when the ward, in his present condition, is living at home with other children.... A judicial determination also benefits the guardian, who otherwise might suffer from lingering doubts concerning the propriety of his decision.[19]

The guardian, in this case, Roe's father, doubtless "thanked" the justices for helping him with his "lingering doubts" by overriding his judgment, and that of the doctors, by ruling that a violent and insane person could not be treated against his will, increasing the odds that Roe's mental illness would become chronic.

The Court finally laid down six criteria for deciding how a judge should decide whether to force treatment. One of these criteria was an open invitation for judges making these decisions to ignore express statements made by the *patient* before he became ill:

> If the ward has expressed a preference while not subjected to guardianship and presumably competent, ... such an expression is entitled to great weight in determining his substituted judgment unless the judge finds that either: (a) simultaneously with his expression of preference the ward lacked the capacity to

make such a medical treatment decision, or (b) the ward, upon
reflection and reconsideration, would not act in accordance with
his   previously   expressed   preference   in   the   changed
circumstances in which he currently finds himself.[20]

But what are a patient's preferences?   How would a judge
know that the patient "would have changed his opinion after
reflection or in altered circumstances"?   This is worse than
guessing what Saikewicz *might* have wanted; the Court here
encouraged a judge to overturn a patient's "expressed preferences
... made while competent" based on what a judge decided that
patient *would* have done.

The sixth criterion for "substituted judgment" is perhaps the
most ludicrous of all:

Sixth, the prognosis with treatment must be examined.   The
likelihood of improvement or cure enhances the likelihood that
an incompetent patient would accept treatment, but it is not
conclusive.[21]

After all, a sane person might prefer insanity — you just can't
tell!   Or perhaps the justices that wrote this opinion were a little
unsure themselves of which was preferable: sanity or insanity.

The effect of this decision was to make it impossible for Roe's
family to try to help him back to sanity.   They gave up their efforts.
According to the attorney who represented Roe's parents, "It blew
the family to pieces.   The husband and wife divorced."   Roe
became "a semi-street person and has been constantly involved
with the law with minor infractions."[22]

Massachusetts was just one state, and there were lawsuits
brought in both state and federal courts during this same period that
reached different conclusions.   By 1983, a survey of the fifty states
plus the District of Columbia found that twenty-five jurisdictions
allowed a mental patient to refuse medication (except for certain
emergency situations), six recognized no such right, and twenty
jurisdictions determined whether a patient was free to refuse
medication based on the patient's legal competency.[23]

This was not the end of the story.   In *Washington* v. *Harper*
(1990), a Washington State man with a history of bipolar disorder
and violence challenged involuntary medication with antipsychotic
drugs as a violation of his rights under the due process clause of the

Fourteenth Amendment. Harper filed suit in Washington courts, lost at the trial court, but won in the Washington Supreme Court, which decided in 1988 that involuntary treatment required not only the procedural protections which Washington law provided, but also that the state must prove by "'clear, cogent, and convincing' evidence that the administration of antipsychotic medication was both necessary and effective for furthering a compelling state interest."[24]   This is an extraordinarily high standard to meet (although not impossible), and Washington State appealed to the U.S. Supreme Court.

The U.S. Supreme Court overruled the Washington Supreme Court, deciding that the procedural protections of Washington's process were sufficient to meet the due process requirement:

> The Policy under review requires the State to establish, by a medical finding, that a mental disorder exists which is likely to cause harm if not treated. Moreover, the fact that the medication must first be prescribed by a psychiatrist, and then approved by a reviewing psychiatrist, ensures that the treatment in question will be ordered only if it is in the prisoner's medical interests, given the legitimate needs of his institutional confinement. These standards, which recognize both the prisoner's medical interests and the State's interests, meet the demands of the Due Process Clause.[25]

The Court made this decision based on a balancing of the needs of a prison, and of the liberty interest that a prisoner had in refusing treatment.[26]   While less rigidly individualistic than the *Guardianship of Roe* decision from Massachusetts, it left open the question of whether this would be the same situation with a mental patient who was not in a prison.

Two years later, in *Riggins* v. *Nevada* (1992), the Court ruled that a person undergoing trial for murder had the right to refuse an antipsychotic drug, because he was attempting to make an insanity plea part of his defense.   The Court ruled that involuntary administration would have been permissible if it "was medically appropriate and, considering less intrusive alternatives, essential for the sake of Riggins' own safety or the safety of others." But simply to make Riggins sane for trial was not enough reason, and the Court heard testimony that the drug might induce confusion. From the standpoint of the defendant, and even from the standpoint of making sure that the courts made the right decision about guilt, this certainly seems like a legitimate reason for a defendant on trial for his life to refuse the drug.[27]

Because *Washington* v. *Harper* was quite specific to the case of a convicted felon serving a prison sentence, and was justified based on the needs to maintain security and order within a prison, it left open questions about the right to refuse treatment in other contexts. A number of other state supreme courts followed Massachusetts's lead in *Guardianship of Roe*, and other states changed their statutes or regulations to conform in anticipation of suits. At least fourteen states required formal hearings, with "substituted judgment" requirements for involuntary medication of mentally ill patients.

The effects of this right to refuse treatment were surprisingly broad and yet, at least by some measures, surprisingly meaningless. Psychiatric hospital staff now spent many hours preparing for formal hearings. The Massachusetts Department of Mental Health budgeted $800,000 for attorneys to handle these cases — and yet "in 98.6% of the cases, the court ruled the individual should be medicated." Delays in medication while waiting for legal approval slowed down treatment and increased risks for patients and staff. Patients who could not be medicated against their will (or at least, the legal paperwork had not yet been completed), could still be locked up in seclusion or strapped down for the safety of themselves and others.[28] In other cases, as we will see in a later chapter, the effect was often to make it simpler for hospitals to release mentally ill people to the streets, devoting their energies to those who were willing to be treated.

Alone, the right to refuse treatment would not have been a serious problem for mental hospitals and for the mentally ill. Hospitals would have, at least in some cases, had to make more use of physical restraints for the violently mentally ill. To the extent that patients were not stabilized, it would have delayed the opportunity for patients to return to the community, at least for those for whom this was a possibility. But as with so many of these changes, the right to refuse treatment did not stand alone.

The courts, by calling into question the authority of the federal and state governments to involuntarily hospitalize and treat mental patients, forced a substantial revision of the existing state laws. Many of these decisions found that mental patients were deprived of Constitutional rights by the commitment laws. Once the courts had defined what those rights included, the authority of the state legislatures to correct defective statutes was quite limited.

Had the courts recognized the sometimes fuzzy and imprecise nature of the problems involved with determining appropriate treatment of the mentally ill, the consequences of these decisions might not have been so destructive. Ingo Keilitz observed, with respect to the 1986 publication of "Guidelines for Involuntary Civil Commitment," some points that applied to the entire civil libertarian approach:

> A basic premise of the "Guidelines" is that the tendencies to view complexities of the involuntary civil commitment process in abstract, polar terms — e.g., personal liberties versus treatment needs, doctors versus lawyers, the legal model versus the medical model, or the police power of the state versus its *parens patriae* function — are stultifying and counterproductive. Perhaps theoretically and historically useful, such dichotomies do not fit the realities facing the public mental health system today....[29]

Abstract principles sound so beautiful in a classroom, but the enormous range of real world problems and people mean that rigid definitions and policies, even if right most of the time, often destroyed lives when they were wrong.

16.   CALIFORNIA MARCHES OFF THE CLIFF

When it came to mental illness commitment laws, California led the way down; most other states followed them into the ground, with destructive effects. While a few other states already had quite restrictive civil commitment laws, California's actions are generally agreed to have been the model that most other states followed in the 1970s and 1980s. The Lanterman-Petris-Short Act of 1967 (LPS), effective in 1969, was full of good intentions. The statute explained its goal as:

(a) To end the inappropriate, indefinite, and involuntary commitment of mentally disordered persons, developmentally disabled persons, and persons impaired by chronic alcoholism, and to eliminate legal disabilities;

(b) To provide prompt evaluation and treatment of persons with serious mental disorders or impaired by chronic alcoholism;

(c) To guarantee and protect public safety;

(d) To safeguard individual rights through judicial review;

(e) To provide individualized treatment, supervision, and placement services by a conservatorship program for gravely disabled persons;

(f) To encourage the full use of all existing agencies, professional personnel and public funds to accomplish these objectives and to prevent duplication of services and unnecessary expenditures;

(g) To protect mentally disordered persons and developmentally disabled persons from criminal acts.[1]

The statute defined a mentally ill person as "gravely disabled" if he or she was "unable to provide for his or her basic personal needs for food, clothing, or shelter" or was found incompetent after indictment for "felony involving death, great bodily harm, or a serious threat to the physical well-being of another person."[2] The motivations for the law reflected the anti-psychiatric beliefs of Szasz and Laing, the deviant labeling theory of sociologists, and the institutional critics who believed that mental hospitals caused insanity.

A strange coalition of mental health professionals supported LPS's passage. Psychologists and social workers, who had traditionally been left out of managing the mentally ill, found the new law gave them enhanced status relative to psychiatrists. Many psychiatrists were either indifferent to the changes, or were actively supportive, because while LPS made long-term involuntary commitment much more difficult, it also made short-term commitment for up to seventeen days (three days for observation, fourteen days for intensive treatment) easier. Mental hospital staff labor unions, on the other hand, saw LPS as a threat to their financial interests, and fought against it,[3] as did legislators who represented districts where state mental hospitals were major employers.[4] Most important of all, the California legislature saw the opportunity to both save money and show themselves as progressive civil libertarians in one step. *The Dilemma of Mental Commitments in California*, a 1966 study that led to Lanterman-Petris-Short, promised that "state hospitals as we know them, will no longer exist."

California's pressing fiscal problems certainly played a part in LPS's passage, as did the support of Governor Ronald Reagan — although Reagan supported expansion of the community mental health system as a necessary companion to LPS.[5] The political ambitions of members of the lower house's Subcommittee on Mental Health Services were also a factor. Having successfully reformed how the state cared for the mentally retarded (and this was a system in need of reform), they introduced similar progressive reforms for the mentally ill.[6]

After LPS's passage, California's courts heard many appeals

from those placed under conservatorship by their county of residence. In some cases, the courts upheld those conservatorships and involuntary commitments; it was not difficult to see why. One example was Bernice Cabanne, who a court-appointed psychiatrist described as unable to provide for her own food, clothing, or shelter. "He testified that she told him that someone was trying to kill her on the way to the examination. He also testified that during the examination she was hallucinating by talking to voices and by stating that she saw a dragon fly by the window."[7]

In another case before the California Court of Appeals, one Margaret L. with a history of more than twenty hospitalizations was found by a psychiatrist to be suffering from "a combination of schizophrenic-type symptoms and symptoms like mania and depression." The psychiatrist described Margaret L.'s delusions:

> She told various professionals, including myself, that her father and brother had been involved in the Watergate scandal. She also had the delusional belief that she was Peggy Sue and was being raped because of that. She claimed that John Fitzgerald Kennedy was her attorney. She said she had been involved in the Manson trial. She claimed that her family had forced her to be a child prostitute for the Kennedys. And again, she made additional charges of being molested and raped in a facility. ... Ms. L[.] repeatedly believes that she's being raped, that has continued through the years. In every facility that she's been at she's reported people coming into her room to [rape her] at night.[8]

In other cases, the courts did not uphold the commitments. These decisions sometimes focused on whether the law met the Fourteenth Amendment's due process requirement. In *Conservatorship of Roulet* (1978), the county argued that because commitment was a civil matter, it only required a preponderance of evidence. The California Supreme Court disagreed, holding that because a person could be confined to a mental hospital for up to a year, to meet due process requirements, the county needed a higher standard of proof: "clear and convincing evidence" of being gravely disabled. This was more than the traditional civil law standard of a preponderance of evidence, although not the "evidence beyond a reasonable doubt" required by the standard of criminal law.[9]

Similarly, *In re S.* (1977) concluded that a 14-year-old minor could not be committed to a mental hospital without the same due process protections that LPS provided to an adult. The California Supreme Court based this due process requirement in part on a U.S. Supreme Court decision involving a 15 year old who had been sent to reform school until 18 for making an obscene phone call. While both cases involved the state depriving a minor of his liberty, *In re S.* was not a criminal conviction, but an attempt by a parent to obtain treatment for a mentally ill child.[10]

Sometimes the courts sided with the mentally ill person because of the precise definition of "gravely disabled" contained in LPS. Humboldt County, on the north coast of California, sought conservatorship over one Elsie Smith:

> At intermittent periods for the last five years, appellant has attended the Eureka Church of God in Eureka, California. In June 1985, appellant began an around-the-clock vigil outside the church. At the times she would enter the church, she would make a disturbance and interrupt services. The pastor of the church made several attempts to counsel her about receiving help, but his advice was ignored. The pastor also contacted the police on several occasions when appellant's behavior was particularly disruptive. On these occasions, the officers arrested appellant and took her to jail or to a nearby mental hospital.

At trial, a psychiatrist described Smith as suffering a paranoid delusions concerning Eureka Church of God, and considered her gravely disabled because of the conflict that her delusions caused when she disrupted church services. The California Court of Appeals decided that this did not meet the legal requirement of "gravely disabled" because even though Smith was without income or assets, she was still able "to provide for his or her basic personal needs" through the kindness of others. She had not committed a felony that threatened great bodily injury to others, and she had found people prepared to help her with food, clothing, and shelter:

> At times, she engages in displays of disruptive behavior, interrupting church services. Her fixation on the church results in her sleeping on the sidewalk in front of the church at night, and on one past occasion this may have caused her to become sick. She has no income, no savings and no permanent home.

However, the record also reveals that the psychiatrist believes that she is able to obtain food, clothing and shelter, and that appellant regularly receives offers of help and does at times accept assistance.[11]

LPS also provided a method for civilly committing those who had committed the most serious felonies, and had been found incompetent to stand trial. This failed to handle cases of criminals who were competent to stand trial, but remained dangerous after release. In response to this, in 1985, California passed the Mentally Disordered Offender Act, providing that criminals whose crimes were related to their mental disorder — but presumably legally sane — could be civilly committed under similar provisions to LPS.

Mentally disordered offenders could be civilly committed, but could they refuse medication? Kanuri Surgury Qawi received a four-year sentence for a felony assault, two misdemeanor assaults, and two misdemeanor batteries. He was paroled after two years. Because of continual parole violations and stalking a woman he claimed was his wife (which was news to her), prosecutors invoked the Mentally Disordered Offender Act. A psychiatrist diagnosed Qawi as paranoid schizophrenic, which in light of the delusions associated with his previous crimes, does not seem to be a stretch.

Qawi's statements and actions while locked up led evaluators to conclude that he "represented a substantial danger of risk of physical harm to others." As the decision observed:

[I]n several examinations, evaluators have described Qawi as "clearly delusional and grandiose" and have noted that he "expresse[s] some persecutory beliefs regarding his continued incarceration," including that "the State of California had no intention of ever letting him out of the hospital."

Qawi's suit sought to discontinue administration of antipsychotic medications, arguing that had a right to refuse, as did other mental patients committed under LPS. The California Supreme Court acknowledged that while most mental patients committed under LPS had a right to refuse medication, as did most patients committed under the Mentally Disordered Offenders Act, specific evidence that a patient was *currently* a threat to others in an institutional setting provided sufficient justification for forced medication. The mental hospital director had not introduced such evidence with respect to Qawi.[12]

One of the virtues of federalism is that it provides fifty laboratories in which different states may try out different approaches to public policy questions. If one state's laws work well, other states should look at the success, and copy it, perhaps adapting it to local conditions or needs. But as often seems to be the case, when California's experiment failed, it was copied nonetheless, perhaps because of the constraints that the civil liberties decisions of the courts had imposed on the states. When California adopted LPS, only five other states had so severely limited civil commitment. Ten years after LPS, "every state and Puerto Rico had modified its commitment code."[13] LPS set the standard followed by every other state that modified its commitment law in the following decade.[14]

Frank Lanterman recognized in his later days what a disaster the act that bears his name had become. He told his secretary, late in life, "I wanted the LPS Act to help the mentally ill. I never meant for it to prevent those who need care from receiving it. The law has to be changed."[15]

California was a leader in deinstitutionalization, but unlike many other states that were doing so under the threat of legal action, California's errors were voluntary — a well-intentioned effort to improve the quality of mental health care based on some assumptions that turned out to be incorrect. The Lanterman-Petris-Short Act turned out to be enormously influential, not because the net effect was so wonderful, but because California throughout the 1960s and 1970s was regarded in other parts of the United States as a center of enlightened and progressive thinking. The destructive effects of LPS took a few years to become completely obvious, but by then, many other states had followed California over the cliff.

17.   RON & ORTHOMOLECULAR TREATMENT

By 1979, my mother, now a widow, was grasping at whatever straws she could find to explain Ron's condition. In 1966, when Ron was about 19, he was in a Tijuana bar. A fight broke out; the police officers who broke up the fight were a bit indiscriminate. One of them knocked Ron unconscious with his nightstick. Did that cause a brain injury? For a while, she had some hopes that Ron's mental illness might be related to hypoglycemia; at least one doctor explored the possibility that there was a connection. (This isn't as bizarre as it sounds; the symptoms of hypoglycemia can include hallucinations.)

Psychoanalytic psychiatry tried to put the blame for schizophrenia on family dynamics. As the genetic evidence that a tendency towards schizophrenia is inherited accumulates, the more absurd the family dynamics argument seems. Adoption, for example, doesn't seem to change the odds of children from schizophrenic families getting it — suggesting that family dynamics doesn't matter.[1] I shudder to think of how many parents have spent their lives overwhelmed with guilt for a child's schizophrenia — a position that increasingly seems as plausible as blaming madness on the full Moon.

At some point, Ron ended up in New York City a second time, staying in some kind of halfway house for the mentally ill, although we don't really know all the details. When he returned to California in 1979, my mother again took him into her house in the small desert town of Lenwood, a suburb of Barstow. Ron's behavior was obviously bizarre, and in some businesses in Barstow, if he showed up, he would be asked if he had business there; if not, he was asked to leave.

It was not just businesses that recognized that there was something wrong with Ron. I vividly recall one crisp, clear winter morning going out for a walk in Lenwood, while Ron was also out for a walk. I came up behind Ron, and noticed that there were two black men in their 20s some distance away, with Ron closer to them than to me. Ron yelled something at them. I could not hear what he said, but from their facial responses, I suspect that it was a racial slur; they were very angry. I feared that Ron was about to get beaten up, and I speeded up in the hopes of being able to explain to them that Ron was crazy. As they approached Ron, their expressions changed. Whatever anger these two men felt about what Ron had said evaporated as they realized that he was not right in the head.

On one of my visits to my mother and Ron, we were working in the back yard with a shovel. Ron was again talking of taking off for New York City; my mother was not happy about this plan, because of concern for his safety. Ron took a swing at her. It was only a glancing blow, so she wasn't injured, but it was enough to show his disapproval. I picked up the shovel to make sure that it wouldn't be available for him to use again, and my mother and I retreated into the house. I stood in the laundry room, in a narrow space between the back door and the washing machine, and called 911.

In the meantime, Ron had figured out that we were calling the police, came back into the house, and in a rage, attempted to get to me as I talked to the 911 operator. I was terrified of Ron, and his apparent rage. I held up the shovel to keep him away from me, and tried to push him away. He then ran out of the house again, and disappeared.

Shortly thereafter, a sheriff's deputy arrived, and we explained the situation to him. A few minutes later, the deputy found Ron somewhere in the area, and took him into custody. After a few hours in a Barstow jail, Ron must have realized that something was wrong with him, because he now recognized that he belonged in jail for attacking our mother.

After a couple of days locked up in San Bernadino, Ron agreed to a voluntary transfer to a hospital in Beverly Hills run by Dr. Harvey M. Ross. My mother was at that point involved with establishing a chapter of the National Alliance for the Mentally Ill in Barstow. Because of her contacts with other parents helping their mentally ill children, she had read some of the claims for orthomolecular treatment. Dr. Ross was one of the psychiatrists using this approach for treating schizophrenia.

For a while, the orthomolecular theory of schizophrenia advanced by the Canadian psychiatrists Hoffer and Osmond seemed like it might be an explanation — and at least for some schizophrenics, a cure.   Hoffer and Osmond believed that schizophrenia was a biochemical problem caused by the inability of schizophrenics to metabolize adrenochrome (an adrenalin byproduct). The orthomolecular theory has now been cast aside by biochemists looking into the causes of schizophrenia, but recent research does suggest that at least one possible cause is the enzyme catechol-O-methyl transferase, which is involved in the metabolizing of adrenalin.[2]   Perhaps Hoffer and Osmond were wrong on the details, but at least headed down the right path.

Ron spent about six weeks in a hospital in Beverly Hills where Dr. Ross was either a part-owner or was on staff; I was never very clear on the relationship. I don't know all the details of what Ron's treatment involved.   I do know that much of it was the orthomolecular therapy promoted by Hoffer and Osmond: no caffeine, no sugar, high doses of niacin, as well as Haldol, an antipsychotic drug widely used at the time, in spite of some nasty side effects.

Previously, when Ron was released from a mental hospital, Ron was calm. But this was a heavily drugged calm; his mind operated slowly, and while he was able to hold a conversation of sorts, it was often not a terribly sensible conversation. There was never any question that he was suffering some sort of mental disorder.   It would have been obvious to anyone having a conversation with him that there was something wrong.

Upon release from Dr. Ross' hospital, Ron was dramatically improved. Over the next few months, I visited my mother and Ron several times. Ron was able to hold serious and perfectly sensible conversations. He was quiet and somewhat reserved, but no more so than many other people. Had I not known of his previous history, I would have had no occasion to suspect that he was suffering from mental illness; perhaps he was just very shy.

The change was more than just how he appeared; in 1981, he enrolled at Barstow College. I remember reading a paper that he wrote for a freshman English Composition class about his experiences working as a mover, many years before.   It was humorous and well organized. He took calculus, psychology, and art history, and he made the Dean's List both semesters.

For about six months, everything went well for Ron. He regularly took the bus from Barstow to Dr. Ross' office in Beverly Hills (about a 2 ½ hour drive by car), but eventually, it seemed more sensible to arrange for Ron to get a counselor closer to home. Then the San Bernadino county bureaucracy decided that Ron needed to be under the care of one of their psychiatrists, if he was going to talk to a counselor on their dime.

Ron's situation definitely declined from there. He was transferred from psychiatrist to psychiatrist, with predictable results. There wasn't any clear point of collapse, but the progress that he had made seemed to reach a plateau.

Was orthomolecular therapy the right approach? Ron certainly benefited from it, and while he was not completely well, he was certainly much better off than he had been for many years. I suspect that the bureaucratic requirements about seeing the county's psychiatrist short-circuited what might have been, if not a complete recovery, at least the potential for Ron to become a self-sufficient member of society again. Unfortunately, the psychiatric profession was still dominated by psychoanalysts who regarded orthomolecular therapy as, at best, unproven, and at worst, a form of quackery. This assumption by the psychiatrists that treated Ron meant that he was unable to continue the program that seemed to be the most effective.

18.   HOMELESSNESS & URBAN DECAY (1975 – PRESENT)

The most visible result of deinstitutionalization of the mentally ill — although it was not at first recognized as such — was homelessness.   Because homelessness has many possible definitions, it might be good to first define our terms.   A person who has no fixed address, living in parks, sleeping in a cardboard box, is clearly "homeless."   A person who has temporary housing in a homeless shelter is pretty clearly homeless.   Some distinguish these two situations by calling the former the "unsheltered homeless."

The lines start to become a bit hazier as you move up the ladder of stability.   Many activists in the 1980s considered persons living in single-room occupancy (SRO) hotels to be homeless.   These were skid-row hotels, and many of the occupants were transient, sometimes moving from SRO to the street when (as often happened), an individual or a family ran out of money before the end of the month.

Is a person who is staying temporarily with friends because they do not have a home actually homeless?   What distinguishes this from roommates or subletting, if the homeless person is giving money to his friends?   A person who is living in their car meets most people's definitions of homelessness — but how do you distinguish this from someone who is living in a motor home or camper, traveling the country?   People in both situations are doing so voluntarily — and people in both situations *may* be doing so because more traditional living arrangements are more expensive than they can afford.

Attempts to count the homeless suffer from this definitional problem.   Another problem was that the transient nature of the homeless made it difficult to accurately count those who were *willing* to be counted. Paranoia meant that many of the mentally ill homeless were unwilling to cooperate with census takers. While political activists in 1983 claimed that there were 2.2 million homeless Americans, the flaws underlying this number were so severe that only journalists and politicians took it seriously.[1]   A Department of Housing and Urban Development survey in 1984 concluded that nationally, those without a place to stay numbered 250,000 to 350,000.[2]   A National Bureau of Economic Research report in 1986 estimated that there were 279,000 homeless in 1983.[3] Estimates using different methodologies for 1987 suggested 567,000 to 600,000 Americans were homeless.[4]

While the Census Bureau made an attempt to count homeless in 1990 and 2000 as part of the decennial population count, by the Bureau's own admission, these counts were necessarily incomplete. Census marshals were understandably afraid to enter abandoned buildings, and counted only those in homeless shelters and on the streets overnight. In addition, some advocates for the homeless, who had long exaggerated the number of homeless in America, actively attempted to prevent a count in 1990. The 1990 Census Bureau count was 228,621; in 2000, the figure had risen to 280,527.[5] The actual number of homeless was almost certainly higher than that — but probably less than a million.

Regardless of how you define homelessness, there does seem to be agreement (except from a few hopeless ideologues) that homelessness increased at about the same time as deinstitutionalization, and that this was not a coincidence. While economic factors doubtless played some role, studies in big cities around the United States in the 1980s found that those staying in homeless shelters were disproportionately mentally ill.[6]

Attempting to compare the results of these studies has some serious problems because there was no standard methodology. In some studies, those evaluating the homeless were psychiatrists; other studies relied on the opinions of homeless shelter managers. For some studies, "major mental illness" included not only schizophrenia and bipolar disorder, but also clinical depression.[7] Still, even analysts who believe that deinstitutionalization was a good step agree that the dramatic expansion of the homeless population was because so many mentally ill persons were either released from mental hospitals, or in the new system, had never been hospitalized.[8]

Variations in surveying techniques and definitions of mental illness used by the different studies makes trend analysis impossible; it does appear that the percentage of the homeless with severe mental illness increased in the 1980s. Adding to the complexity of the categorization problem is that over time, ever larger percentages of the homeless population had substance abuse problems.[9]

Unlike schizophrenia and bipolar disorder where the direction of causality is obvious, it is not immediately clear how many are homeless because of depression, and how many have sunk into severe depression because of being homeless. The overlap between the mentally ill and substance abusers is also a complicated puzzle to unravel. Some psychoses are caused or aggravated by drug abuse; mentally ill people are also prone to substance abuse to deal with their symptoms.

The data from early 1980s surveys had a sad consistency to it. Of 179 homeless men and women who received psychiatric examinations in a Philadelphia shelter in 1981, 40 per cent were found to have "major mental disorders." One-third of those examined were diagnosed as schizophrenic, and another one-fourth had a primary diagnosis of substance abuse. A Boston shelter study of 78 residents in 1983 again found that 40 per cent had major mental disorders, and another 51 per cent had less severe psychiatric problems. Only 9 per cent had no diagnosable mental disorder — and they were largely dependents (both children and spouses) of the 91 per cent with either major or minor mental problems. In New York, studies completed in 1981 and 1982 of those living on the streets found about half had serious psychiatric disorders. A survey of 345 subjects seeking food assistance in 1983 Phoenix found that about 30 per cent had spent some time in a mental institution. Studies of women's shelter residents in Washington, D.C. and Baltimore in 1981-2 produced similar results. Schizophrenia and other forms of psychosis tended to be most common among the chronically homeless.[10]

The disproportionate levels of severe mental illness among the homeless are not surprising. Living in cars, in homeless shelters, or sleeping on park benches, is at least quite unpleasant, and often far worse than that. Many of the difficulties are obvious to anyone who has ever gone camping: cold, rain, snow, or excess heat; a shortage of facilities for showering; difficulties in sleeping out of doors because of fear of violence. Even sleeping in a car makes only a slight improvement, as anyone who has ever slept in a car when it is freezing outside can attest. Other difficulties are less obvious: finding toilets; no way to store perishable food; the difficulty in protecting one's belongings from theft. It isn't surprising that many, if not most, homeless people are mentally ill. Anyone who remains homeless if he or she had any possible way out of such a situation would *have* to be a bit crazy.

By the late 1980s, the causal relationship between mental illness and homelessness was sufficiently obvious that only a few ideologues disputed that the major cause of people living on the street wasn't Ronald Reagan, but serious mental problems, often compounded by substance abuse. Nationwide, something that called itself the "new asylum movement" argued that as bad at the old institutions had been, patients at least had not been sleeping on steam grates in freezing weather.[11] It didn't have much success.

Why do people freeze to death in America? In 1982, Rebecca Smith, who had been in a mental hospital, and refused to go back, lived in a cardboard box on the streets of New York. She refused all assistance. While New York City authorities were attempting to get a court order to bring her in out of the cold, she froze to death.[12] She was not alone, by any means, nor was the problem restricted to New York City. A Veterans Administration doctor reported a shocking increase in amputations for frostbite among homeless, mentally ill veterans in the early 1980s.[13]

In 1985, New York City Major Ed Koch, concerning about freezing deaths in subfreezing weather (such as Rebecca Smith), ordered police officers to take into custody anyone lying in the streets. The New York chapter of the ACLU sent out a "freeze patrol" to hand out leaflets letting people know that they had a right to refuse to be taken to shelter.[14]

Joyce Brown, aka Billy Boggs, a homeless person living on the streets of New York City in 1987, became something of a poster child for where this abstract theory of Constitutional rights led. Her behavior was clearly psychotic: "She urinated and defecated on the streets,... ran recklessly into heavily trafficked streets, and exposed herself when assistance was offered."[15] Other aspects of her behavior were, at least, eccentric, such as tearing up money that passers-by gave her. Psychiatrists diagnosed her as paranoid schizophrenic.[16]

Brown was sleeping on a steam grate in freezing weather, and the city authorities hospitalized her against her will. The New York Civil Liberties Union filed suit, arguing that her essential dignity as a human being was denied by her involuntary hospitalization, and that she should not be forced to take psychiatric medications against her will. Rather than seeing her living conditions as a sign of mental illness, the NYCLU characterized it as "a fearless, independent life style"[17] and the courts agreed. As Judge Lippman, who first heard the NYCLU's suit against Brown's involuntary treatment described her situation:

> Who among us is not familiar with the tattered, filthy, malodorous presence of the wretched homeless? ... The blame and shame must attach to us, not to them. The predicament of Joyce Brown and the countless homeless raises questions of broad social, economic, political and moral implications not within the purview of this court.[18]

The courts upheld Brown's right to refuse treatment. The hospital concluded that there was no point in holding Brown against her will, if they were not allowed to treat her mental illness. Brown's brief time hospitalized appears to have done her some good, but eventually, the core problem of mental illness returned, and less than two months later, reporters again found her living on a steam grate, "shouting obscenities at passersby," and begging for money.[19]

Mayor Koch's concern about homeless people freezing to death on the streets may have been impressionistic, but there was data to support it. At the same that deinstitutionalization was in full swing, hypothermia deaths in America were on the rise. In 1974, the death rate was $0.164/100,000$ people. By 1979, the death rate had doubled to $0.322/100,000$. Hypothermia death rates continued to rise, peaking at $0.411/100,000$ in 1989, before dropping back below $0.2/100,000$ in the late 1990s. Not every person who died of hypothermia was mentally ill, but a detailed study of hypothermia deaths in Washington, DC in the years 1972-82 found that one-third were severely malnourished, with "most discovered in abandoned buildings or vehicles. Four-fifths had not been reported missing. One-half had high blood ethanol levels."[20] It is difficult to read these characteristics, which sound suspiciously like those of mentally ill homeless people in America, and not suspect that the increase in hypothermia death rates was partly because of deinstitutionalization.

Another component of the failure was that the institutionalized mentally ill had been disproportionately without families to assist them in a non-institutional setting. In 1960, 73 per cent of mental patients had no current spouse. While these numbers reflect the large percentage of elderly senile mental hospital patients in the pre-Medicare times, it does not seem implausible that the severely mentally ill were also likely to be alone when released. Economic considerations alone would have made life for single deinstitutionalized mental patients difficult, simply because they would have no partner with whom to share living expenses. Without someone closely monitoring their behavior, it is surprisingly easy for a patient who stops taking anti-psychotic medications to spiral downward and out of control. I have seen it happen to Ron more than once.

Yet while many of the advocates for community mental health centers (CMHCs) in the early 1960s were aware that the deinstitutionalized were unlikely to fare well when returned to the community, they showed no awareness of the likely consequences. Instead, the statutes and regulations largely ignored the needs of those who were in state mental hospitals.[21]   If the CMHC movement had not been so openly and bluntly directed at emptying out the state mental hospitals, this refusal to confront the problems of the psychotics might have made sense. As it was, it opened the door to a catastrophe.

It has been fashionable for some years to blame the failure of CHMCs to handle deinstitutionalization as a failure of funding. Certainly, the ambitious plans to build 2,000 CHMCs did not happen, partly because of insufficient funding. Senator Patrick Moynihan, who had been part of President John Kennedy's interagency task force that created this ambitious goal, claimed that the large population of homeless Americans was the result of this funding shortfall.

Contrary to Moynihan's 1980s hindsight enhanced explanation, funding shortages were not the reason that the federal government failed to build the 2000 centers that had been the original goal. By 1967, even members of Congress sympathetic to the CHMC concept admitted that only a few communities had a dense enough population to support such centers. Even had Congress funded building those centers, there was a severe shortage of professionals to staff these centers.

More important than the shortage of funds to build CMHCs was the problem of operating funds. The CMHC Act had envisioned federal funding of operating budgets as a temporary matter, until such time as fees from clients, health insurance reimbursements, and state and local subsidies took their place. The difficulty in finding permanent operating budgets for CMHCs made the 2000 center goal impossible.[22]

The radical political sentiments of the time also seduced at least some CMHCs into taking a broader, environmental view of their mission. The mission was no longer simply helping mental patients in the community; it was alleviating poverty and racism so that there would be fewer clients in the future. Whatever the merits of this argument with respect to depression and neuroses, there was no realistic possibility that these laudable social goals would have prevented schizophrenia, bipolar disorder, or any of the other biochemically-based mental illnesses.[23]   (Reducing drug abuse would have made a difference, but this was not initially a major concern of the community mental health movement.)   Perhaps indicative of how experience transformed perspectives on this, Robert E. L. Faris and H. Warren Dunham's *Mental Disorders in Urban Areas* (1939) had first made a statistical case that poverty and social disorder caused mental illness.[24] By the 1960s, Dunham had decided that mental illness had a biological origin, and the resulting incapacities caused poverty.[25]

Ronald Reagan's election in 1980 led to an attempt at reducing SSDI (Social Security Disability Insurance) and SSI (Supplemental Security Income) payments. Partly this was driven by a desire to solve a budget problem, but also, the Reagan Administration believed that freeloaders were abusing these programs.[26] There is absolutely no question in my mind that the problem of freeloaders was real.

I knew four people who were receiving SSDI and SSI checks in the late 1970s for mental illness, including my brother Ron. One was Joan, whom I mentioned earlier in this book. While clearly mentally ill, she was, in my opinion, capable of working. She was not very motivated, especially once she had a regular check every month.

A second recipient was a young man whom I will call Mark. He was receiving SSDI and SSI checks because he was mentally disabled. In two years of regular contact with him, I saw absolutely no indications of any mental illness whatsoever. He worked off the books about twenty hours a week, while waiting to inherit his father's substantial estate.

A third young man I will call Joe. Joe was supposedly disabled by a hip problem and some mental illness. I never saw that Joe's hip slowed him down. His behavior was at times somewhat inappropriate, but he was not disabled in any real sense. He worked the same off the books job as Mark. Of these four people, one was clearly unable to work (Ron), and three, while certainly not completely well, were capable of working some sort of job — and two of them (Mark and Joe) were doing so.

The Reagan Administration's efforts to correct this problem were built on the assumption that fraud was rampant in the system. Inevitably, when it came time for government agencies to review eligibility of recipients, their decisions hit the mentally disabled especially hard. While the mentally disabled were only 11 per cent of those receiving SSDI, they were 30 per cent of those cut from the rolls.[27]

It is possible that this disproportionate culling of the mentally ill from SSDI was because mental disability was easy to fake, especially compared to paralysis, or a lost limb. It is more likely that many of the mentally ill SSDI recipients simply lacked the capability to challenge the review process, and had no family member or friend to speak on their behalf. It is almost a Catch-22 of mental disability: how mentally ill was someone who could successfully appeal the decision to stop his SSDI check?

Those who styled themselves as advocates for the mentally ill had a point: if someone was severely mentally ill, how could they advocate for themselves against courts and bureaucracies? But a mentally ill person needed more assistance than just a lawyer at a commitment hearing, or someone to keep government checks flowing. They needed a level of assistance and supervision in the community that was simply not possible on an occasional basis.

Along with homelessness and its destructive effects on the mentally ill, homelessness led to a hard to measure, but nonetheless obvious decline in the quality of life for the rest of the society. Public libraries became, in many urban areas, day shelters for the mentally ill. This should be no surprise to anyone living in big cities over the last thirty years. What is surprising is how, even in the early 1980s, when the problem of homelessness was still being blamed on "Reaganomics" rather than deinstitutionalization, the public library problem was recognized as primarily caused by mental illness. A 1981 *New York Times* article detailed how public libraries around the country were dealing with what the article called "problem patrons":

> The Library of Congress in Washington has recently been patronized by a man wearing a yellow plastic wastebasket over his head, an elderly woman who sped to the stacks of telephone books in search of someone who had put a curse on her, a woman who smelled so foul she cleared one whole section of the main reading room, and a man the librarians came to call Robin Hood. He wore a quiver of arrows, and spent his time at the microfilm screen reading *The Los Angeles Times*.[28]

In 2007, Chip Ward, assistant director of the Salt Lake City public library system, wrote a devastating account of how the mentally ill homeless changed the library environment. While incorrectly blaming deinstitutionalization on the Reagan Administration, his first-hand accounts leave no question as to the severity of the mental illness afflicting many of those he saw:

> Ophelia sits by the fireplace and mumbles softly, smiling and gesturing at no one in particular. She gazes out the large window through the two pairs of glasses she wears, one windshield-sized pair over a smaller set perched precariously on her small nose. Perhaps four lenses help her see the invisible other she is addressing. When her "nobody there" conversation disturbs the reader seated beside her, Ophelia turns, chuckles at the woman's discomfort, and explains, "Don't mind me, I'm dead. It's okay. I've been dead for some time now." She pauses, then adds reassuringly, "It's not so bad. You get used to it." Not at all reassured, the woman gathers her belongings and moves quickly away. Ophelia shrugs. Verbal communication is tricky. She prefers telepathy, but that's hard to do since the rest of us, she informs me, "don't know the rules."
>
> Margi is not so mellow. The "[obscenity deleted] Jews" have been at it again she tells a staff member who asks her for the umpteenth time to settle down and stop talking that way. "Communist!" she hisses and storms off, muttering that she will "sue the boss." Margi is at least 70 and her behavior shows obvious signs of dementia. The staff's efforts to find out her

background are met with angry diatribes and insults. She clutches a book on German grammar and another on submarines that she reads upside down to "make things right."

Mick is having a bad day, too. He hasn't misbehaved but sits and stares, glassy-eyed. This is usually the prelude to a seizure. His seizures are easier to deal with than Bob's, for instance, because he usually has them while seated and so rarely hits his head and bleeds, nor does he ever soil his pants. Bob tends to pace restlessly all day and is often on the move when, without warning, his seizures strike. The last time he went down, he cut his head. The staff has learned to turn him over quickly after he hits the floor, so that his urine does not stain the carpet.[29]

A friend, Norma Kennemer, worked at the main branch of the Santa Rosa, California public library in the 1980s and 1990s. She was awash in similar stories of mentally ill homeless people who would urinate in the corners of the library, make frightening noises, sleep at the tables, and generally create an environment that would have been grounds for at least expulsion, if not arrest and commitment, in any American public library in 1960. The library staff was obligated to work with such "patrons" until their actions became clearly criminal. She recounted what happened when she observed that one of these mentally ill patrons was sitting at a table with his pants down to his knees. Her supervisor was obligated by library rules to attempt to first resolve the problem without the police. He approached this exposed "patron" and diplomatically asked, "Sir, are you appropriately attired for the library?"

Why was it necessary for librarians to take such a kid glove approach? Attempts to resolve behavioral problems led to lawsuits, such as happened in Morristown, New Jersey. The behavior and offensive smell of a homeless person named Kreimer led to the adoption of a code of conduct, prohibiting loitering, "unnecessary staring," following others around the library, and requiring those using the library to conform to community standards of cleanliness. The ACLU filed suit against this discriminatory code. At trial, Judge Sarokin ruled that the rules were discriminatory, and the ban on annoying other patrons violated Kreimer's right to freedom of speech:

The greatness of our country lies in tolerating speech with which we do not agree; that same toleration must extend to people, particularly where the cause of revulsion may be of our own making. If we wish to shield our eyes and noses from the homeless, we should revoke their condition, not their library cards.[30]

Wiser heads prevailed on appeal: the Court of Appeals concluded that the rules were not unconstitutional, and reversed Sarokin's decision.[31] Nonetheless, the cost of fighting this suit was substantial, with Morristown paying $230,000 to Kreimer as a settlement for this violation of his rights — and by the time they were finished, Morristown had spent more than one million dollars.[32] The cost of fighting such lawsuits by the ACLU certainly discouraged codes of conduct.

The problems of urban life degradation were not limited to libraries. In the 1990s, I had occasion to visit the University of California San Francisco's Hastings Law School library, which was located in the area called the Tenderloin, a rough area just north of Market Street. Homelessness was widespread in San Francisco, but especially concentrated in the Tenderloin. While mental illness was not the only cause, it did not require professional training to conclude that many of the homeless on the streets were showing signs of psychosis.

One consequence of this was the smell of urine on the sidewalks was overpowering, to the point that I had to hold my nose to avoid nausea. There was a shortage of public restrooms at least partly because businesses were reluctant to allow non-patrons to use their facilities. Why were they reluctant? Because many of the homeless were dirty, smelly, and behaved in ways that were frightening to both their customers and employees. Sometimes that fear was not prejudice, but a realistic appraisal based on past experiences.

San Francisco was an especially obvious example, but throughout the last three decades, I have visited dozens of large American cities, and seen this same depressing degradation in urban conditions (and one that was not present until the late 1970s). Obviously mentally ill homeless people lived under conditions of personal filth, either unable to access shower and laundry facilities, or unconcerned about the need for it. This picture I took in September of 2004 in downtown Philadelphia captures one of those tragedies:

The picture is grainy, and it fails to capture the terror on the face of this man who had climbed up on a scaffold, but it was quite obvious as I stood there, watching this little tragedy playing itself out. I do not know what demons drove him up there, but within a few minutes, a police officer (in the yellow rain slicker) was trying to talk him down. I passed by on my way to an appointment, and half an hour later, the police were still trying to talk him down. I talked to Philadelphia residents as we watched. Those I spoke to recognized the core of the problem (mental illness) and none of them found this scene surprising. For those of us who are old enough, this is tragedy enough: that it *was* no longer surprising.

Homelessness, while it has multiple causes, exploded in the late 1970s, largely because of deinstitutionalization. Some were institutionalized mental patients who were now supposed to make their way in the world; some were like my brother Ron, who were clearly too ill to care for themselves. The disability checks that the government provided would have been barely adequate for those who were completely sane. For the severely mentally ill, the situation was, unsurprisingly, a disaster. The consequences degraded urban life to a level that is difficult for those under forty to understand; they do not remember a time when the streets of American cities were not filled with homeless, often clearly mentally ill people, begging and dying.

19.   INDOOR TRAGEDIES (1975 – PRESENT)

Along with mentally ill people who lived and died on the streets, there were other tragedies that took place indoors. Wisconsin psychiatrist Darold Treffert described the consequences of Wisconsin's involuntary commitment law, struck down for vagueness in *Lessard* v. *Schmidt* (E.D.Wis. 1972):

In one, two young women drew a crowd as they stood on a street corner staring at one another for hours on end. Police took the young women to a nearby station for questioning, and the women continued to stare, mutely, at one another. Police released the women because despite their behavior, they did not display suicidal or homicidal tendencies and could not be committed.

Just 30 hours later, police found the two women again, "writhing and screaming in a self-made pyre they lit for each other in a suicide pact," Treffert said. One of the women died, and the other was critically injured.

In another case, a woman with anorexia was admitted to a hospital after she had been involved in a family disagreement and refused to eat. She had lost a great deal of weight but refused to submit to a psychiatric exam, and since a judge felt her condition was not dangerous in an immediate sense, she was allowed to go home. "She died from starvation three weeks later," Treffert recalled.[1]

In 2002, reporters at the Portland *Oregonian* examined the deaths of at least ninety-four Oregon mentally ill residents over a

3½ year period that they believed could be fairly attributed to a failure of Oregon's public mental health system. These ninety-four deaths were those that were easy to find, and the reporters were convinced the problem was more widespread. At least twenty-eight of those deaths involved failures to involuntarily commit persons who appeared to qualify. In some cases, judges refused to commit; in others, there was a reluctance of mental health workers to use Oregon's extraordinarily demanding commitment law. Two examples demonstrate where the strict civil libertarian approach failed.

Mary Boos of Portland graduated from the University of Oregon, but in retrospect, her descent into paranoid schizophrenia was already underway. Her break with reality happened slowly enough that friends and family could see that something was wrong, but it was not immediately obvious what. By the time she was prepared to tell her parents why she was unable to hold a job, she unleashed an "eight-hour rant" about the CIA and FBI and their persecution of her. She refused to leave her home.

A caseworker who knew that Oregon's law made involuntary commitment extraordinarily difficult recommended to Boos' parents that they stop supporting her. Eventually, she would be evicted, and the caseworker believed that her response would be violent, thus providing a basis for involuntary commitment. Instead, Boos traveled around the country, looking for clues as to why government agencies were after her. She came to the attention of authorities while sitting in the lobby of the Pentagon. In South Carolina, her problems were so severe that a mental health worker apparently broke the rules, and successfully committed Boos to a hospital. After two weeks of treatment, she was well enough to write to her parents and acknowledge that mental illness had nearly destroyed her.

Back in Portland, she seemed on the road to recovery, but the side effects of Haldol were so severe that her doctor switched her to another antipsychotic, but one that failed to keep her symptoms under control. From there, it was a series of steps downward, in and out of court. A court-appointed attorney argued that Boos' problems, while serious, did not represent an imminent danger. This was true. It took ten months for Mary Boos to starve herself to death inside her apartment.[2]

Corrine Reed of Coos Bay, Oregon in her forties developed a delusional disorder. She was convinced that the sizzling sound that she heard was her body on fire. She attempted suicide at least once, and started starving herself to death, in the belief that food and water aggravated the fire. She was involuntarily committed for a year, made significant progress, and then was released.

As with so many of her homeless counterparts, Corrine Reed felt so good that she stopped taking the medicine that had helped bring her back to sanity; the spiral downward resumed. Reed was certainly ill enough to be again involuntarily committed, but a combination of errors prevented this from happening. Her caseworker apparently did not understand Oregon's commitment laws. Her psychiatrist failed to grasp the seriousness of her condition. The operator of the foster home *may* have been too focused on the money the state paid for Reed's care to see that Reed was in far too bad a shape for such a facility. In the end, Corrine Reed starved herself to death — something that could not have happened if Reed had been institutionalized earlier in the process.[3] Oregon's very strict involuntary commitment laws were not the only cause of Reed's death, but her caseworker's perception that this was not an option was certainly part of why Reed died.

Another component that aggravated the problems of mental patients who were now back in the community was substance abuse. Alcohol and drug abuse aggravated existing mental illness.[4] At least inside a mental hospital, the opportunities for alcohol and drug abuse were limited. On the street, with a disability check and no supervision, unsurprisingly, substance abuse took serious problems and made them more serious.

Many advocates for deinstitutionalization argue that the policy was good, but was only badly implemented. Dear and Wolch, for example, argue for a host of public policy changes designed to assist the deinstitutionalized to become self-sufficient, without ever recognizing that most of the mentally ill homeless are not capable of caring for themselves.[5]

It was not simply that the government did not provide the services required; in many cases, the deinstitutionalized mentally ill, once they had stopped taking their medications, were not *interested* in many of those services, even such basic services as shelter. It had been fashionable in the early 1960s to blame a "lack of initiative, apathy, withdrawal" of schizophrenics on "institutionalism": the tendency of institutional regimentation to reduce inmates to a lowest common denomination. By the early 1980s, it was becoming clear that schizophrenics who had never been institutionalized suffered these problems as well.[6]

Aggravating the problem of the mentally ill who had been returned to the community was a shortage of community mental health service funding and workers. Some of the shortage of funding for community mental health services was an unwillingness of state and local governments to adequately fund a replacement for state mental hospitals. This is not surprising; advocates of deinstitutionalization in the early 1960s at least partly sold the idea to state legislators as a cost-cutting maneuver. Even in those cases where governments may have been willing to spend the money, the decentralization of services complicated providing them.

Money was not the only problem. Working with the severely mentally ill is a demanding and stressful job, and even if the government provides funding to hire workers, it is not necessarily the case that qualified workers will be available in the locations where they are most needed. A social worker or psychiatrist in a low-density area simply cannot meet the needs of as many clients as one who is able to work in a hospital setting, where the clients are physically concentrated. A state mental hospital provided a single institutional setting in which to group all the different workers involved in helping the mentally ill.[7]

Not only did a mental hospital make it more efficient to provide necessary services, it also made it difficult to lose track of those in need of help. Social workers did not need to hunt down mentally ill people wandering the streets. Patients with a hospital bed required no one to assist them in finding housing, or to navigate the complexities of Medicaid. The state mental hospital, even when it operated only as a custodial institution, at least meant that a mentally ill person did not have to search for a homeless shelter for the night[8]; nor would a hospitalized mental patient freeze to death, or die of tuberculosis.

Within a few years, the emptying out of public mental hospitals that were, at least, custodial, required state and local governments to create homeless shelters for many of the same people. In one of those ironic twists, deinstitutionalization meant that many of the buildings at New York's Creedmoor Psychiatric Hospital gradually emptied out. By 1984, some of those buildings were again in use, but as a homeless shelter for mentally ill men. This was a curious way to recreate an institution that was far less effective than its ancestor.[9]

At least some state mental hospitals, such as the Alabama state mental hospital in *Wyatt* v. *Stickney*, had been grossly inadequate even as custodial institutions. Even if the per patient cost of community treatment had been comparable to mental hospital treatment (which seems most unlikely) holding funding at the same level would have meant that deinstitutionalized mental patients would have received completely insufficient care. Not only was community mental health funding in short supply, there were also shortages of trained psychiatric professionals even before deinstitutionalization.

There was also a shortage of psychiatrists *willing* to work with the mentally ill in a non-institutional setting. Sometimes, this was based on fear. When Ron first started to behave oddly, we contacted a psychiatrist that we knew. We didn't think we could get Ron to go talk to a psychiatrist at his office, and the psychiatrist was unwilling to come to our house to talk to Ron, out of fear of injury. There had been a number of recent incidents in which psychiatrists had been badly hurt in those situations. As even a 1984 American Psychiatric Association report admitted, psychiatrists willing to work with the chronically mentally ill were in short supply.[10]

The indoor tragedies were a logical consequence of deinstitutionalization. In many cases, these were mentally ill people who had not yet become homeless. Sometimes they had enough resources to remain independent. In other cases, facilities paid for by the government failed to adequately look out for their charges. A generation earlier, journalists had bewailed the bad job that public mental hospitals were doing with their charges; now, the problem was decentralized, and it was much less obvious where and what the failure was.

20. RON ON HIS OWN

Somewhere along the way, Ron seemed to be doing well enough that our mother accepted some well-meaning advice from counselors that she should allow Ron to be on his own. Ron was still attending Barstow College, so it didn't seem like a ridiculous idea. It was 1982; my wife and I were living in the San Francisco Bay Area, and my mother decided to move into a retirement apartment building near us. She kept in touch with Ron by phone, and he seemed to be doing okay. I talked to Ron by phone a few times during that same period, and while he sounded a bit too flippant at times, there wasn't anything that clearly indicated that he was unable to care for himself. But within a year, friends of our mother at the Barstow Public Library (where my mother had worked) reported that Ron was *not* doing well.

My mother headed down to Barstow to see for herself. Ron didn't recognize her, and wouldn't let her into the house. The pastor of the church my mother and father had attended nearby reported to the police that Ron was acting quite strangely, such as answering the door naked. The neighbors' concern about Ron was enhanced by the recent suicide of another schizophrenic who lived in the area, who had thrown herself in front of a train.

Ron was again hospitalized in San Bernadino for observation, and again, advocates for the mentally ill were there to make sure that he wasn't held against his will. My mother told the judge she was willing to take care of him, and so Ron, again stabilized by antipsychotic medications, went back to Barstow.

It was a very encouraging sign that after his release, Ron actually went out looking for a job. He started out working for a restaurant, doing kitchen cleanup at 5:30 AM, and then took a job at Carl's, Jr. in Barstow. Carl's at the time had a policy of attempting to hire the mentally handicapped in some capacity, and they were willing to ignore Ron's many years of unemployment because they understood his situation; he was someone recovering from a serious mental illness.

Ron held that job for about eight months, moving from clean up to cooking sandwiches. When he left, it wasn't because he imagined dark conspiracies and quit, or behaved oddly and was fired, but because he had found a better job. He went to work as an electronics technician at the Marine Corps Logistics Base in Barstow. The job that they gave him tended to be more on the mechanical side of things at first, but it was still a job that required him to work without a lot of supervision, making decisions, and fixing things. Ron was very happy to have a professional job again. It seemed for a while as though Ron was on the way to recovery.

It did not last. My mother went on vacation for two weeks. During that time, it appears that Ron lost track of which of his medications he was supposed to be taking. The orthomolecular diet also had no room for caffeine, and is there anything more common to the American workplace than coffee? (In my industry, we have an expression: "An engineer is a device for converting coffee into software.") Soon, he was looking at co-workers in ways that made them uncomfortable. His boss assumed that he was taking illegal drugs. Ron explained the situation, and soon thereafter, Ron quit rather than be fired.

I still don't know if finding out that Ron had a history of mental illness sealed his fate with that boss or not. I can see why his co-workers, who thought he was behaving oddly because of drug abuse, would have been even more worried if they thought he was slipping back into mental illness, as it appears that he was. But the net effect was that Ron ceased to work in 1985, and several years of success as a part-time college student came to an end. This picture, taken in 1988 at Halloween, captures the exterior expression of an interior in chaos.

RON AND JACK-O'-LANTERN 1988

Four years passed, with my mother living back in Barstow. She kept on eye on Ron, made sure he took his medications, and acted as his conservator with respect to his disability payments. This involved making sure that the checks were deposited, and performing the substantial clerical work required to keep Medicaid processing bills for Ron's medicines and treatment. This involved a lot of time on the phone. To expect that Ron, or most other psychotics, could have handled these responsibilities by himself was itself a form of madness.

My mother did not give up hope that Ron could return to work. Like the nineteenth century's psychiatrists who believed that labor was a therapeutic activity in itself, my mother believed that Ron would benefit from putting his skills as an electronic technician to use. In 1989, my sisters Susan and Carolyn, who were living in the Portland area, found a mental illness rehabilitation program that purported to combine therapy with an electronics training program. This sounded like a very good match for Ron's needs and previous experience. And so Ron moved to Portland.

What happened next is very troubling. As a general rule, I think there is a lot of lot of merit to allowing private sector organizations to play a contracted role in performing governmental functions. But sometimes this approach does not work, and when it fails, the exact reasons can be difficult to unravel. Some organizations fail to do their duty because greed gets in the way. If the government is writing checks, and fails to do a good job of verifying that the clients are getting what the government has paid for, it is unsurprising that people will end up in the business of fleecing the government.

Sometimes, it is not greed, exactly, that comes into play. Not everyone who ends up in social services (in either private sector firms or governmental agencies) is completely competent at it. There are people who are doing their best, and that is just not good enough. When the clients that you are supposed to be helping are psychotic, good intentions may not be enough.

Worst of all, helping someone who is hearing and seeing things that are not there would try the patience and skills of the most dedicated and most skilled. Agencies that are in the business of helping the mentally ill are not in a position to hire only the best and the brightest. There are millions of severely mentally ill Americans, and the staff required to assist them is going to include a lot of people who are middle of the pack, and a few who are simply incompetent. There is no way to avoid this, and the private sector has no monopoly on failures like this.

My sister Susan lived nearby, and her reports of what happened were very disappointing. The program that Ron found himself in, the supposed electronics training program, was nothing of the sort. He and other mentally ill persons were doing menial labor, stuffing envelopes, packaging small parts, for sub-minimum wage pay. It was not in any sense a training program. While there might have been some merit to it, it was certainly not what my mother had understood Ron would be doing. Adding to the disappointment, Ron was only two classes away from his A.A. degree at Barstow College when he moved to Portland, and most of those classes did not transfer to Portland Community College.

Ron shared a two-bedroom apartment with another mentally ill person in the program, who was clearly not in as good a shape as Ron was. His roommate almost never left his bedroom. Ron had seen inside it; it was filled with coffee cans filled with human excrement. Cockroaches filled the place; and in spite of the program's claim that it did weekly inspections to see how its charges were doing, Susan was unable to get them to ever go over and take a look at the unsanitary conditions in which Ron was living. I won't claim that Ron, once he had declined into mental illness, was going to be mistaken for Felix Unger of *The Odd*

Couple, but this was grotesque.

Ron moved to another of these private, but government-funded group homes, one where conditions were not quite as bad. It was institutional, and while circumstances were again unsanitary, it seems to have been as much Ron's fault as the lack of attention from the staff. Ron was clearly unable to properly care for himself, and the staff was not doing it, either.

A third group care facility was deplorable for a different reason. Ron did not live in the facility, but was again housed in an apartment that theoretically the group home inspected periodically to provide some minimal level of supervision and therapy. But Ron's caseworker apparently felt that it would be invading Ron's privacy to show up and ask to see him. A number of the caseworker's other clients committed suicide over the course of several months. I guess she didn't invade their privacy, either. So what if Ron didn't show up for appointments to talk to a counselor? The policy of this group home was not to remind him, or attempt to get him to show up.

Ron was supposed to remember to show up for his medicines. It was rather like those in charge did not realize that they were running a care facility for the severely mentally ill, or did not care that much what the outcome would be. Perhaps aggravating the problem is that many of those working in counseling and monitoring positions in this organization were themselves recovering mental patients.

The situation wasn't working for Ron, at least as my mother saw it, and so she moved to the Portland area where she could provide more direction and assistance. This is one of the sad parts of what happens to many mentally ill people. It should not be a great surprise to find out that strangers do not care about the needs of a mentally ill person as much as the patient's family. Of course, parents care the most of all. At the same time, family members lack objectivity. They see their son, or brother, or spouse through the prism of past experiences. It's unavoidable, and sometimes it means that family makes mistakes about the best strategy for helping. What makes a patient's family fight with the system to see a mentally ill relative properly cared for also can make it difficult to clearly see the best course of action.

Throughout the more than three decades that my brother has been mentally ill, there have been times when social workers saw my mother's efforts to help Ron as counterproductive, and sometimes they have been right. But there is no social worker who ever had the interest, the energy, or the time to devote to championing Ron's cause as strongly as my mother. I am convinced from reading the legal struggles that have taken place over this issue that my mother is not unique; there are a lot of parents who have done their best to help mentally ill children, and they have been stymied by patient privacy laws and advocates for the civil rights of the mentally ill.

Whatever method a government agency creates to deal with mental illness needs to have the flexibility to deal with this. There are clients with a family who cares, and clients with a family who never want to hear from their mentally ill relative again. There are clients with relatives who remain calm, no matter how trying the circumstances, and there are clients whose relatives are emotional basket cases. Figuring out when to listen to family members, and how much weight to give to their concerns, is a challenge because every client is different, and so is every family.

Dr. Mary McCarthy was Ron's psychiatrist during part of this time that he lived in Portland. She made the observation to our sister Carolyn that Ron's family did not all agree about what was the best way to help him, but that we all cared about what happened to him. In her view, even genuine disagreements about the best course of action were better than having no one who cared at all.

There is no question that mental hospitals in the period after World War II were often warehouses where the mentally ill were locked up and forgotten. But based on the facilities that took a fair amount of money from various levels of government to "care" for Ron, it did not appear that deinstitutionalization changed this very much. Deinstitutionalization just moved the neglect from large institutions run directly by the government, to smaller institutions where the government paid private sector employees to provide the neglect.

My mother was convinced that she needed to provide direct supervision and assistance to Ron, and so my mother and Ron bought a mobile home in the Portland suburbs. My cousin Michael and I loaded up a 24-foot truck with the contents of my mother's apartment (how did she get so much stuff into a one bedroom apartment?), and drove to Portland. Ron moved in, and did a lot of the work required to get the mobile home in shape.

Ron was now receiving injections of Prolixin that kept his schizophrenia in check. These shots were every two weeks — a very long acting medication. Ron was not well, but he was not attacking strangers, or acting excessively bizarre, and he was able to perform some chores around the house. He enrolled at a community college, and took classes in computer programming and calculus, and seemed to be doing pretty well. Unfortunately, Ron had acquired a number of friends during his time living in these group homes whose lives revolved around smoking and drinking coffee (common forms of self-medication and recreation among the mentally ill). Ron had a car, and soon his friends were showing up on campus, trying to persuade Ron to leave class early, so that he could drive them to a coffee shop. This created problems with the college, and soon, Ron dropped out of college again.

As is often the case, there were unpleasant side effects from the Prolixin, and eventually Ron was no longer willing to accept the shots. He went back onto pills. Soon, he was not swallowing the pills but putting them in his cheek, and spitting them out later. His behavior became increasingly strange. Ron became unable to help with the maintenance on the mobile home. Our mother was too old to take care of it herself, so she put the mobile home on the market, and started looked for an apartment where the landlord would be responsible for the maintenance.

My sister Susan bought a house on Cedar Street in Hillsboro, and rented it to Ron and my mother. Ron was still not doing well; he had some good days, and some bad ones. Ron went through three different psychiatrists, one of whom, Mary McCarthy, went quite a bit beyond the others in her level of concern, even calling him at home to see how he was doing. But in spite of this level of concern, Ron's mental health was declining.

Open Gate, which was the organization now theoretically helping Ron, insisted that he move into a place of his own, apparently convinced that he would do better without our mother's supervision. My mother prepared to move to a retirement apartment in Riverside, California. Likely because of his bad experiences in other group housing, Ron was not happy about the situation. Perhaps because of this, perhaps for other reasons, Ron stopped taking his medicines, and Open Gate was either unable to persuade him to resume, or unaware that he had stopped.

Ever since Ron has become mentally ill, rocks had become a major focus of conversation. He collected quite non-descript rocks, and attached great meaning and significance to them; these meanings were beyond the rest of us to understand. (He knew where he had found every one of those rocks.) While our mother was packing up her belongings for the move back to Southern California, Ron became quite insistent on finding one of those rocks. Our mother told Ron where the rock was, and for reasons that made no sense (at least to us), he grabbed her by the throat and in the struggle she hit her head on a desk. At about the same moment, our sister Susan rang the doorbell, probably causing Ron to let go.

Ron ran from the house, convinced that he had killed our mother. Many hours later, the police found Ron in a muddy field, confused. They took him back to the Cedar Street house, and helped him get back inside, where he was convinced that the police would find our mother's dead body. She wasn't there, of course, and apparently the report from earlier in the day of Ron's attack on her had not filtered down to these police officers, so they left him in the Cedar Street house.

The next day, my sister Susan arrived at Cedar Street, intending to change the locks on the doors — and found Ron at home. She went to a neighbor's house, and called the police, who came out and arrested Ron. But even this was a bit more complicated than it should have been. As Susan explained it:

> The policeman who came to the neighbor's house in response to my call was surprisingly patient and helpful. He said, "I can't go in there and arrest him unless he was menacing you." I said something like, "Well, he had hurt our mother, and she's afraid of him, and so am I. He's off his meds, and ...." The policeman repeated, "Was he menacing?" The neighbor caught my eye and I finally got it. "Yes," I said. "He was menacing me." It was only the magic word "menacing" that caused the police officer to arrest Ron. Even so, Ron would not have been hospitalized had I not shown the judge the photos of Mom's throat, black and blue from Ron's hands.

Because of this violent attack on a family member, the criminal justice system was finally able to hospitalize Ron.

Ron's problems during this period all come down to this: it is surprisingly easy to forget to take a daily medication. Think of the last few times that you were taking an antibiotic pill to deal with an infection. Did you ever forget to take one? Almost all of us have done so, but missing one dose, or even two, was not a disaster. For

Ron, as with many of the severely mentally ill, forgetting to take his medication for several days would start him down a path to out of control madness. The paranoia would identify the pills as poison, and what started as forgetfulness would soon turn into a willful refusal. The spiral down from there could be very rapid.

21. CRIME (1972 – PRESENT)

Along with the enormous increase in quality of life problems, deinstitutionalization also led to an increase in crime. Most of the mentally ill who were deinstitutionalized, or who had never been institutionalized in the first place, were not a hazard to others. Those that were dangerous, however, often became newspaper stories across America.

John Linley Frazier was one of the first examples of how California's emerging concern for civil liberties of the mentally ill led to disaster. Like many other schizophrenics, the first clear evidence appeared when he was in his early 20s. He fixated on ecology, and after a traffic accident, became convinced that God had told him that he would die if he drove again. Frazier was now on a mission from God: to rid the Earth of those who were altering the natural environment. Frazier's mother and wife recognized how seriously ill he was, and tried to obtain treatment for him, but he refused it.

Frazier's behavior became increasingly disturbed, and he warned that "some materialists might have to die" in the coming ecological revolution. The following Monday, Frazier climbed the hill from the cowshed where he was living near Santa Cruz, and murdered "Dr. Victor M. Ohta, his wife, their two young sons, and the doctor's secretary."[1] He blindfolded them, tied them up, shot each of them, and threw them into the pool. Then he set fires throughout the house to return it back to the environment. Frazier's bizarre behavior and statements to family and friends soon led to his arrest. He was found legally sane, convicted, and sentenced to life in prison.[2] (The legal definition of insane is considerably narrower than the psychiatric or popular definition of insane.

There are times that it seems that juries convict even clearly insane defendants, out of fear that they might be released after being declared "cured.")

Edmund Emil Kemper III was a sexual sadist who killed his paternal grandparents at age 15, in an attempt to punish his mother, who was having increasing difficulties handling him. California hospitalized him until he was 21, and then released him on parole in 1969. Over a bit less than a year, starting in May of 1972, Kemper shot, stabbed, and strangled eight women, including his mother. He dismembered his victims, had sex with their dead bodies, and engaged in cannibalism. After repeated phone calls to the police to persuade them that he was the killer, he was arrested, found legally sane, convicted, and sentenced to life in prison.[3]

Herbert William Mullin was another of the schizophrenics whose illness arrived just as California was moving towards a supposedly more humane and less restrictive approach to mental illness. In high school, Mullin showed some odd behaviors, more obviously frightening in retrospect, but until 1969, just before Mullin's 22nd birthday, it was not obvious that he was mentally ill. Mullin was persuaded to voluntarily enter Mendocino State Hospital, on California's north coast on March 30. Six weeks later, having refused to participate in treatment programs, and under no legal obligation to remain, he left.

Mullin had trouble holding jobs. He would, as many schizophrenics do, refer to "hearing voices," which understandably frightened employers, even at the menial jobs that Mullin was able to hold. In October of 1969, Mullin was again hospitalized, but this time against his will, in San Luis Obispo County's psychiatric ward. A few weeks later, he was discharged "on the condition that [he] would continue to receive treatment at the Santa Cruz Community Mental Health Outpatient Clinic." He did so, but then moved to Hawaii, where he again asked for mental illness treatment.

Back he went to California, where his parents picked him up at San Francisco Airport. His behavior so scared them that within thirty miles of the airport, his parents stopped to call the Mountain View Police Department. Mullin was again hospitalized against his will at Santa Cruz General Hospital for a few weeks, and again discharged "less noisy and belligerent" than when he entered — but not well. Like many of the severely mentally ill, he lived in cheap hotel rooms in San Francisco, before moving back home with his parents in Santa Cruz in 1972.

Mullin's parents tried to find long-term hospitalization for their son, who was clearly dangerous to others. But California's hospitals were busily emptying out; they were not looking to take new patients. In light of Mullin's history of voluntarily entering, then leaving mental hospitals, it might not have mattered, without involuntary commitment.

In four months of late 1972 and early 1973, Mullin murdered thirteen people in the Santa Cruz area. Why? To prevent the San Andreas fault from rupturing, and causing a catastrophic earthquake. Mullin had created an entire theology built around his belief that murder decreased natural disasters. Mullin was found legally sane (although both prosecution and defense agreed that he was seriously mentally ill), and guilty of ten murders.[4]

Patrick Purdy, a mentally ill drifter, used his Social Security Disability payments to buy guns, while having a series of run-ins with the law. Six successive felonies were plea-bargained down to misdemeanors. His actions and remarks to the judge in at least one case should have been enough to have him committed: he was shooting at "Communist trees." But instead, the short and unhappy life of Patrick Purdy ended when he went onto a schoolyard in Stockton, California with a rifle, murdered five children, and wounded twenty-nine others, before taking his own life.[5]

Laurie Wasserman Dann was another of the tragedies. Federal prosecutors held back for a few days indicting her for a series of harassing and frightening phone calls. During those few days, she went on a rampage, killing one child in an elementary school, wounding five children and one adult, and distributing poisoned cookies and drinks to fraternities at Northwestern University. She had a history of odd behavior going back at least two years, riding the elevator in her apartment building for hours on end.[6]

Buford Furrow was a member of a neo-Nazi group in Washington State. A series of conflicts with his wife soon led her to take him to a mental hospital:

> Furrow arrived at the hospital drunk and told staff members he was thinking about committing suicide and shooting people at a nearby shopping mall.

> At one point hospital employees persuaded him to surrender his keys. Later, Furrows angrily demanded the keys' return and

threatened two nurses with a knife.

"He was about two feet away," said Kirsten Brown, one of his victims. "I was afraid he was going to stab me. He said, 'Give me the f-- keys . . . or I will cut you up.'"

Eventually, a King County sheriff's deputy persuaded Furrow to surrender. While in custody, he told a sheriff's deputy, "Sometimes I feel like I could just lose it and kill people."

He was charged with first-degree assault and spent nearly six months in jail awaiting trial. Last April, he agreed to plead guilty to second-degree assault and received an eight- month jail sentence -- roughly the time he had already served while awaiting trial.

In pleading guilty, Furrow acknowledged having long-standing fantasies about killing himself and others. "The defendant (Furrow) also detailed how he has cut himself numerous times with knives, some of the cuts requiring multiple stitches to close the wound," said one court document filed in the case.

So what did the judge do? He released Furrow. Within a few months, he went to Los Angeles, and did what he had told the hospital staff he fantasized about doing. He shot up a Jewish community center, wounded five people there, and murdered an Asian-American mail carrier nearby.[7]

Larry Gene Ashbrook was another mentally ill person who gave plenty of warning. Letters to local papers "referred to encounters with the CIA, psychological warfare, assaults by co-workers and being drugged by police." In one letter, Ashbrook "said he thought he was a suspect in some Fort Worth area murders, including a 1985 sexual mutilation slaying" for which another man had already been executed. Neighbors had long noticed his bizarre behavior, such as exposing himself in response to laughter that he thought (incorrectly) was at him. A few weeks later, he went into a Fort Worth, Texas Baptist Church. He screamed insults about their religion, killed seven people inside then killed himself.[8]

In April of 2007, David W. Logsdon of Kansas City, Missouri, beat to death a neighbor, Patricia Ann Reed, and stole her late husband's rifle. Using Reed's credit card and car, Logsdon bought ammunition and magazines for the rifle, and drove to the Ward Parkway Center Mall, where he shot and killed two people at random, wounding four others.[9] Only good luck and the arrival of police, who shot Logsdon to death, prevented a larger massacre.

According to Logsdon's sister, Logsdon had a history of mental illness and alcoholism. His family contacted police over Logsdon's deteriorating mental condition and physical conditions in Logsdon's home. The police took Logsdon to a mental hospital for treatment in October of 2005, concerned that he was suicidal. He was released six hours later with a voucher for a cab and a list of resources to contact.

In this case, the problem was not that the law prevented Logsdon from being held. Instead, a shortage of beds in Missouri public mental hospitals was apparently the cause of Logsdon's early release. In addition, Missouri in 2003 had eliminated mental health coordinator positions in its community mental health centers as a cost-cutting measure.[10]

Logsdon's criminal history went back a long ways; in 1981, it appears Logsdon murdered Steve Foster, husband of a woman with whom Logsdon was having an affair, and persuaded witnesses to lie about the circumstances, to make it appear to be a suicide. Even though the coroner's report concluded that suicide was not possible, the evidence was insufficient for a grand jury to indict Logsdon.[11]

Russell Eugene Weston Jr. was the gold standard of violent mental illness. After he shot two police officers at the U.S. Capitol, he explained to the court appointed psychiatrist his actions:

"He described his belief that time was running out and that if he did not come to Washington, D.C., he would become infected with Black Heva," wrote Sally C. Johnson, the psychiatrist who examined Weston last fall. Weston called this imaginary ailment the "most deadliest disease known to mankind" and said it was spread by the rotting corpses of cannibals' victims, Johnson wrote.

Weston told Johnson he went to the Capitol to gain access to what he called "the ruby satellite," a device he said was kept in a Senate safe. That satellite, he insisted, was the key to putting a stop to cannibalism.

Weston explained that the two "cannibals" he had shot to
death, police officers "Jacob J. Chestnut and John M. Gibson,"
were "not permanently deceased." Weston just needed access to
the satellite controller so that he could turn back time.

Before this incident, Weston had been involuntarily
hospitalized for fifty-three days in Montana after threatening a
neighbor, but then released. According to Weston's parents, he had
been losing the battle with schizophrenia for two decades when he
went to the Capitol.[12]

Jennifer Sanmarco is one recent example of a woman "going
postal." An employee of the Post Office, she was removed from
her Goleta, California workplace by the police in 2003 because she
was acting strangely, and placed on psychological disability. She
moved to Milan, New Mexico, where her neighbors described her
as "as crazy as a loon." Her behavior there included going to the
gas station naked, harassing employees of businesses, and: "A
Milan businessman said he sometimes had to pick her up and bring
her inside from the cold because she would kneel down and pray,
as if in a trance, for hours." She returned to the Goleta mail sorting
facility in January of 2006, and murdered five employees, before
taking her own life.[13]

When I was first writing this chapter, America was mourning a
tragedy at Virginia Tech, where Cho Seung-Hui murdered thirty-
two students and faculty before taking his own life. His
psychological problems had been evident for some months before
this massacre, and he was briefly hospitalized after a stalking
incident. The special judge appointed to determine whether Seung-
Hui should be involuntarily committed concluded that he was a
danger to himself, but allowed Seung-Hui to commit himself. The
next day, Seung-Hui left the hospital, and soon he was back on
campus, living in a world of paranoid schizophrenia, culminating in
the largest gun mass murder in U.S. history.[14]

Many other spectacularly horrifying crimes followed that one.
Jiverly Wong murdered thirteen people before killing himself at a
Binghamton, New York immigrant-assistance center in April 2009.
Letters by Wong to local news media demonstrate what "Dr. Vatsal
Thakkar, assistant professor of psychiatry at NYU's Langone
Medical Center" described as "major mental illness, quite possibly
paranoid schizophrenia."[15]

Rep. Gabrielle Giffords (D-Ariz.) was one many people shot at a town hall meeting in Tucson in January of 2011. The alleged shooter, Jared Lee Loughner, had a history of police contacts involving death threats, and was expelled from college for bizarre actions that clearly established that he was mentally ill. A series of disturbing web postings and YouTube videos also confirmed that Loughner's grasp on reality was severely impaired.[16] Court-ordered psychiatric evaluations concluded that Loughner was suffering from schizophrenia, and was incompetent to stand trial.[17]

Nor were these problems specific to the United States and its "gun culture" as some contended. Europe, which also started down the same road towards deinstitutionalization, although a few years later than the United States, has suffered many similar mass murders by persons who were obviously mentally ill, or whose crimes made so little sense that mental illness was the obvious explanation. Christian Dornier, 31, under treatment for "nervous depression," murdered fourteen people in three villages in eastern France.[18] He was later found innocent by reason of insanity.[19] Eric Borel, 16, murdered his family with a hammer and a baseball bat, and then went on a shooting rampage in the nearby town of Cuers, France in September, 1995. He killed twelve in total beside himself.[20] In March 2002, Richard Durn murdered eight local city officials and wounded nineteen others in Nanterre, a suburb of Paris. Durn had a master's degree in political science and "a long history of psychological problems." After his arrest, he was described as "calm but largely incoherent," but then leaped to his death through a window. He was chronically unemployed.[21]

In April 2002, 19-year old Robert Steinhaeuser went into a school from which he had been expelled in Erfurt, Germany and murdered eighteen people before killing himself.[22] In April of 2011, Wellington Menezes de Oliveira went into a school in Rio De Janeiro, Brazil, murdering twelve children, before killing himself. He suicide note was unclear, but a police officer described de Oliveira as a "hallucinating person."[23] Later the same month, Tristan van der Vlis went into a shopping mall in Alphen aan der Rijn, the Netherlands, and shot six people to death. In spite of very strict Dutch gun licensing laws, van der Vlis had a gun license in spite of a history of brief mental illness hospitalization and suicide attempts.[24]

Along with the spectacular cases, there were many minor tragedies, soon forgotten outside the family and friends of their victims. In 1983, the 17-year-old daughter of my landlord was murdered in San Francisco's Golden Gate Park. The killer had a long history of mental problems, some of which had sent him to prison, but none of which had caused his hospitalization. As so often happens, this tragedy led to another. The continuing legal battles over the killer's sanity soon led Claire's grief-stricken father to sneak a gun into the courtroom, and open fire.[25]

While most of these murders involved guns, there were many others that did not, often completely unknown outside the community where they happened because the body count was low. Here's one that I know about only because I used to live in Rohnert Park, California, and a friend forwarded it to me. A 33 year-old paranoid schizophrenic named Hoyt was arrested outside his mother's home, holding a sword. Inside, his mother lay dying of sword wounds. A relative of the dead woman described a problem that was not news to me, after all the struggles we had gone through with my brother:

> A distraught Cooper suggested that the family's efforts to get Ezra Hoyt timely and proper help were frustrated by the mental health system.
>
> "It's the way the social services system works -- or doesn't work," he said. "All we're told, of course, is that nothing can be done until until he becomes a threat to himself or others."
>
> Cooper said family members had worried that Hoyt wasn't taking medication for the illness with which he'd been diagnosed about five years ago.
>
> "He's over 18, he can't be forced to stay on his medications until something happens," Cooper said. "Well, something has happened."[26]

San Joaquin (California) District Attorney Thomas Testa complained to a reporter in 2005 that "he has prosecuted too many murderers with previously diagnosed mental health problems and is tired of it." He listed four recent cases:

- Wayne Osborg Jr., 32, was convicted and sentenced to two consecutive life sentences in August for bludgeoning two men when he didn't show up at a treatment home for his mental illness.

• Khanh Duy Phan, then 34, was convicted in March 2004 for decapitating his 18-month-old daughter and sentenced to state prison for 26 years to life.

• Peter Nhim, then 18, was convicted in October 2004 of second-degree murder in the stabbing death of a 9-year-old family friend.

• Robin Rials, then 17, pleaded guilty to first-degree murder in March 2004 but avoided prison after a judge ruled she was insane when she set fire to an abandoned trailer where a man slept.[27]

Some of the "minor" tragedies are colorful, but it is still the color of blood and the smell of suffering. In May of 1998, San Francisco put 21-year-old Joshua Rudiger on probation and ordered him to enter a live-in treatment center in San Francisco after shooting a former friend with a bow and arrow. Authorities knew that Rudiger was mentally ill; he had been confined to Atascadero State Hospital for six months, diagnosed as suffering from schizophrenia and bipolar disorder. Then the hospital declared him cured, and able to stand trial for the bow and arrow incident. Rudiger never showed up at the treatment center, nor did anyone go looking for him. In one of the more disturbing understatements of the day, Carmen Bushe, the head of community services for San Francisco's Probation Department observed, "It's perhaps not necessarily a cohesive system.... It needs to be reviewed and looked at very, very closely." When Rudiger next came to the attention of police, it was for slashing the throats of four homeless people, killing one, and drinking the blood of the others.[28] When arrested, Rudiger told police that he was a 2,600 year-old vampire. Yet the jury concluded that he was legally sane, because he knew what he was doing, and that he knew it was wrong. Rudiger was sentenced to 23 years to life.[29]

Rudiger's mental problems started at age four, and like Patrick Purdy, his life was a disaster from the very beginning. But some of these tragedies were people who made it to adulthood before mental illness showed itself. Richard Baumhammers was an immigration attorney — and yet something went wrong sometime in his 20s. He believed that someone had poisoned him on a trip to Europe. He "had been treated since 1993 for mental illness and had voluntarily admitted himself to a psychiatric ward at least once...." When the final break happened, he killed five people.[30] A jury found him legally sane, and convicted him of first-degree murder. The court sentenced Baumhammers to death.[31]

In 1986, Juan Gonzalez was arrested for shouting threats on the street, "I'm going to kill! God told me so!" At the hospital, doctors diagnosed him as suffering from a "psychotic paranoid disorder," gave him some antipsychotic medicines to take, made an appointment for outpatient treatment, and released him after two days. Within a few days he went on a rampage on the Staten Island Ferry with a sword, killing two people, and wounding nine. If not for the presence of a retired police officer who disarmed Gonzalez at gunpoint, the death toll might have been much higher.[32]

Having killed two people, Gonzalez was finally considered too dangerous to release, and the courts ordered his involuntary commitment to a mental hospital. He repeatedly contested his commitment. In March of 2000, the courts granted Gonzalez unsupervised leave from the hospital, with a number of conditions on his actions for five years.[33]

When the *New York Times* did a detailed study of rampage killers in 2000, they pointed out that there was often plenty of warning:

> An examination by The New York Times of 100 rampage murders found that most of the killers spiraled down a long slow slide, mentally and emotionally. Most of them left a road map of red flags, spending months plotting their attacks and accumulating weapons, talking openly of their plans for bloodshed. Many showed signs of serious mental health problems.
>
> ...
>
> The Times' study found that many of the rampage killers... suffered from severe psychosis, were known by people in their circles as being noticeably ill and needing help, and received insufficient or inconsistent treatment from a mental health system that seemed incapable of helping these especially intractable patients. ...

The Times found what it called "an extremely high association between violence and mental illness." Of the 100 rampage murderers, forty-seven "had a history of mental health problems" before committing murder, twenty had been previously hospitalized for mental illness, and forty-two had been previously seen by professionals for their mental illness. While acknowledging that mental illness diagnoses "are often difficult to pin down... 23 killers showed signs of serious depression before the killings, and 49 expressed paranoid ideas."[34]

I could go on at great length with example after example, both those that made national headlines, and those that did not. Along with the cases that ended in death, there are vast numbers of lesser incidents involving either mentally ill offender, or mentally ill victims. The Treatment Advocacy Center maintains a searchable database of these "minor" tragedies.[35] There is no shortage of these tragedies that have one common element: a person whose exceedingly odd behavior, sometimes combined with criminal acts, would likely have led to confinement in a mental hospital in 1950, or 1960, before they graduated to murder. After deinstitutionalization, these people remained at large until they killed. The system then took them out of circulation, but a bit too late for their victims.

That's a strong claim, but there is a clear statistical relationship between institutionalization and murder rates. Violent crime rates rose dramatically in the 1960s, most worrisomely, in the murder rate.[36]

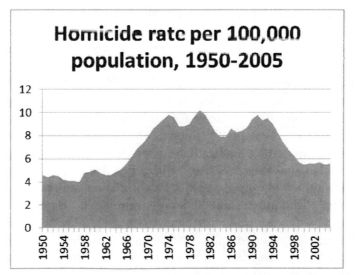

Homicide rate per 100,000 population, 1950-2005

Sociologists came up with a variety of explanations for why the murder rate more than doubled between 1957 and 1980. An obvious explanation was that the Baby Boomers (the children born in the ten years after World War II) were reaching their peak violent crime years of adolescence. Some conservatives blamed the civil liberties revolution of the Warren Court for rendering the criminal justice system impotent to deal with crime, and the expansion of drug abuse by the Flower Power generation of the 1960s.

What caused the decline in violent crime — and specifically murder — in the 1990s? This was variously ascribed to the Baby Boom Echo generation passing out of its peak violent crime years, and to increasingly tough sentencing for violent crimes. These were possibilities, but proving or disproving these claims was not easy.

One claim — that gun control laws passed in 1993 and 1994 caused the decline — was easy to disprove. Most of the improvement in murder rates from 1991 to 1998 was from a decline in *non-gun* murders, which fell 46.1 percent, while gun murders fell only 28.3 percent over the same period. (It is hard to imagine how gun control could reduce non-gun murders, and even harder to imagine that it could reduce non-gun murders *more* than gun murders.) Multivariate correlation studies, in some cases, by advocates of restrictive gun control laws, acknowledged that neither of the federal laws passed during this period made any statistically significant changes in murder rates.[37]

Professor Bernard E. Harcourt points out that the rise in murder rates in the 1960s, and their decline in the 1990s correlated with the change in the percentage of the population that was institutionalized: those who were confined to either a mental hospital or prison. According to Harcourt, sociologists examining the expansion of imprisonment in the 1990s, the so-called "incarceration revolution," missed the even more important component of institutionalization: mental hospitals. When adding mental hospital inmates to prisoners, Harcourt found an astonishingly strong negative correlation between the institutionalization rate, and the murder rate: -0.78. Harcourt found that even when adjusting for changes in unemployment and the changing fraction of the population that was at their peak violent crime ages, the negative correlation remained strong, and did a better job of predicting both the 1960s rise and the 1990s decline in murder rates than other models.[38]

When Harcourt used state level data for institutionalization and murder rates, and controlled for more variables, the statistically significant negative correlation remained for most states. A few states (such as Florida) showed no significant correlation between institutionalization rates and murder rates, meaning that there was no apparent connection. No state, however, showed a significant *positive* correlation; nowhere did increasing the institutionalization rate clearly cause an increase in murder rates.[39]

Another study, using quite different methodology, came to similar conclusions. Steven P. Segal's study of the effects of civil commitment law on murder rates used a variety of types of data to examine the interaction between how strict involuntary commitment laws were, along with socioeconomic, demographic, and geographic data on a state by state basis. He concluded that 25 percent of the variation in homicide rates was associated with "social-economic-demographic-geographic-and-political indicators." This is not surprising. He also concluded that "[l]ess access to psychiatric inpatient-beds and more poorly rated mental health systems were associated with increases in the homicide rates of 1.08 and 0.26 per 100,000, respectively." But an even bigger difference was the difference in the breadth of the different state involuntary civil commitment (ICC) laws. "Broader ICC-criteria were associated with 1.42 less homicides per 100,000." In short, states where involuntary commitment was easy, had roughly a third less murders than states where it was very hard.[40]

It is not difficult to see why the deinstitutionalization of the mentally ill would cause a rise in violent crime rates, including murder. When Massachusetts opened Worcester Hospital in the early nineteenth century, the law limited its admissions to "the violent and furious." Dr. Samuel B. Woodward, who was Worcester Hospital's first superintendent, noted that, "More than half of those manifesting monomania and melancholia [roughly equivalent to paranoid schizophrenia and psychotic bipolar disorder in modern terms] are said to exhibit a propensity to homicide or suicide."[41] The opening of state asylums in Vermont in 1836 and New Hampshire in 1840 "contributed to the decline in such spouse and family murders during the 1850s and 1860s."[42] Accounts of mass murder (usually involving family members) appear often enough in this period to understand why concerns about insanity could lead to hospitalization.[43]

During the period before deinstitutionalization, the mentally ill seem to have been *less* likely to be arrested for crimes than the general population. Studies in New York and Connecticut from the 1920s through the 1940s showed a much lower arrest rate for the mentally ill. But this started to change as deinstiutionalization took effect.[44]

As early as 1976, studies of deinstitututionalized New York City mental patients showed that their arrest rates for rape, burglary, and aggravated assault were disproportionate for their community.[45] A study of San Mateo County, California, mental hospital patients found dramatically higher rates of arrest for murder, rape, robbery, aggravated assault, and burglary compared to the general population of the county: for murder, 55 times more likely to be arrested for murder in 1973, and 82.5 times more likely in 1972. Differences in arrest rates for rape, robbery, aggravated assault, and burglary were less dramatic, but even here, the differences were enormous. Overall, mental patients were about nine times as likely to be arrested for this group of serious felonies as the general population of the county in which they lived.[46] Reexamination of the San Mateo County data revealed that even patients with no pre-hospitalization arrests were five times as likely to be arrested for violent crimes as the general population.[47] Studies in Denmark and Sweden similarly show psychotics are disproportionately violent offenders.[48] Recent surveys in the United States also show "violence and violent victimization are more common among persons with severe mental illness than in the general population."[49]

Yet a more detailed examination, published as I write this, suggests that mental illness alone is not the cause, but one of several risk factors that in combination increase violence rates. Mental illness and substance abuse seem to be an especially dangerous combination.[50] It is important to remember, however, that even though this is a disproportionately violent population, most people suffering a psychotic disorder (even those who are actively psychotic) are not violent.[51]

In an era when involuntary commitment was relatively easy, many of the mentally ill prone to violence were hospitalized before becoming violent, or on the first violent action after it became apparent that there was a mental illness problem. The connection between insanity and crime was apparent,[52] even though the mentally ill were less frequently arrested for crimes than the general population.

Deinstitutionalization created a revolving door, in which those who had engaged in minor crimes might be briefly held for observation, but were then again released to the community. Ron has been arrested innumerable times over thirty years, for a variety of actions, some of which were just odd behavior, and some of which were attacks on family members or complete strangers. (Fortunately, no one that he has attacked has ever been seriously injured.)

Some of the violent mentally ill leave a human debris trail behind them. Deinstitutionalization, by making it more likely that the violent mentally ill are on the street, instead of institutionalized, has certainly contributed to the perception of the mentally ill as dangerous, adding to the stereotype problems with which the non-violent mentally ill struggle.

Once a mentally ill offender ends up in the criminal justice system for the most serious crimes, such as murder or rape, sympathy for their mental illness declines quite dramatically. As some of the examples given above demonstrate, juries and judges find people who were clearly mentally ill to be legally sane.

It also seems likely that some mentally ill persons are not recognized as such at trial. A 1998 review of the existing surveys of mental illness found that "6 to 15 percent of persons in city and county jails and 10 to 15 percent of persons in state prisons have severe mental illness."[53]   While it might be argued that prison conditions cause this disproportionate level of mental illness, the somewhat similar rates for jail inmates, most of whom are confined for periods of days to weeks, suggests that mental illness is the cause of incarceration, not the result.

Deinstitutionalization played a substantial role in the dramatic increase in violent crime rates in America in the 1970s and 1980s. People who might have been hospitalized in 1950 or 1960 when they first exhibited evidence of serious mental illness instead remained at large until they committed a felony. When the crime is serious enough, the criminal justice system usually sends these mentally ill offenders to prison, not a mental hospital.

The result is a system that is bad for the mentally ill: prisons, in spite of their best efforts, are still primarily institutions of punishment, and are inferior places to treat the mentally ill. It is a bad system for felons without mental illness problems, who necessarily are sharing at least some facilities with the mentally ill, and are understandably afraid of their unpredictability. It is a bad system for the victims of those mentally ill felons, because in 1960, that mental patient was much more likely to have been hospitalized before victimizing someone else. It is a bad system for the taxpayers, who foot the bill for expensive trials and long prison sentences, instead of the much less expensive commitment procedures and perhaps shorter terms of treatment.

22. THE PENDULUM SWINGS BACK

By the mid-1980s, it was apparent, at least to some in the mental health care field, that there needed to be something in between releasing severely mentally ill people to the streets, and institutionalization, especially because the courts had repeatedly made institutionalization so difficult.[1] By the late 1990s, the extent of the problem was becoming apparent outside of the mental health field. Books and articles appeared, often the result of advocacy by the National Alliance for the Mentally Ill, the Treatment Advocacy Center, and families of mentally ill persons like my brother who had fallen through the cracks.

In state after state, sympathetic legislators responded to both organizational lobbying and the requests of family members who had seen the consequences of deinstitutionalization up close. My mother, for example, testified at California legislative hearings in 1997. She explained that the failure of the current system was that until Ron actually became violent, and not just a little violent, the police were powerless to hospitalize him. The police did promise to show up promptly if they were needed, but as our mother explained, "Just try calling 911 when you are lying unconscious on the floor."

OUR MOTHER TESTIFYING BEFORE A CALIFORNIA LEGISLATIVE COMMITTEE HEARING

However, while some legislators were sympathetic, others were not, and in many states the effort to reform the system was maddeningly slow. In some cases, legislators were sympathetic to the ACLU's concerns about due process; in other cases, the cost of building state mental hospitals seemed daunting, since so many of the old facilities had been demolished or allowed to decline to a point where they were no longer restorable.

One proposed strategy that avoided at least part of the problem of building mental hospitals was involuntary *outpatient* commitment (IOC). The theory was that a person who was mentally ill might be "forced to undergo mental health treatment or care in an outpatient instead of an institutional setting." This might include psychotherapy, or medication, and of course, this meant yet another set of battles with civil libertarians.[2]

Every state is a laboratory, and different states experimented with IOC at different times. North Carolina was an early adopter, beginning in 1984.[3] North Carolina's law allowed a court to order such treatment for those who were not in imminent danger, but were "in need of treatment... to prevent further disability or deterioration which would predictably result in dangerousness."[4] Unlike some of the later adopters, North Carolina's goal appears to have been not to widen the power of the government over mentally ill persons, but to narrow it, by substituting involuntary outpatient commitment for hospitalization.[5] By the 1990s, the IOC experiment had also been tried in Iowa, Ohio, Tennessee, and the District of Columbia.

In North Carolina, different studies came to somewhat different conclusions. IOC appears to have made little difference, probably because the courts were reluctant to use this new procedure. In addition, community mental health professionals were reluctant to treat involuntary patients. Many of them lacked knowledge of how to use IOC.[6] Tennessee also failed to see progress, probably because the mental health workers there were not vigorously using the IOC law. (Why? No one seems to know.)

New York State tried the experiment next, starting with a trial program at Bellevue Hospital in New York City in 1994. Like most of the other states that had tried this approach, the results were sufficiently positive to justify expanding the program, in spite of complaints from civil libertarians.[7] Success in a trial does not always lead to wider use, but there was a particular tragedy that led New York State to expand this coercive model. On January 3,

1999, Andrew Goldstein, a 29-year-old schizophrenic from Howard Beach, pushed Kendra Webdale in front of an oncoming subway train in midtown Manhattan, killing her. Webdale was an aspiring writer from upstate New York. As her brother explained, "She was the kind of person who would have helped the kind of person who did this."[8]

This wasn't the first person murdered in this way; it wasn't even the first such New York City murder by a mental patient pushing someone under a subway train. An escapee from a state psychiatric hospital had done something similar in 1995.[9] But unlike that 1995 escapee, Goldstein had a long history of hospitalization, followed by release.

The first symptoms of schizophrenia appeared when Goldstein was 16, but did not disable him until he was in college. Like many other mentally ill Americans, Goldstein received a disability check, which gave him just enough money to survive at the most basic of lifestyles.[10] Like many other schizophrenics, Goldstein was well above average in intelligence, a graduate of the elite Bronx High School of Science.[11]

Goldstein had only one previous criminal offense on his record. Acquaintances described Goldstein as lonely, gentle, and not prone to violence.[12] His hospital records revealed a different story: a patient who often attacked staff in doctor's offices and hospitals, and was described in those records as violent and dangerous.

Even by the existing standards, Goldstein should have been subject to involuntary commitment. Goldstein himself had repeatedly sought hospitalization, only to be turned away.[13] Goldstein had been hospitalized five times in 1998, and was released three weeks before attacking Webdale.[14] Shortly before killing Webdale, Goldstein stopped taking his medications because of the side effects.[15]

Goldstein provided a shocking example, and Kendra Webdale was such a sympathetic victim that soon there were editorials in the *New York Times* calling for the state to take a more active role in caring for the deinstitutionalized mentally ill.[16] New York Governor Pataki signed the bill providing for an involuntary outpatient commitment law in August,[17] and it took effect in November of 1999.[18]

The definition of who was eligible for Assisted Outpatient Treatment (AOT) (as New York called its IOC program) sounds like it was written with an awareness of the battles the New York

Civil Liberties Union had fought to prevent involuntary commitment. That care in drafting paid off; a series of challenges to Kendra's Law failed to strike it down.[19] The target population was those who, without continued help, might relapse and become a threat to themselves or others. They were not *yet* in that category, but were at risk of becoming so.

The criteria were specific, and appear to have been written with the "compelling governmental interest" and "narrowly tailored" requirements of strict scrutiny in mind. Those criteria included a history of non-adherence to treatment where such failure had "been a significant factor in his or her being in a hospital, prison or jail at least twice with the last 36 months" or "resulted in one or more acts, attempts, or threats of serious violent behavior towards self or others within the last 48 months."[20] Kendra's Law also included many other changes intended to improve the provision of mental health services to outpatients, as would be necessary to take care of an increased number of patients who would be subject to it.

In the first four years of the program, 10,078 persons in New York State were referred to the program. Of those, mental health officials filed 4,041 petitions seeking IOC status; 3,766 of those petitions were granted.[21] These numbers suggest that mental health officials took some care to make sure that IOC was appropriate, since more than half of the referrals did not lead to IOC.

A critic of Kendra's Law, while concerned about the loss of constitutional rights of the mentally ill, also complained that, "Kendra's Law wastes expensive investigative and judicial resources, especially if only about one of every four result in an order."[22] One presumes that if IOC referrals led to a *high* percentage of IOC orders, the complaint would be about the lack of due process.

Of those placed on IOC, 64 percent were renewed at the end of six months; this is not a surprising situation for people with long-term mental illness problems. Of those persons under IOC who were not renewed, 76 percent were because "the individual has improved and is no longer in need of court-ordered services" and another 10 percent were institutionalized.[23]

By a number of measures, persons subject to IOC were better off in terms of functioning and self-care. But the improvements were not evenly distributed across all categories. For the criteria that most people would consider the most directly relevant to a mentally ill person's individual well-being, such as "Maintain adequate diet," "Handle finances," and "Avoid dangers," the improvements had the least impressive gains.[24]

With respect to public safety, however, the improvements were much larger. The percentage of IOC patients that threatened suicide fell from 15 percent at the start to 8 percent by the first six-month renewal. Those physically harming others also fell from 15 percent to 8 percent, with comparable improvements in the categories, "Threaten Physical Harm," "Damage or Destroy Property," and "Verbally Assault Others." There were also substantial reductions in "hospitalization, homelessness, arrest and incarceration" as result of IOC.[25]

Civil libertarians who objected to involuntary hospitalization were no happier with commitment being on an outpatient basis. Among the more astonishing claims of critics was that schizophrenics were just as capable of making rational decisions as the general population.[26] A cynic might note that one of the criticisms by lawyers of Kendra's Law is that it failed to provide increased funding for lawyers to participate in challenging the IOC process.[27]

My mother's testimony before a California legislative committee in 1997 did not immediately lead to a new law, but the example from New York of Kendra's Law, in combination with a mass murder in Nevada City, California, led to passage of "Laura's Law." Like New York, California's law was named after a victim, Laura Wilcox, a 19-year-old college student who was one of three victims murdered in January 2001 by Scott Thorpe. Thorpe was a psychiatric patient convinced that the FBI was conspiring to poison his food.[28]

Unlike New York's Kendra's Law, California's legislature made Laura's Law optional on a county-by-county basis; only one of California's fifty-eight counties initially chose to spend the money to implement it.[29] As a San Francisco *Chronicle* columnist pointed out in 2008, after yet another tragedy in the streets:

> Why is it that the city is unwilling to fund Laura's Law, which forces severely mentally ill people to take their medications? The law has been passed in California, but it has to be funded by individual counties.
>
> The reason, according to City Hall sources, is that it is too expensive.

More expensive than a man dead on the street?

Put a price on that.[30]

The value of IOC was sufficiently clear that other states
followed along, with Florida passing an IOC law in 2004. A pilot
program in Seminole County reduced by 43 percent the number of
days that mentally ill persons within the program were hospitalized
or jailed, saving about $14,000 per patient over an eighteen month
period. Unfortunately, there seems to be no information about
reductions in mortality to patients or improvements in living
conditions.[31]

A review of all studies of IOC published in English concluded
that it was most effective with patients suffering from psychotic
disorders who were subject to such orders for six months or more.
Unsurprisingly, IOC was effective only if community mental health
services were available. IOC was no panacea; a one-year follow-
up study in North Carolina found that "few patients in any group
did well on measures of compliance with medication, appointments
kept and absence of disruptive symptoms." (This is one of the
reasons that my brother has often done better on long-term, injected
antipsychotics, rather than oral medications.) However, those
patients subject to IOC did much better than patients who had been
involuntarily committed or who had been held for 72-hour
observation. Those who had been involuntarily committed were
likely the most severely ill. The IOC patients may have done better
because they were not as severely ill.[32]

In Iowa, a five-year retrospective study found that IOC patients
did much better, with reduced hospital and emergency room
treatment, compared to a matched set of control subjects not
subject to IOC.[33] Studies across the industrialized world found that
IOC patients were less likely to be hospitalized, half as likely to be
involved in acts or threats of violence, far less likely to be victims
of crime (23.5 percent of patients within a year vs. 42.4 percent of
patients in the control group), and enjoyed improved quality of
life.[34]

In several states, a factor that seems to have contributed to the
limited used of IOC was that mental health professionals did not
know about the program, or did not know how to go about using it.
Perhaps not surprisingly, a 2001 survey concerning involuntary

commitment (both inpatient and outpatient) found that large numbers of psychiatrists did not fully understood the commitment laws of the states in which they practiced. In general, they erred on the side of believing the law to be narrower than it actually was. Especially with respect to IOC, error rates were quite high, with only 52.6 percent of psychiatrists correctly answering questions about whether IOC was allowed.[35]

Somewhat surprisingly, when psychiatrists were asked their opinions about expanding legal authority for involuntary commitment, the results were decidedly mixed. Some answers suggest that the respondents were split as to whether existing statutes should be loosened to allow involuntary commitment, while other answers suggest that psychiatrists generally supported involuntary commitment where a patient is described as "mentally ill and could benefit from treatment": the old *parens patriae* standard, under which the government looked out for the interests of those who were too ill to look out for themselves.[36]

An increased willingness to use involuntary *inpatient* commitment also became apparent by the mid-1990s. Wisconsin had been one of the states that had led the way down with *Lessard* v. *Schmidt* (1972). In 1996, after twelve years of discussion, the Wisconsin legislature added what became known as the "fifth standard" for involuntary commitment. In addition to being an imminent hazard to oneself, or to others, or gravely disabled, Wisconsin provided for involuntary commitment "if a lack of treatment will cause deterioration of a person's mental and physical health, or cause him or her to suffer severe mental, emotional, or physical harm resulting in loss of independent functioning or loss of control over thoughts and actions, and if the person is incapable of understanding the advantages and disadvantages of accepting treatment and its alternatives."

Inevitably, a court case challenged the new law. A schizophrenic identified in court documents as Dennis H. was committed at the request of his father (a physician). Dennis H. was refusing to eat or drink, and had already suffered kidney failure as a result of a previous episode. The Wisconsin Supreme Court upheld the new "fifth standard." Dennis H. was not in *imminent* danger because of his condition, but it was clear that his mental illness made it likely that he would deteriorate to a point where he was at risk if something wasn't done about his condition.[37]

Most of the Wisconsin Supreme Court's decision focused on

whether the fifth standard was clearly unconstitutional or not, and they held to a traditional, judicial restraint view of what determines constitutionality. "A court does not evaluate the merits of the legislature's economic, social, or political policy choices, but is limited to considering whether the statute violates some specific constitutional provision."[38] The Wisconsin Supreme Court thus returned to a more traditional view of the state's duty towards the mentally ill: "The state has a well-established, legitimate interest under its *parens patriae* power in providing care to persons unable to care for themselves, and also has authority under its police power to protect the community from mentally ill persons determined to be dangerous."[39] Wisconsin was again prepared to violate Dennis H.'s personal sovereignty so that he would not die from the intersection of his physical and mental illnesses.

As I write this chapter, there has certainly been a sea change in attitudes about the *legal* aspects of the state's responsibility to care for the mentally ill, as evidenced by the Wisconsin Supreme Court's willingness to recognize that that the state's authority includes not simply public safety, but the health of mentally ill individuals. It remains uncertain whether the political will exemplified in Wisconsin's "fifth standard" can spread across the country. If it does, it will be because Americans have started to recognize that all the beautiful theory that underlay deinstitutionalization was fundamentally at odds with the real world.

23.   RON CALMS DOWN

Like many other schizophrenics, as Ron moved into his 50s, he calmed down. It is not clear that his mental illness declined, but he certainly became less frightening and aggressive as he aged. After the incident in which Ron knocked our mother down, he spent two days in jail, and ten days being stabilized in a hospital. From there, he spent two weeks in a halfway house, then to Lukedorf, where he lived in a group home for about a year. This group home was a very nice facility, and they kept Ron sufficiently medicated that he was not a danger to himself or to others.

RON OUTSIDE A HALFWAY HOUSE IN TIGARD, 1999

After that year, Lukedorf put him into a two-bedroom apartment that he shared with others suffering from mental illness. The first roommate was quiet and not a problem. A later roommate, however, was frightening, and destroyed some of Ron's possessions, some of which were pretty minor (some frying pans) and some of which were family heirlooms. Ron had an aquarium; while visiting our mother in Riverside, the roommate turned off the filter pump, killing Ron's fish. It may not sound like much, but when you have nothing else, even these little things mean a lot.

My sisters Susan and Carolyn found the roommate pretty frightening; in August 2002, they helped Ron to find an apartment of his own. But Lukedorf at that point refused to continue providing any supervision of Ron's medicines, because he was no longer living in one of their apartments. After much effort, Susan and my mother persuaded Lukedorf to continue providing Ron's medicines, and making sure that he took them.

Because Ron had shown some unwillingness to take his medicines, Lukedorf threatened to have the Oregon government take away Ron's driver's license. Now, you may find it surprising that a mentally ill person had a driver's license. Oddly enough, Ron's driving record over these many years was not noticeably worse than you might expect for a sane person. He had a couple of minor, non-injury accidents, but over a period of more than four decades, this is not terribly startling.

Still, Ron had received notification that his license was about to be suspended because of Lukedorf's efforts at enforcing medication compliance. He slid his car into a hedge in the rain in the early morning. He walked two blocks home to make a call to report the accident. (Ron had no phone available to him at the scene of the accident.) Nonetheless, the police considered this "leaving the scene of an accident." While these charges were eventually dropped, his license suspension that had already been planned took effect a few days after the accident.

Ron managed to do okay (no arrests, no mental hospital lockups) for several months. Ron was talking to himself and slapping the sidewalk with his hand. Portland police officers approached and asked him if he had been drinking. He responded that he drunk a beer the previous week; they assumed (understandably enough) that he was being a troublemaker. At some point, the officers knocked Ron to the ground, and sent him to the mental ward of St. Vincent's.

Certainly, Ron has never shown a great deal of ability to deal with police since he became mentally ill. Nor do I find it implausible that the police officers questioning Ron were afraid for their safety, once they realized that he was mentally ill. Ron was soon transferred to the VA hospital. While there, Ron agreed to go back on injected Prolixin again, at my mother's request.

At about this time, my sister Carolyn moved from the Portland area to a coastal city some hours away. A year later, my mother moved there as well with Ron, who liked the small town flavor. That's where they live today. Ron is a senior citizen now, and spends much of his time walking around town, drinking coffee in several shops that he frequents. He provides assistance to my mother around the house, cooking, and doing various household maintenance jobs. When it came time to install a ceiling fan, Ron was able to do that just fine. He is a keen observer of the world around him, even though he does not talk much.

Because Ron lives in a small town of only a few thousand people, I believe that most residents know who Ron is. Certainly, when Ron and I walk around town together, many people know his name. They may not know exactly what is wrong with Ron. It would be very easy to misinterpret some of his quirks as retardation, not mental illness. I suspect that there is no fear of Ron, in spite of his oddness, because it is a small town, and Ron's quirks have not led to violence there.

I wish that there were a happy ending to Ron's story. I wish that I could tell you that he recovered, and put his intelligence to some productive use. I wish that I could tell you that he was able to get married and raise a family. But that is not the case. He is still largely reliant on my mother to deal with the various agencies with which he must interact: Social Security and the Veterans Administration in particular. While my mother is much like the Eveready Bunny, and remains active into her 90s, this will not continue forever, and the burden of watching over Ron will fall on my siblings who live nearest him.

It would be very comforting to blame Ron's current condition on deinstitutionalization. It would be very nice to believe that, if the laws hadn't changed, that Ron would have been hospitalized in 1973, and come out a year or two later, right as rain. But I don't know that this is so. He might have been hospitalized in 1973 and spent his whole life inside a mental hospital.

What I do know is that Ron has been one of the lucky ones. He didn't freeze to death or die of pneumonia. He didn't spend thirty years sleeping in parks, or living in a cardboard box in a big city. He wasn't murdered on the streets of San Francisco by another homeless person, or by angry teenagers in Santa Cruz who decided to rid their town of "street people." With enormous effort by my mother, Ron has had food, shelter, and adequate medical care. Many others in Ron's category have not been so fortunate.

24.   WE CAN PAY NOW OR WE CAN PAY LATER

A cynic would suggest that the enormous struggle to fix America's mental illness policy reflects a heartless lack of concern by the public. But there's quite a bit more to the story. In spite of how common severe mental illness is, there are a surprising number of people who have been lucky that no family member or friend has fallen under this juggernaut.

This ignorance of mental illness is not limited to those who are poorly educated. Even people with positions of some influence are often startlingly unaware. I remember being utterly shocked to hear two national television correspondents discussing a criminal case in 2007 with a clear misunderstanding of what mental illness is; they gave the impression that they thought mental illness was an invention of defense lawyers to excuse horrifying crimes.

Another problem is that the severely mentally ill, unlike many other beneficiaries of government programs, seldom write to their elected representatives or vote. At best, their families and friends may form an organized force, if someone takes the time to promote such a mass movement (as the National Alliance for the Mentally Ill began to do in the 1980s).

What needs to be done? First of all, the sterile definition of individual rights that produced the absurd situation of the ACLU arguing for the "dignity" of Joyce Brown to live in filth and degradation on the streets of New York needs to be called out for what it is: a theoretical construct that has little to do with the real world. In the interests of the mentally ill, *and* the society at large, we need to be willing to civilly commit those who are *clearly* unable to care for themselves or who have *clearly* lost touch with reality. This process might be an outcome of minor criminal behavior that gives clear evidence of mental illness, or evidence of hallucinations or delusions that give good reason to worry that a person's mental health is in serious decline.

The exacting standards imposed by *Addington* v. *Texas* (1979), which created a requirement for commitment just a bit short of that required for criminal commitment, were clearly in error. The goal of involuntary commitment, on either an outpatient or inpatient basis, is not punishment, but to help those unable to recognize that they are unable to help themselves. A preponderance of evidence, as in other civil proceedings, should be the standard. Mere eccentricity should not be the basis for locking someone up against his will; nor has this been the standard throughout American history. Taxpayers will not tolerate unnecessary hospitalizations, and it is hard to imagine that public mental hospital doctors are going to waste resources on people who are not seriously mentally ill.

In the period before deinstitutionalization, there must certainly have been abuses of the power to commit, with inhumane results, because human nature guarantees that power will be abused. It has, however, left little in the way of evidence. Our choice is not between the abuse of power and utopia. Our society's widespread *failure* to hospitalize the severely mentally ill has produced a *different* set of suffering from the bad old days. The suffering today is that which comes from neglect of the mentally ill, and it leaves footprints that can be seen on a daily basis in America's largest cities: in homelessness; in death by exposure; in crimes committed by and against the homeless mentally ill; in the general squalidness of modern urban life.

Secondly, in the interests of costs, and because confining anyone against their will has potential for abuse, hospitalization should remain a relatively short-term solution for most of those who are no longer able to make rational decisions. Involuntary outpatient commitment programs have generally been a successful low cost method of supervising mentally ill people who are in need of post-hospitalization supervision. Hospitalization, even long-term commitment, must remain an option, however, for those who are unable to care for themselves in an unsupervised setting.

Third, our society needs to be prepared to spend some money. Because of the social costs associated with the severely mentally ill, it is not clear that deinstitutionalization actually saved much money. Fixing the problem now, however, will likely require significant capital expenditures. In some states, the existing public mental hospital system lacks the capacity to care even for those who are prepared to check themselves in for treatment. States went on an orgy of state mental hospital closings in the 1970s; the statistical evidence is strong that the strongest cause of such closings was implementation of deinstitutionalization, not the availability of CMHCs or reduced state expenditures on the mentally ill.[1] Building new public mental hospitals or rebuilding existing ones will be a major capital investment. (Mental health courts, a diversion program for mental ill criminal offenders, are an approach for those who have not yet committed the more serious offenses.)[2]

In some cases, this capital investment may reduce operating costs in other parts of the system. A member of the Idaho state legislature, Rep. Carlos Bilbao, gave me an example several years ago at a men's prayer breakfast. Bilbao's district includes rural Gem County, just west of where I live. Police in Emmett, the county seat, took a young man into custody on a Saturday night. He appeared to be suffering some type of mental illness, but what to do with him presented a serious problem.

There were so few vacant beds in mental hospitals in Idaho that night that the police were unable to find anywhere to place him closer than the state mental hospital in Blackfoot, 286 miles away. This meant transporting him more than four hours *by ambulance* on Saturday night. On Monday morning, an ambulance brought him back to Emmett for a hearing to decide whether he could be held for observation. When a judge ordered him held for observation, it was another four hour plus trip by ambulance back to the state mental hospital at Blackfoot.

If you have ever seen the bill for an ambulance ride, you can guess what Gem County was going to pay for thirteen hours of transport. How many events like this would it take for Gem County, population 16,513, to exhaust its indigent mental health budget? A little excess capacity in the public mental hospital system might have meant an hour's ride each way to Boise, an enormous savings in the county's mental health budget, which could help to pay for the cost of the state expanding its mental hospital system.

Rep. Bilbao told me that just a few years earlier, there were mental patients *handcuffed to desks* in some police stations while police tried to figure out an appropriate disposition. Many county jails were simply not safe places for a mentally ill person, and in many parts of rural Idaho, general hospitals do not have locked facilities for patients who are there against their will.

As we have previously discussed, the mentally ill are a significant fraction of those held in prisons and jails across the United States. An increased willingness to hospitalize the dangerously mentally ill *before* they commit a serious felony will reduce the number of prison cells that need to be built. Advocates for the treatment of the mentally ill argue that community mental health treatment is far less expensive than prison, for several reasons. As an example, Pennsylvania estimates it costs $51,100 per year to incarcerate a mentally ill prisoner. (Mentally healthy prisoners cost Pennsylvania about $28,000 per year, which is a bit higher than the national average cost for inmates in state prisons of $22,650.) Advocates claim that outpatient mental health care costs about $10,000 to $20,000 per year. This seems like a very vague figure, but it does seem likely that outpatient care is cheaper than a prison cell, where the prisoner will also be receiving mental health treatment.[3]

Mentally ill prisoners are not just more expensive per day to lock up; they are likely to be locked up longer. New York City found that in 1997, mentally ill jail inmates spent an average of 215 days in jail, compared to 42 days for sane prisoners.[4] This is not surprising; an extremely disturbed person is likely to have a hard time persuading others to bail them out, or to have the resources to make their own bail. Since many mentally ill people are homeless, judges are likely to regard them as flight risks. To the extent that a mentally ill person awaiting trial appears unpredictable, judges may also be reluctant to risk public safety by releasing them on bail.

It should be apparent that many of these same issues apply to mentally ill persons serving time in prisons: it would be surprising indeed if parole boards gave preference to the release of mentally ill felons, both out of concern for public safety, and concern for an inmate's welfare once released. To the extent that we can identify and treat mental illness early in a patient's decline and *prevent* a mentally ill person from entering the criminal justice system, there is enormous potential to save money.

Fourth, one consequence of *O'Connor* v. *Donaldson* (1975) was that doctors, even those who were employees of state mental hospitals, could be held *personally* liable for decisions that they made concerning involuntary commitment. This produces a variety of risk-reduction actions by mental health professionals that are not good for public safety.

As an example, in February of 2007, Jason Hamilton of Moscow, Idaho, made a suicide attempt by overdosing on prescription drugs. During his mental health evaluation to determine if he should be committed, he told a psychologist that he would never overdose in the future: he would use "guns or bombs" and take "a whole bunch of people with him." Because there was no imminent threat, he was not committed. Three months later, Jason Hamilton went on a mass murder spree killing three people, then himself, in Moscow, Idaho. Diana Pals, "president of the Idaho Mental Health Counselors Association" explained that, "The commitment laws just don't allow people to be committed easily in Idaho."[5]

I suspect based on the lack of response that I received to questions about the Hamilton case, that at least part of what drives a reluctance of mental health professionals to pursue civil commitment is not just weaknesses in the laws, but liability concerns. If the director of a state mental hospital could be held *personally* liable for damages for holding a mental patient pursuant to a court order (as happened in *O'Connor* v. *Donaldson*), think of the risks for a private doctor who is not a public employee who seeks involuntary commitment. No mental health professional should be at risk as a result of any good faith effort concerning commitment. There should be clear evidence of negligence or willful misconduct before a commitment results in personal liability.

Deinstitutionalization degrades and often shortens the lives of the mentally ill. It has coarsened public life as homelessness has become more common, and the mentally ill haunt public libraries, building lobbies, and public parks. It has increased the danger of random criminal attacks by the small fraction of the mentally ill population that turns violent. While the degradation of public life may not have a definite price tag on it, it is certainly not free, even if you only limit yourself to the cost of cleaning urine stains off the public library's carpets, and having the police remove unruly "patrons" who are arguing with creatures that aren't there.

Over the years, I've learned that many people have an abstract concern about the suffering of the mentally ill people that they see begging on sidewalks, filthy, muttering to themselves. How far does that abstract concern go? Will it lead to pressure on legislators to do something about these deplorable conditions? Not usually. Fear of crime, however, is a powerful motivator. In stories about mental illness, journalists often emphasize that mentally ill people are no more dangerous than others, apparently with the goal of ending stereotypes and discrimination against the mentally ill. The continual repetition of this false statement by journalists suggests that many Americans believe the stereotype.

I am not happy about using this fear of the mentally ill to break the logjam. Prejudice against mentally ill persons is certainly increased by this fear. But it is a fear based on reality. It is also a fear that has the best hope for improving circumstances for both the society as a whole, and for the mentally ill who have fallen by the wayside.

It is impossible to determine, except experimentally, what the actual costs will be, because there are so many possible paths that a mentally ill person may take through the social welfare and criminal justice systems. Consider the following scenarios for mentally ill people today, and in an improved and more humane system.

Today: Mr. Jones is 24 years old. He has been working since college at a mid-level professional job. Friends and family notice that he is withdrawing. Worse, he starts to say things that make no sense, and his behavior becomes increasingly bizarre. They suspect mental illness, but Mr. Jones declines to see a doctor about this: "They are going to poison me!" Mr. Jones' behavior at work also becomes increasingly bizarre, and his job performance declines. His employer suspects Mr. Jones of drug abuse and comes up with an excuse to fire him. Over a period of several months, he exhausts his savings, moves into his car, and becomes homeless.

Mr. Jones may never end up in the criminal justice system, although he will likely be a continual drain on public services. Police officers will frequently spend time with Mr. Jones: checking to see if he is unconscious or dead; dealing with public nuisances he commits, such as public urination. If he becomes enough of a nuisance, police may quite unlawfully "encourage" him to move to another jurisdiction. (I have seen this happen.)

There is a good chance that Mr. Jones' bizarre behavior in public will lead to at least a few arrests. Over the remaining forty years of his life, Mr. Jones may be in jail as much as six months of his life, awaiting trial, or being punished for minor criminal acts. Mr. Jones may well end up an expense to the coroner's office and the potter's field if he dies of exposure, disease, or violence.

More frequently, the costs associated with our societal neglect of mentally ill people like Mr. Jones will fall on individuals and non-profit organizations that must confront the ugliness that results when mentally ill people are reduced to living in cardboard boxes, begging and sometimes menacing passers-by for money, digging through trash cans for food, and using alleys as toilets. The expansion of homeless shelters in the 1980s and 1990s means that many cities spend tens of thousands to hundreds of thousands of dollars a year to provide temporary shelter to a population that includes large numbers of the mentally ill. What is especially ugly is that many Americans under forty years of age are unaware that these problems used to be extraordinarily rare.

Less common, but hardly rare, is the scenario where Mr. Jones commits a more serious crime because of his mental illness. As previously mentioned, a large fraction of jail and prison inmates are mentally ill.[6] It may be robbery, or rape, or aggravated assault. His mental illness may not be recognized at trial. Perhaps it is recognized, but neither judge nor jury wants to find him not guilty by reason of insanity out of fear that Mr. Jones will be released a few months from now. Mr. Jones may spend five or ten years in prison. Even if his mental illness is recognized and treated in prison, few people expect that he is not going to come out worse for the experience.

There is a *small* chance that Mr. Jones will become one of those wrenching stories that we examined earlier. His hallucinations and delusions will take him into a world of zombies, or secret government conspiracies, or neighbors plotting against him. He eventually decides that he has no choice, and kills one or two people. Perhaps he kills dozens. A murder trial involving a mentally ill defendant can easily cost hundreds of thousands of dollars, as defense attorneys (almost always public defenders) and prosecutors spend vast quantities of the public's money on mental health evaluations, expert testimony, pre-trial motions, and then a trial. Regardless of the final decision about whether Mr. Jones is sane enough to try, he is going to be locked up for most of the rest of his life, at a cost exceeding two million dollars. In spite of his obvious mental illness, he may well be found guilty, and executed. Because of the expense of death penalty appeals, the cost to the

taxpayers of executing Mr. Jones will likely be *higher* than if he is
given life in prison.

Let us now consider a hopeful tomorrow: Mr. Jackson's family
and friends notice delusionary thinking, and evidence of
hallucinations. After a very strange set of answers to police, Mr.
Jackson is hospitalized first for observation. A judge talks to Mr.
Jackson a few days later, and concludes that he needs treatment.
After two months of stabilization, Mr. Jackson is released, and
treated on an outpatient basis. There is some evidence that early
treatment with antipsychotic medications may prevent the most
destructive effects of schizophrenia.[7] In the rosiest of scenarios,
Mr. Jackson recovers enough to return to work. This is not the
likely case, but in our hopeful tomorrow it has more potential than
in our hopeless today.

More likely, Mr. Jackson does not fully recover. I have talked
to a few schizophrenics who have recovered, at least in part. They
are able to work, although generally not at as high an income level
as they did before. They have difficult days, and they have good
ones. They are not a drain on the society, or at least they are not
completely dependent on the government for their care.

Perhaps Mr. Jackson does not recover even in part. He remains
disabled, but takes his medicine consistently enough that he does
not need to be hospitalized again. This is roughly equivalent to
what happens today, where some psychotics are successfully
treated in an outpatient setting, and remain in that setting their
entire lives. This scenario may be a bit more expensive because of
Mr. Jackson's stabilization time in the hospital, but over a forty-
year life, it is not a big difference in costs.

A less hopeful alternative is that like many schizophrenics
today, Mr. Jackson forgets to take his medications, and
occasionally ends up back in the hospital, because a social worker,
friend, or family member sees that something has gone wrong. He
might spend a year in total of the remaining forty years of his life in
hospitals. Compared to Mr. Jones, the homeless man living in his
car, this is going to cost some money. Compared to Mr. Jones' ten
years in prison for aggravated assault and mayhem, a year of
hospitalization and thirty-nine years of outpatient treatment saves
money, and some victims.

There is only one scenario that is going to be clearly more
expensive in our hopeful tomorrow: Mr. Jackson is hospitalized for
psychosis, and his problems are so severe that he spends much of

his life inside the mental hospital. But someone with such severe mental illness is almost certainly going to be a major expense to our criminal justice system in the hopeless today, along with causing a few tragedies.

Until the general public fully understands the nature of what deinstitutionalization has done to America, there will not be the public will to correct this well-intentioned, but disastrous error. It is time to admit that the theories and intentions behind deinstitutionalization were a mistake. They were well-intentioned and beautiful theories, but they do not have much to do with the real world. It is time to admit that reality is not optional when it comes to public policy.

NOTES

Introduction

1 Tom H. Watkins, *The Hungry Years: A Narrative History of the Great Depression in America* (New York: Macmillan, 2000), 68-72.

2 Jim Tull, "Homelessness: An Overview," in Padraig O'Malley, ed. *Homelessness: New England and Beyond* (Amherst, Mass.: University of Massachusetts Press, 1992), 33-34.

3 Committee on Health Care for Homeless People, U.S. Institute of Medicine, *Homelessness, Health, and Human Needs* (Washington: National Academy Press, 1988), 50-52.

4 George Romero, *The Rescue* (Arcadia, Cal.: Lotus Vision Publishing Co., 2010), 315-23 is one of the many credulous but not credible conspiracy theories.

Chapter 1: Ron's Breakdown

1 L.M. Brzustowicz, K.A. Hodgkinson, E.W. Chow, W.G. Honer, A.S. Bassett, "Location of a major susceptibility locus for familial schizophrenia on chromosome 1q21-q22," *Science* [April 28, 2000] 288(5466):678-82, abstract available at http://www.ncbi.nlm.nih.gov/entrez/query.fcgi?cmd=Retrieve&db=PubMed&list_uids=2024 7438&dopt=Citation, last accessed August 16, 2006.

2 Irwin G. Sarason and Barbara R. Sarason, *Abnormal Psychology: The Problem of Maladaptive Behavior*, 10th ed. (Upper Saddle River, N.J.: Prentice-Hall, 2002), 359-69.

3 Nashaat N. Boutros, Malcolm B. Bowers, Jr., and Donald Quinlan, "Chronological Association Between Increases in Drug Abuse and Psychosis in Connecticut State Hospitals," Journal of Neuropsychiatry and Clinical Neurosciences [February 1998] 10:48-54, available at http://ncuro.psychiatryonline.org/cgi/content/full/10/1/48, last accessed August 16, 2006.

4 Louise Arsenault, Mary Cannon, John Witton, Robin E. Murray, "Causal Association Between Cannabis and Psychosis: Examination of the Evidence," *British Journal of Psychiatry* [2004] 184:110-117; Cécile Henquet, Marta Di Forti, Paul Morrison, Rebecca Kuepper and Robin M. Murray, "Gene-Environment Interplay Between Cannabis and Psychosis," *Schizophrenia Bulletin* [August 22, 2008] 34:6:1111-1121; John McGrath, Joy Welham, James Scott, *et al.*, "Association Between Cannabis Use and Psychosis-Related Outcomes Using Sibling Pair Analysis in a Cohort of Young Adults," *Archives of General Psychiatry* 67:5 [May 2010] 440-447; Kathleen Doheny, "Pot And Psychosis: Possible

Link?" *CBS* *News*, July 26, 2007, http://www.cbsnews.com/stories/2007/07/26/health/webmd/main3102653.shtml?source=mo stpop_story, last accessed August 25, 2007.

5 Stanley Zammit, Peter Allebeck, Sven Andreasson, Ingvar Lundberg, and Glyn Lewis, "Self reported cannabis use as a risk factor for schizophrenia in Swedish conscripts of 1969: historical cohort study," *British Medical Journal* 325:1199 [November 23, 2002], abstract available at http://www.bmj.com/content/325/7374/1199, last accessed May 14, 2011; Louise Arsenault, Mary Cannon, Richie Poulton, Robin Murray, Avshalom Caspi, Terrie E. Moffitt, "Cannabis Use In Adolescence And Risk For Adult Psychosis: Longitudinal Prospective Study," *British Medical Journal* [November 23, 2002], 325:1212-1213, last accessed May 14, 2011.

6 M. M. Vardy and S. R. Kay, "LSD psychosis or LSD-induced schizophrenia? A multimethod inquiry," *Archives of General Psychiatry* 40:8:877-83 [August 1983], abstract available at http://www.ncbi.nlm.nih.gov/pubmed/6870484, last accessed May 14, 2011; Max Rinkel, H. Jackson DeShon, Robert W. Hyde, and Harry C. Solomon, "Experimental Schizophrenia-Like Symptoms," *American Journal of Psychiatry* 108:8:572-578 [February, 1952].

7 E. Dyck, "Flashback: psychiatric experimentation with LSD in historical perspective," *Canadian Journal of Psychiatry* [June 2005] 50(7):381-8, abstract available at http://www.ncbi.nlm.nih.gov/entrez/query.fcgi?db=pubmed&cmd=Retrieve&dopt=Abstract Plus&list_uids=16086535&query_hl=3&itool=pubmed_docsum, last accessed August 16, 2006.

Chapter 2: What Is Mental Illness?

1 "Antidepressants and Suicide," in Linda Wasmer Andrews, ed., *Encyclopedia of Depression* (Santa Barbara, Cal.: Greenwood Press, 2010), 1:35-36; Robert Grieco and Laura Edwards, *The Other Depression: Bipolar Disorder* (New York: Taylor & Francis Group, 2010), 129-30.

2 Evelyn J. Bromet and Herbert C. Schulberg, "Special Problem Populations: The Chronically Mentally Ill, Elderly, Children, Minorities, and Substance Abusers," 67-68, in David A. Rochefort, ed., *Handbook on Mental Health Policy in the United States* (Westport, Conn.: Greenwood Press, 1989).

3 R. J. Wyatt, I. Henter, M. C. Leary and E. Taylor, "An economic evaluation of schizophrenia-1991," *Social Psychiatry and Psychiatric Epidemiology* 30:5 [September 1995], 196-205, abstract available at http://www.springerlink.com/content/wj15686263364413/, accessed August 16, 2006.

4 J.P. McEvoy, "The Costs of Schizophrenia, *Journal of Clinical Psychiatry*, 68 Suppl. 14:4-7 (2007), abstract available at http://www.ncbi.nlm.nih.gov/pubmed/18284271, last accessed June 9, 2012.

5 National Quality Measures Clearinghouse, "Schizophrenia: percent of patients with severe symptoms or side effects and no recent medication treatment change to address these problems," February 25, 2008, http://www.qualitymeasures.ahrq.gov/summary/summary.aspx?ss=1&doc_id=418, last accessed February 29, 2008; U.S. Social Security Administration Office of Policy, "Annual Statistical Supplement, 2006," Table 5.A4, http://www.socialsecurity.gov/policy/docs/statcomps/supplement/2006/5a.html#table5.a4, last accessed March 9, 2008; Samuel L. Baker, "U.S. national health spending, 2005," August 26, 2007, http://hspm.sph.sc.edu/Courses/Econ/Classes/nhe00/ last accessed March 9, 2008.

6 R. J. Wyatt, I. Henter, M. C.Leary and E. Taylor, "An economic evaluation of schizophrenia-1991," *Social Psychiatry and Psychiatric Epidemiology* 30:5 [September 1995], 196-205, abstract available at http://www.springerlink.com/content/wj15686263364413/, accessed August 16, 2006.

7 Paula M. Ditton, Bureau of Justice Statistics, "Mental Health and Treatment of Inmates and Probationers," (Washington: U.S. Department of Justice, 1999), NCJ 174463.

8 Jason C. Matejkowski, Sara W. Cullen, and Phyllis L. Solomon, "Characteristics of Persons With Severe Mental Illness Who Have Been Incarcerated for Murder," *Journal of the American Academy of Psychiatry and the Law* 36:1[2008]74-86, http://www.jaapl.org/cgi/reprint/36/1/74, last accessed May 14, 2011.

9 *The Homeless Mentally Ill: A Task Force Report of the American Psychiatric Association* (Washington: American Psychiatric Association, 1984), 204-8; Sarason and Sarason, *Abnormal Psychology*, 354-9.

10 Lamb, *Homeless Mentally Ill*, 204-8.

11 Sarason and Sarason, *Abnormal Psychology*, 354, 359.

12 Lamb, *Homeless Mentally Ill*, 204-8; Sarason and Sarason, *Abnormal Psychology*, 350.

13 Lamb, *Homeless Mentally Ill*, 204-8; Sarason and Sarason, *Abnormal Psychology*, 359-64.

14 Blackwood, "Are Some Genetic Risk Factors Common to Schizophrenia, Bipolar Disorder and Depression?", 73-83; Hamid Mostafavi Abdolmaleky, Kuang-hung Cheng, Stephen V. Faraone, *et al.*, "Hypomethylation of *MB-COMT* promoter is a major risk factor for schizophrenia and bipolar disorder," *Human Molecular Genetics* 15:21 (2006) 3132-45; there are hundreds of other recent studies examining the connection between these two mental illness.

15 International Schizophrenia Consortium, "Common polygenic variation contributes to risk of schizophrenia and bipolar disorder," *Nature* 460[August 6, 2009] 750-1.

16 Kristen J. Brennand, Anthony Simone, Jessica Jou, *et al.*, "Modelling Schizophrenia Using Human Induced Pluripotent Stem Cells," *Nature* 473[May 12, 2011]:221-7.

17 J. Allan Hobson and Jonathan A. Leonard, *Out Of Its Mind: Psychiatry in Crisis* (Cambridge, Mass.: Perseus Publishing Group, 2001), 188-9.

18 Hreinn Stefansson, Roel A. Ophoff, Stacy Steinberg, *et al.*, "Common variants conferring risk of schizophrenia," *Nature* 460 [August 6, 2009] 744-5.

19 Douglas Fox, "The Insanity Virus," *Discover*, June, 2010, 58-64; Robert H. Yolken, "Infectious Agents and Schizophrenia," in Stacey Knobler, *et al., The Infectious Etiology of Chronic Diseases: Defining the Relationship, Enhancing the Research, and Mitigating the Effects* (Washington: National Academies Press, 2004), 62-65.

20 Frank P. Ryan, "Human Endogenous Retroviruses In Health And Disease: A Symbiotic Perspective," *Journal of the Royal Society of Medicine*, 97:560-565 (December 2004).

21 Sarah Rosenfield, "Psychiatric Epidemiology: An Overview of Methods and Findings," 46-7, in Rochefort, *Handbook on Mental Health Policy in the United States.*

22 Sarason and Sarason, *Abnormal Psychology*, 355.

23 Rosenfield, "Psychiatric Epidemiology," 46-7.

24 Sarason and Sarason, *Abnormal Psychology*, 354.

25 Hobson and Leonard, *Out of Its Mind*, 238-9.

26 Rosenfield, "Psychiatric Epidemiology," 46-7.

27 Hobson and Leonard, *Out of Its Mind*, 202-3.

28 Sarason and Sarason, *Abnormal Psychology*, 378.

29 A. G. Jolley, S. R. Hirsch, E. Morrison, A. McRink, and L. Wilson, "Trial of brief intermittent neuroleptic prophylaxis for selected schizophrenic outpatients: clinical and social outcome at two years," *British Medical Journal* 837:1136 [October 13, 1990], http://www.bmj.com/content/301/6756/837.abstract, last accessed May 14, 2011.

30 Joint Commission on Mental Illness and Health, *Action for Mental Health: Final Report of the Joint Commission on Mental Illness and Health* (New York: Basic Books, 1961), 4.

31 "llness," *ScienceDaily*, October 1, 2003, http://www.sciencedaily.com /releases/2003/10/031001061055.htm, last accessed February 29, 2008. Generally, see Robert Lubow and Ina Weiner, eds., *Latent Inhibition: Cognition, Neuroscience, and Applications to Schizophrenia* (Cambridge, Eng.: Cambridge University Press, 2010).

32 Hobson and Leonard, *Out Of Its Mind*, 83-84.

Chapter 4: Colonial America (1607-1775)

1 Gerald N. Grob, *The Mad Among Us: A History of the Care of the America's Mentally Ill* (New York: The Free Press, 1994), 6-7.

2 Michael Dalton. *The Country Justice: Containing The Practice, Duty And Power Of The Justices Of The Peace....* (London: William Rawlins and Samuel Roycroft, assigns of Richard and Edward Atykins, 1690), ch. 147, in *Archives of Maryland*, 153:350.

3 Henry F. Buswell, *The Law of Insanity In Its Application to the Civil Rights and Capacities and Criminal Responsibility of the Citizen* (Boston: Little, Brown & Co., 1885), 1-13.

4 Buswell, *The Law of Insanity*, 15-18.

5 *Public Records of the Colony of Connecticut,* 11:318. Sarah Frazier of Connecticut, who killed an Indian woman with an ax, was found not guilty by reason of "distraction" in 1724. Joshua Hempstead, *Diary of Joshua Hempstead of New London, Connecticut* (New London, Connecticut: New London County Historical Society, 1901), 139, 141-2.

6 *Public Records of the Colony of Connecticut,* 11:318. In 1761, Benajah again requested assistance from the legislature in caring for his son, and they gave him twenty pounds more. *Ibid.*, 11:590-1.

7 State of Pennsylvania, *Official Documents, Comprising The Department And Other Reports Made To The Governor, Senate And House of Representatives Of Pennsylvania* (Harrisburg, Penn.: Edwin K. Meyers, 1893), 8:107.

8 Duane Hamilton Hurd, *History of Norfolk County, Massachusetts...* (Philadelphia: J.W. Lewis & Co., 1884), 1:312.

9 *Public Records of the Colony of Connecticut,* 11:111-12.

10 James W. North, *The History of Augusta, From the Earliest Settlement to the Present Time...* (Augusta, Me.: Clapp & North, 1870), 87.

11 Hempstead, *Diary of Joshua Hempstead,* 359, 233.

12 Lloyd Vernon Briggs, *History of the Psychopathic Hospital, Boston, Massachusetts* (Boston: Wright & Potter Printing Co., 1922), 3.

13 Mary Ann Jimenez, "Madness In Early American History: Insanity In Massachusetts From 1700 To 1830," *Journal of Social History* [Fall 86] 20:1, 25-26.

14 Boston [Mass.] Registry Department, *A Report of the Record Commissioners of the City of Boston, Containing the Records of Boston Selectmen, 1736 to 1742* (Boston: Rockwell and Churchill, 1886), 15:366, Boston [Mass.] Registry Department, *A Report of the Record Commissioners of the City of Boston, Containing the Records of Boston Selectmen, 1736 to 1742* (Boston: Rockwell and Churchill, 1887), 17:97.

15 Clifford K. Shipton, *New England Life in the Eighteenth Century* (Cambridge, Mass.: Harvard University Press, 1995), 216-19.

16 Jimenez, "Madness In Early American History," 25-26.

17 Maine Historical Society, *Collections and Proceedings of the Maine Historical Society,* 2nd ser., 5:99-101 (1894).

18 Jimenez, "Madness in Early American History," 25-26.

19 *Public Records of the Colony of Connecticut,* 4:285-6, 5:503; Gerald N. Grob, *Mental Institutions in America: Social Policy to 1875* (New York: The Free Press, 1973), 12-13; Grob, *Mad Among Us,* 16-17; Albert Deutsch, *The Mentally Ill in America: A History of Their Care and Treatment from Colonial Times,* 2nd ed. (New York: Columbia University Press, 1949), 40-50. Deutsch's work has been widely criticized as presenting a darker account of Colonial treatment of the mentally ill than his own evidence shows; see Grob, *Mental Institutions in America,* 12 n. 9.

20 Duane Hamilton Hurd, *History of Middlesex County, Massachusetts...* (Philadelphia: J.W. Lewis & Co., 1890), 1:611.

21 Josiah Henry Benton, *Warning Out in New England: 1656-1817* (Boston: W.B. Clarke Co., 1911), 114-15.

22 Providence (R.I.) City Council, *The Early Records of the Town of Providence* (Providence, R.I.: Snow & Farnham, 1899), 15:39.

23 Edward Field, ed., *State of Rhode Island and Providence Plantations at the End of the Century: A History* (Boston: Mason Publishing Co., 1902), 3:416.

24 Field, *State of Rhode Island and Providence Plantations*, 3:416; Providence (R.I.) City Council, *The Early Records of the Town of Providence* (Providence, R.I.: Snow & Farnham, 1893), 2:55.

25 Providence (R.I.) City Council, *The Early Records of the Town of Providence*, 2:104.

26 Grob, *Mad Among Us*, 13-15.

27 *"The same Evening* Joseph Watson *a* Lunatick..." *South Carolina Gazette*, January 1, 1737.

28 "Extract of a letter," *Pennsylvania Gazette*, August 22, 1765.

29 "Hannah Abraham," *Pennsylvania Gazette*, August 20, 1767, "James Lewis," August 30, 1753, "Tamer Way," January 22, 1783.

30 Grob, *Mental Institutions in America*, 13-31; Grob, *Mad Among Us*, 18-19.

31 James V. May, *Mental Diseases: A Public Health Problem* (Boston: Richard G. Badger, 1922), 34.

32 Grob, *Mental Institutions in America*, 13-31; Grob, *Mad Among Us*, 18-19.

33 Benjamin Franklin, *Some Account of the Pennsylvania Hospital From Its First Rise to the Beginning of the Fifth Month, Called May, 1754* (Philadelphia: United States' Gazette, 1817), 4-5.

34 May, *Mental Diseases*, 35-36; D. Hayes Agnew, Alfred Stille, Lewis P. Bush, Charles K. Mills, Roland G. Curtin, *History and Reminiscences of the Philadelphia Almshouse and Philadelphia Hospital* (Philadelphia: Detre & Blackburn, 1890), 1:78.

35 Franklin, *Some Account of the Pennsylvania Hospital*, 3.

36 Grob, *Mental Institutions in America*, 13-31; Grob, *Mad Among Us*, 18-19.

37 Franklin, *Some Account of the Pennsylvania Hospital*, 45.

38 Franklin, *Some Account of the Pennsylvania Hospital*, 65-66.

39 Deutsch, *Mentally Ill in America*, 31-38.

40 Grob, *Mad Among Us*, 9-12; Mary de Young, *Madness: An American History of Mental Illness and Its Treatment* (Jefferson, N.C.: McFarland & Co., 2010), 74-75.

41 Grob, *Mad Among Us*, 14.

42 Grob, *Mental Institutions in America*, 39-47; Deutsch, *Mentally Ill in America*, 77-81.

43 Robert Jean Campbell, *Campbell's Psychiatric Dictionary*, 8th ed. (New York: Oxford University Press, 2004), 296.

44 Deutsch, *Mentally Ill in America*, 419-20.

45 Jack D. Marietta and G.S. Rowe, *Troubled Experiment: Crime and Justice in Pennsylvania, 1682-1800* (Philadelphia: University of Pennsylvania Press, 2006), 112-14, 35, 164.

46 May, *Mental Diseases*, 36-37.

47 Shomer S. Zwelling, *Quest For A Cure: The Public Hospital In Williamsburg, 1773-1885* (Williamsburg, Va.: Colonial Williamsburg Foundation, 1985), 8-12.

48 Grob, *Mental Institutions in America*, 37.

49 G. Lewis, A. David, S. Andreasson, P. Allebeck, "Schizophrenia and city life," *Lancet*,   [July   18,   1992]   340(8812):137-40,   abstract   available   at http://www.ncbi.nlm.nih.gov/entrez/query.fcgi?cmd=Retrieve&db=PubMed&list_uids=1352 565, last accessed September 13, 2006; M. Marcelis, F. Navarro-Mateu, R. Murray, J.P. Selten, J. Van Os, "Urbanization and psychosis: a study of 1942-1978 birth cohorts in The Netherlands," *Psychological Medicine*, [July 1998] 28(4):871-9, abstract available at http://www.ncbi.nlm.nih.gov/entrez/query.fcgi?cmd=Retrieve&db=PubMed&list_uids=9723 142, last accessed September 13, 2006; E. Fuller Torrey and Judy Miller, *The Invisible Plague: The Rise of Mental Illness from 1750 to the Present* (New Brunswick, N.J.: Rutgers University Press, 2001), 122.

50 Torrey and Miller, *The Invisible Plague*, 291-2.

51 Herbert Goldhamer and Andrew W. Marshall, *Psychosis and Civilization: Two Studies in the Frequency of Mental Disease* (Glencoe, Ill.: The Free Press, 1953). Torrey

and Miller, *The Invisible Plague,* 295-297, discusses the many problems with Goldhamer and Marshall's use of the data.

52 Torrey and Miller, *The Invisible Plague,* 120-123, 298-9.

53 Briggs, *History of the Psychopathic Hospital,* 4.

54 Deane Merrill, "Estimated Population of American Colonies, 1630-1780," http://merrill.olm.net/mdocs/pop/colonies/colonies.htm, last accessed September 10, 2009.

55 Torrey and Miller, *The Invisible Plague,* frontispiece and 124-47.

Chapter 5: The State Mental Hospital (1775-1900)

1 Grob, *Mental Institutions in America,* 39-47; Deutsch, *Mentally Ill in America,* 77-81; D. Hack Tuke, *The Insane in the United States and Canada* (London: H.K. Lewis, 1885), 7-14. See also Laurel Thatcher Ulrich, *A Midwife's Tale: The Life of Martha Ballard, Based on Her Diary, 1785-1812* (New York: Vintage Books, 1991), 259-60, for a discussion of how a Maine midwife treated someone whose mind was "considerably disordered" with medicines. It was apparently no more effective than Rush's treatment, but less torturous.

2 Brattleboro (Vt.) Vermont Asylum for the Insane, *The Vermont Asylum for the Insane: Its Annals for Fifty Years* (Battleboro, Vt.: Hildreth and Fales, 1887), 1-8.

3 Tanaquil Taubes, "'Healthy Avenues of the Mind': Psychological Theory Building and the Influence of Religion During the Era of Moral Treatment," *American Journal of Psychiatry* 155:8[August 1998], 1002; Grob, *Mad Among Us,* 29-30.

4 William Henry Octavius Sankey, *Lectures on Mental Diseases* (London: John Churchill and Sons, 1866), 214-17; Alexander Morison, *Cases of Mental Disease, With Practical Observations on the Medical Treatment for the Use of Students* (London: Longman & Co., 1828), 7.

5 Sankey, *Lectures on Mental Diseases,* 219-29; Philippe Pinel, D. D. Davis trans., *A Treatise on Insanity. In Which Are Contained the Principles of a New and More Practical Nosology of Maniacal Disorders* (Sheffield, Eng.: W. Todd, 1806), 48-109.

6 Deutsch, *Mentally Ill in America,* 90-113; Grob, *Mental Institutions in America,* 65-67; T. Romeyn Beck, "Statistical Notices of Some of the Lunatic Asylums of the United States," *Transactions of the Albany Institute* (Albany, N.Y.: Webster & Skinners, 1830), 1:63-64.

7 Tuke, *Insane in the United States and Canada,* 7; Morison, *Cases of Mental Disease,* is filled with examples of treating mental illness with various medications intended to address underlying physical causes. Similarly, James Cowles Prichard, *A Treatise on Insanity and Other Disorders Affecting the Mind* (Philadelphia: E.L. Carey & A. Hart, 1837), 185-204, covers the established methods of treating mental illness by curing the underlying physical causes. Significantly, Prichard at 202 observes that "in a great proportion of maniacal cases there are symptoms of disturbance in the natural functions, and that diseases of the thoracic and abdominal viscera co-exist with that morbid state of the brain on which madness immediately depends," a position consistent with modern understanding of bipolar disorder.

8 Grob, *Mental Institutions in America,* 51-64; Deutsch, *Mentally Ill in America,* 106-7, 139-41; Grob, *Mad Among Us,* 46-7.

9 T. Romeyn Beck, "Statistical Notices of Some of the Lunatic Asylums of the United States," 1:60-64, 82; New York Hospital Society, *Charter of the Society of the New-York Hospital and the Laws Relating Thereto, with the By-laws and Regulations of the Institution, and Those of the Bloomingdale Asylum for the Insane* (New York: Daniel Fanshaw, 1856), 21.

10 Beck, "Statistical Notices," 1:71.

11 Briggs, *History of the Psychopathic Hospital,* 12.

12 Tuke, *Insane in the United States and Canada,* 50-52.

13 Deutsch, *Mentally Ill in America,* 107-13.

14 Grob, *Mad Among Us,* 41-44.

15 Thomas G. Morton, "Reminisces of Early Hospital Days," *Philadelphia Medical Times,* December 26, 1885, 227.

16 Thomas S. Kirkbride, *On the Construction, Organization, and General Arrangements of Hospitals for the Insane: With Some Remarks on Insanity and Its Treatment*, 2nd ed. (Philadelphia: J.B. Lippincott & Co., 1880), 248. This is from a later work by Kirkbride, but Grob, *Mad Among Us*, 69-70 indicates that this was Kirkbride's early view as well.

17 Robert Waln, Jr., "An Account of the Asylum for the Insane, established by the Society of Friends, near Frankford, in the vicinity of Philadelphia," *Philadelphia Journal of Medical and Physical Science* [1825] 10:238-39.

18 Deutsch, *Mentally Ill in America*, 420-2. See, however, North, *The History of Augusta*, 493-5, for how Henry McCausland was found not guilty of murder by reason of insanity in 1793, and spent thirty-six years in jail (until his death), where he became a tourist attraction. Thousands came to look at him, and hear him tell the tale of how he killed a "wicked woman" and burned down a church. Admission fees helped to cover his costs of confinement.

19 Grob, *Mad Among Us*, 80-81. See Briggs, *History of the Psychopathic Hospital*, 4 for the sequence by which Massachusetts first provided for holding the furiously mad in jail (1798) and then confining them to a hospital or lunatic asylum (1827).

20 *Acts of a General Nature, Enacted, Revised and Ordered to be Reprinted, At the First Session of the Twenty-Ninth General Assembly of the State of Ohio* (Columbus, Ohio: Olmsted & Bailmache, 1831), 29:224.

21 Deutsch, *Mentally Ill in America*, 422-4.

22 Grob, *Mad Among Us*, 52, 94.

23 Torrey and Miller, *The Invisible Plague*, 95-97.

24 Grob, *Mental Illness and American Society*, 47.

25 Isaac Ray, Winfred Overholser, ed., *A Treatise on the Medical Jurisprudence of Insanity* (Cambridge, Mass.: Harvard University Press, 1962), 21-35.

26 Ray, *Treatise on the Medical Jurisprudence of Insanity*, 174.

27 Ray, *Treatise on the Medical Jurisprudence of Insanity*, 178-81.

28 Ray, *Treatise on the Medical Jurisprudence of Insanity*, 339.

29 *Matter of Oakes*, 8 Law Rep. 122 (Mass. 1845).

30 Deutsch, *Mentally Ill in America*, 132-8.

31 Garfield Tourney, "A History of Therapeutic Fashions in Psychiatry, 1800-1966," *American Journal of Psychiatry* 124:6 [December 1967] 786.

32 Deutsch, *Mentally Ill in America*, 132-8.

33 Basil Hall, *Travels in North America, in the Years 1827 and 1828*, 3rd ed. (Edinburgh: Robert Cadell, 1830), 2:194-7.

34 Deutsch, *Mentally Ill in America*, 132-8.

35 Grob, *Mental Institutions in America*, 67-69; Grob, *Mad Among Us*, 99-101; Deutsch, *Mentally Ill in America*, 132-8.

36 Tourney, "A History of Therapeutic Fashions in Psychiatry," 785-7.

37 Deutsch, *Mentally Ill in America*, 138-40.

38 Deutsch, *Mentally Ill in America*, 423.

39 *Hinchman* v. *Richie*, Brightly 143, 152 (C.P. Phila, 1849).

40 [An American Citizen], *The Hinchman Conspiracy Case, in Letters to the New York Home Journal...* (Philadelphia: Stokes & Brother, Arcade, 1849).

41 Deutsch, *Mentally Ill in America*, 423.

42 *Hinchman* v. *Richie*, Brightly 143, 144 (C.P. Phila, 1849).

43 Paul S. Appelbaum and Kathleen N. Kemp, "The Evolution of Commitment Law in the Nineteenth Century: A Reinterpretation," *Law and Human Behavior*, 6:3-4 [1982], 345-7.

44 Buswell, *Law of Insanity*, 25 n. 1; Appelbaum and Kemp, "The Evolution of Commitment Law in the Nineteenth Century," 347-9.

45 Appelbaum and Kemp, "The Evolution of Commitment Law in the Nineteenth Century," 347-9.

46 Appelbaum and Kemp, "The Evolution of Commitment Law in the Nineteenth Century," 349-51.

47 Deutsch, *Mentally Ill in America*, 424-8; Grob; *Mad Among Us*, 133-4.

48 Illinois General Assembly, *Reports Made to the General Assembly of Illinois at its Thirtieth Regular Session* (Springfield, Ill.: D.W. Lusk, 1877), 2(part 1):114.

49 Deutsch, *Mentally Ill in America*, 424-8; Grob; *Mad Among Us*, 133-4.

50 Grob, *Mental Illness and American Society*, 48.

51 George Leib Harrison, *Legislation on Insanity: A Collection of All the Lunacy Laws of the States and Territories of the United States to the Year 1883, Inclusive...* (Philadelphia: privately printed, 1884), 3-9.

52 Edward Jarvis, "Law of Insanity, and Hospitals for the Insane in Massachusetts," *Monthly Law Reporter* 22:[November 1859]387. See also Benjamin Franklin Thomas, *The Town Officer: A Digest of the Laws of Massachusetts In Relation to the Powers, Duties and Liabilities of Towns, and Town Officers* (Worcester, Mass.: Warren Lazell, 1849), 201-206.

53 Massachusetts Commission on Lunacy, *Report on Insanity and Idiocy in Massachusetts* (Boston: William White, 1855), 159-74.

54 Buswell, *The Law of Insanity*, 25-36. Spot checking of the stupefyingly complete collection of state laws in Harrison, *Legislation on Insanity*, confirms Buswell's claim. See also Isham G. Harris, "Commitment of the Insane, Past and Present, in the State of New York," *New York State Journal of Medicine* 7:12 [December, 1907] 487-91, for a detailed account of the increasing formalization of the commitment procedure in that state.

55 Deutsch, *Mentally Ill in America*, 187-90.

56 Deutsch, *Mentally Ill in America*, 187-90.

57 State of New York, *Seventeenth Annual Report of the State Board of Charities* (Albany: Weed, Parsons & Co., 1884), 18-22. *Ibid.*, 12, contains a list of revenue sources for the state hospitals; counties were one of the sources.

58 Grob, *Mad Among Us,* 48-51.

59 Gerald N. Grob, *Mental Illness and American Society, 1875-1940* (Princeton University Press, 1983), 9.

60 Grob, *Mental Illness and American Society*, 9-10.

61 Grob, *Mental Illness and American Society*, 10-11.

Chapter 6: Twentieth Century Commitment Until World War II

1 Grob, *Mad Among Us*, 116-24; Grob, *Mental Illness and American Society*, 10. See Goldhamer and Marshall, *Psychosis and Civilization*, 81-82, for a statistical analysis of the increase in mental hospital admissions of the senile in the twentieth century.

2 State of New York, State Commission in Lunacy, *Ninth Annual Report* (Albany: Wynkoop Hallenbeck Crawford Co., 1898), 289-91.

3 Massachusetts State Board of Insanity, *Fifteenth Annual Report of the State Board of Insanity of the Commonwealth of Massachusetts* (Boston: Wright & Potter Printing Co., 1914), 45. As late as 1909, psychiatry textbooks were careful to state that while the evidence was strong that syphilis caused general paresis, it was by no means completely proven. See William A. White, *Outlines of Psychiatry*, 2ᵈ ed. (New York: The Journal of Nervous and Mental Disease Publishing Co., 1909), 126-7.

4 Grob, *Mad Among Us*, 124-7, 166.

5 Goldhamer and Marshall, *Psychosis and Civilization,* 41.

6 Grob, *Mad Among Us*, 124, 127.

7 Tourney, "A History of Therapeutic Fashions in Psychiatry", 787.

8 Torrey and Miller, *The Invisible Plague,* 288-90.

9 Peter Bassoe, ed., *Practical Medicine* (Chicago: The Year Book Publishers, 1922), 8:165-7.

10 Grob, *Mad Among Us*, 178-80; "The Nobel Prize in Physiology or Medicine 1927," Nobelprize.org, http://nobelprize.org/nobel_prizes/medicine/laureates/1927/, last accessed December 6, 2006.

11 Edward Shorter, *A History of Psychiatry: From the Era of the Asylum to the Age of Prozac* (Chichester, Britain: Wiley, 1997), 209-14; Elliot Valenstein, *Blaming the Brain:*

The Truth About Drugs and Mental Health (New York: Free Press, 1998), 17-19; Grob, *Mad Among Us*, 180-2.

12 Shorter, *A History of* Psychiatry, 214-17; Grob, *Mad Among Us*, 182; Isaac and Armat, *Madness in the Streets*, 194-5.

13 Shorter, *A History of Psychiatry*, 218-222.

14 Grob, *Mad Among Us*, 182.

15 Personal communication from John Simutis describing student nursing experience at Herrick Hospital, Berkeley, California, December 3, 2006; J. Greenhalgh, C. Knight, D. Hind, C. Beverley and S. Walters, "Clinical And Cost-Effectiveness Of Electroconvulsive Therapy For Depressive Illness, Schizophrenia, Catatonia And Mania: Systematic Reviews And Economic Modelling Studies," *Health Technology Assessment* [2005] 9:9; Tarique D. Perera, Bruce Luber, Mitchell S. Nobler, Joan Prudic, Christopher Anderson and Harold A Sackeim, "Seizure Expression During Electroconvulsive Therapy: Relationships with Clinical Outcome and Cognitive Side Effects," *Neuropsychopharmacology* [2004] 29:813–825; Isaac and Armat, *Madness in the Streets*, 217-20.

16 Grob, *From Asylum to Community*, 126-9.

17 Isaac and Armat, *Madness in the Streets*, 194-9.

18 Carl Caskey Speidel, "Studies of Living Nerves. VI. Effects of Metrazol on Tissues of Frog Tadpoles....," *Proceedings of the American Philosophical Society* 83[1940]:349-78.

19 Grob, *Mad Among Us*, 182-6; Isaac and Armat, *Madness in the Streets*, 177-80; Grob, *From Asylum to Community*, 129-33.

20 Isaac and Armat, *Madness in the Streets*, 177-93; Grob; *From Asylum to Community*, 134.

21 Grob, *Mad Among Us*, 167-9; Harriet Sturdy and William Parry-Jones, "Boarding-Out Insane Patients: the Significance of the Scottish System: 1857-1913," 86-114, in Peter Bartlett and David Wright, eds., *Outside the Walls of the Asylum: The History of Care in the Community: 1750-2000* (New Brunswick, N.J.: Athlone Press, 1999).

22 Marie L. Donohoe, "A Social-Service Department in a State Hospital," *Mental Hygiene* 6:1 [January, 1922] 309-10.

23 Grob, *From Asylum to Community*, 158-9.

24 Alexander D. Brooks, *Law, Psychiatry and the Mental Health System* (Boston: Little, Brown & Co., 1974), 751-2.

Chapter 7: Deinstitutionalization As A Theory (1945-1980)

1 *Olmstead* v. *U.S.*, (J. Brandeis, diss.) 277 U.S. 438, 478 (1928).

2 Grob, *Mad Among Us*, 191-7; Gerald N. Grob, *From Asylum to Community: Mental Health Policy in Modern America* (Princeton, N.J.: Princeton University Press, 1991), 15-16.

3 Gerald N. Grob, "Public Policy and Mental Illnesses: Jimmy Carter's Presidential Commission on Mental Health," *Milbank Quarterly* [2005] 83:3, 425-56; Eric A. Plaut and Susannah Rubenstein, "State Care for the Mentally Ill: A Brief History," *State Government*, Autumn 1977, 193; Roy W. Menninger and John Case Nemiah, eds., *American Psychiatry After World War II (1944-1994)* (Washington: American Psychiatric Press, 2000), 162.

4 Julia I. Brooking, Susan A. H. Ritter, and Ben L. Thomas, eds., *A Textbook of Psychiatric and Mental Health Nursing* (New York: Churchill Livingstone, 1992), 325-6.

5 David Mechanic and David A. Rochefort, "A Policy Of Inclusion for the Mentally Ill," *Health Affairs*, 11:1 [1992], 130. Grob, *From Asylum to Community*, 11-12, argues that the screening procedures "proved more effective in theory than in practice" because of vague criteria, inaccurate personal histories, and the very abbreviated nature of the screening. Winfred Overholser, "Mental Hygiene," *Proceedings, American Philosopical Society* 90:4[September 1946] 259, reports that "over 700,000 men or 16 ½ percent" were rejected by the draft for "nervous and mental disorders" but also points out that "many of these disorders did not materially disable the individual for civilian life."

6 Grob, *From Asylum to Community*, 13.

7 Michael J. Dear and Jennifer R. Wolch, *Landscapes of Despair: From Deinstitutionalization to Homelessness* (Princeton, N.J.: Princeton University Press, 1987), 171.

8 Allan V. Horwitz, *Creating Mental Illness* (Chicago: University of Chicago Press, 2002), 40-41; Grob, *Mad Among Us,* 142, 197-202, 243-6.

9 Isaac and Armat, *Madness in the Streets,* 69-73; James M. Cameron, "A National Community Mental Health Program: Policy Initiation and Progress," 125-7, in Rochefort, *Handbook on Mental Health Policy in the United States,* 128; Hobson and Leonard, *Out of Its Mind,* 50.

10 Hobson and Leonard, *Out of Its Mind,* 50.

11 Grob, *From Asylum to Community,* 12-19; Grob, *Mad Among Us,* 194-6.

12 Cameron, "A National Community Mental Health Program," 122-3.

13 Grob, *From Asylum to Community,* 25-41; Horwitz, *Creating Mental Illness,* 48-49.

14 Hobson and Leonard, *Out of Its Mind,* 221.

15 Horwitz, *Creating Mental Illness,* 42-43.

16 Grob, *Mad Among Us,* 224.

17 Grob, *From Asylum to Community,* 171-80.

18 Grob, *From Asylum to Community,* 58-61.

19 Grob, *From Asylum to Community,* 61-63.

20 Joint Commission on Mental Illness and Health, *Action for Mental Health,* 146; Grob, *From Asylum to Community,* 65-66.

21 Grob, *From Asylum to Community,* 98-100.

22 Dear and *Landscapes of Despair,* 61-62; Isaac and Armat, *Madness in the Streets,* 70.

23 Joint Commission on Mental Illness and Health, *Action for Mental Health,* 39-46; Grob, *From Asylum to Community,* 146-49

24 Grob, *Mad Among Us,* 228-31; Grob, *From Asylum to Community,* 150-1.

25 David Mechanic, "Toward the Year 2000 in U.S. Mental Health Policymaking and Administration," in Rochefort, *Handbook on Mental Health Policy in the United States,* 480-1; Sarason and Sarason, *Abnormal Psychology,* 380.

26 George E. Crane, "Tardive Dyskinesia in Patients Treated with Major Neuroleptics: A Review of the Literature," *American Journal of Psychiatry* 124:8 [February 1968 Supp.] 39-48.

27 U.S. Senate, *To Protect the Constitutional Rights of the Mentally Ill,* Hearings before the Subcommittee on Constitutional Rights of the Committee on the Judiciary, United States Senate (88th Cong., 1st sess.), 68.

28 U.S. Senate, *To Protect the Constitutional Rights of the Mentally Ill,* 161.

29 Louis Linn, "The Fourth Psychiatric Revolution," *American Journal of Psychiatry* 124:8[February 1968] 1043-4.

30 Grob, *Mad Among Us,* 127-8.

31 Dear and Wolch, *Landscapes of Despair,* 62; David Mechanic and David A. Rochefort, "A Policy Of Inclusion for the Mentally Ill," *Health Affairs,* 11:1 [1992], 129; Brooks, *Law, Psychiatry and the Mental Health System,* 398, describing abuses at a hospital for the criminally insane; *Morgan* v. *State,* 65 Misc. 2d 978, 319 N.Y.S.2d 151 (Ct. Cl. 1970), quoted at Brooks, *Law, Psychiatry and the Mental Health System,* 407-10.

32 David A. Rochefort, "Mental Illness and Mental Health as Public Policy Concerns," 6, in Rochefort, *Handbook on Mental Health Policy in the United States.*

33 Joint Commission on Mental Illness and Health, *Action for Mental Health,* 46-49.

34 W. Louis Coppersmith, "Deinstitutionalization in Pennsylvania," *State Government,* Autumn 1977, 227.

35 Grob, *Mad Among Us,* 174-5, 202-207.

36 Grob, *Mad Among Us,* 249-50.

Chapter 9: Acid Trips & Anti-Psychiatry (1960-1980)

1 Isaac and Armat, *Madness in the Streets,* 21-24.

2 Isaac and Armat, *Madness in the Streets*, 21-24.

3 Isaac and Armat, *Madness in the Streets*, 24-27.

4 Robert E. L. Faris and H. Warren Dunham, *Mental Disorders in Urban Areas: An Ecological Study of Schizophrenia and Other Psychoses* (New York: Hafner Publishing Co., 1960), 38-62.

5 Faris and Dunham, *Mental Disorders in Urban Areas*, 63-81.

6 Faris and Dunham, *Mental Disorders in Urban Areas*, 124-7.

7 Faris and Dunham, *Mental Disorders in Urban Areas*, xix.

8 Faris and Dunham, *Mental Disorders in Urban Areas*, 163.

9 Faris and Dunham, *Mental Disorders in Urban Areas*, 124.

10 Grob, *Mad Among Us,* 271-4; Paul S. Appelbaum, "The Draft Act Governing Hospitalization of the Mentally Ill: Its Genesis and Its Legacy," *Psychiatric Services* 51:[February 2000]191.

11 Thomas Szasz, *Schizophrenia: The Sacred Symbol of Psychiatry* (New York: Basic Books, 1976), 36-37.

12 Szasz, *Schizophrenia*, 3-15.

13 "Thomas Szasz in Conversation with Alan Kerr," *Psychiatric Bulletin*, 21[1997]:39-44.

14 Isaac and Armat, *Madness in the Streets*, 33-41.

15 Szasz, *Schizophrenia,* 23.

16 Szasz, *Schizophrenia,* xii-xiv.

17 Grob, *Mad Among Us,* 271-4; Appelbaum, "The Draft Act Governing Hospitalization of the Mentally Ill," 191.

18 Hobson and Leonard, *Out of Its Mind*, 52-53.

19 R.D. Laing, *The Divided Self* (New York: Pantheon Books, 1960), 38-39, 177.

20 Isaac and Armat, *Madness in the Streets*, 27-32.

21 Hobson and Leonard, *Out of Its Mind*, 52.

22 Grob, *Mad Among Us,* 271-4; Paul S. Appelbaum, "The Draft Act Governing Hospitalization of the Mentally Ill: Its Genesis and Its Legacy," *Psychiatric Services* 51:[February 2000]191.

23 Isaac and Armat, *Madness in the Streets*, 45-53, 58.

24 Jason Deparle, "Snyder Told His Colleagues Of Being Audited by I.R.S.," *New York Times,*   July   7,   1990, http://query.nytimes.com/gst/fullpage.html?sec=health&res=9C0CE2DC1731F934A35754C0A966958260, last accessed May 15, 2007.

25 Isaac and Armat, *Madness in the Streets*, 45-53, 58.

26 Thomas Scheff, *Being Mentally Ill: A Sociological Theory,* 3rd ed. (Hawthorne, N.Y.: Aldine de Grutyer, 1999), x-xi.

27 Seth Farber, *Madness, Heresy, and the Rumor of Angels: The Revolt Against the Mental Health System* (Chicago: Open Court, 1993), 226-37; Isaac and Armat, *Madness in the Streets*, 58-60.

28 Isaac and Armat, *Madness in the Streets*, 58-60; Mike Fitzgerald, Paul Hamos, John Muncie, and David Zeldin, eds., *Welfare in Action* (London: Routledge & K. Paul, 1977), 202.

29 Zbigniew Kotowicz, *R.D. Laing and the Paths Of Anti-Psychiatry* (London: Routledge, 1997), 80-81.

30 Terence Taylor and Tim Revan, "The Red Army Faction (1980)," in Jonathan B. Tucker, ed., *Toxic Terror: Assessing Terrorist Use of Chemical and Biological Weapons* (Cambridge, Mass.: MIT Press, 2000), 107-108; J. Smith and Andre Moncourt, *The Red Army Faction: A Documentary History* (Oakland, Cal.: PM Press, 2009), 1:109; Martha Crenshaw, ed., *Terrorism in Context* (University Park, Penn.: Pennsylvania State University Press, 1995) 206-7.

31 Torrey and Miller, *The Invisible Plague*, 305-313.

32 Goldhamer and Marshall, *Psychosis and Civilization*, 94-95.

33 *Twenty-second Annual Report of the Trustees of the State Lunatic Hospital at Worcester* (Boston, 1855), 77, quoted at Goldhamer and Marshall, *Psychosis and Civilization*, 95.

34 Isaac and Armat, *Madness in the Streets*, 58-60.

35 Hobson and Leonard, *Out Of Its Mind*, 60-62.

Chapter 10: "Snakepits" To CHMCs: The Theory (1945-1980)

1 Grob, *Mad Among Us,* 169-72, 231-5.

2 Brown, *The Transfer of Care*, 27.

3 Grob, *From Asylum to Community*, 71-73.

4 Isaac and Armat, *Madness in the Streets*, 67-69; Grob, *From Asylum to Community*, 75-76.

5 Grob, *From Asylum to Community,* 76-78.

6 Joint Commission on Mental Illness and Health, *Action for Mental Health,* 6-7.

7 Brown, *The Transfer of Care,* 33-34; Horwitz, *Creating Mental Illness,* 50-51; Grob, *Mad Among Us,* 231-5; Grob, *From Asylum to Community,* 161-5.

8 Grob, *From Asylum to Community*, 76-77, 80-81; W.E. Baxter, American Psychiatric Association, "Central Inspection Board (1947-1960) ARCHIVES FINDING AID" (1985), http://psych.org/MainMenu/EducationCareerDevelopment/Library/Archives/AssociationRec ords/ProgramCentralInspectionBoard.aspx, last accessed July 3, 2011.

9 Grob, *From Asylum to Community*, 159-60, 234.

10 Joint Commission on Mental Illness and Health, *Action for Mental Health,* 39-46.

11 Isaac and Armat, *Madness in the Streets*, 48, 62-63.

12 Grob, *Mad Among Us,* 213-16, 233.

13 Joint Commission on Mental Illness and Health, *Action for Mental Health,* xvi.

14 Isaac and Armat, *Madness in the Streets*, 73-75; Grob, *From Asylum to Community*, 181-208, gives a detailed account of the formation and actions of the Joint Commission.

15 U.S. Senate, *To Protect the Constitutional Rights of the Mentally Ill*, 174.

16 Institute of Medicine, Division of Mental Health and Behavioral Medicine, National Institute of Mental Health, *Mental Health Services in General Health Care: Coordinated Mental Health Care in Neighborhood Health Centers* (Washington: National Academy of Sciences, 1979), 2:v-vii.

17 Joseph P. Morrissey, "The Changing Role of the Public Mental Hospital," 317-20, in Rochefort, *Handbook on Mental Health Policy in the United States.*

18 David Braddock, "A National Deinstitutionalization Study," *State Government*, Autumn 1977, 224.

19 Joint Commission on Mental Illness and Health, *Action for Mental Health*, xv-xvi.

20 Isaac and Armat, *Madness in the Streets*, 73-75.

21 Isaac and Armat, *Madness in the Streets*, 77-78.

22 Joint Commission on Mental Illness and Health, *Action for Mental Health,* xvi-xvii; Grob, *From Asylum to Community*, 210-2, 227-9.

23 "Message from the President of the United States," February 5, 1963, reprinted in Henry A. Foley and Steven S. Sharfstein, *Madness and Government: Who Cares For the Mentally Ill?* (Washington, D.C.: American Psychiatric Press, 1983), 166-7, quoted in Isaac and Armat, *Madness in the Streets*, 77-78.

24 Grob, *From Asylum to Community*, 236-7.

25 Phil Brown, *The Transfer Of Care: Psychiatric Deinstitutionalization And Its Aftermath* (Boston: Routledge & Kegan Paul, 1985), 20-21.

26 Grob, *Mad Among Us,* 235-7; Cameron, "A National Community Mental Health Program," 136.

27 Grob, *Mad Among Us,* 249-50, 255-8; Grob, *From Asylum to Community*, 216-18; *Ibid.*, 209-27 provides a detailed account of the internal decision making process of the Kennedy Administration in how to convert the Joint Commission's report into law.

28 Cameron, "A National Community Mental Health Program," 125-7.

29 Grob, *From Asylum to Community,* 181-2.

30 Grob, *From Asylum to Community*, 160-1.

Chapter 11: Emptying the "Snakepits" (1965 - 1980)

1 Dear and Wolch, *Landscapes of Despair*, 63-64; Grob, *Mad Among Us*, 241-7; Dale H. Farabee and Lillian Press, "Legislative Perspective on Public Mental Health Programs," *State Government*, Autumn 1977, 204.

2 Foley and Sharfstein, *Madness and Government*, 101, quoted in Isaac and Armat, *Madness in the Streets*, 81.

3 Grob, *From Asylum to Community*, 237.

4 Isaac and Armat, *Madness in the Streets*, 82.

5 Isaac and Armat, *Madness in the Streets*, 83-84.

6 Isaac and Armat, *Madness in the Streets*, 86-90; Francoise Castel, Robert Castel, and Anne Lovell, *The Psychiatric Society* (New York: Columbia University Press, 1982), 156-9, provides a more supportive view of what happened at Lincoln, but admits that the radical approach was gradually abandoned after 1975.

7 Rochefort, "Mental Illness and Mental Health as Public Policy Concerns," 6, in Rochefort, *Handbook on Mental Health Policy in the United States*; Cameron, "A National Community Mental Health Program," 128-9.

8 "Advocate Radical Change in Mental Health Care for Black Patients," *Jet*, May 20, 1971, 47.

9 Isaac and Armat, *Madness in the Streets*, 90-100; Leona L. Bachrach, "The Homeless Mentally Ill and Mental Health Services: An Analytical Review of the Literature," 30-31, in Lamb, *Homeless Mentally Ill*.

10 Grob, *From Asylum to Community*, 239.

11 Grob, *From Asylum to Community*, 254-5.

12 Grob, *From Asylum to Community*, 252-3.

13 Isaac and Armat, *Madness in the Streets*, 90-100.

14 Isaac and Armat, *Madness in the Streets*, 90-100.

15 Isaac and Armat, *Madness in the Streets*, 90-100.

16 Grob, *Mad Among Us*, 265-7, 289-90; Grob, *From Asylum to Community*, 267-9; Jonathan Oberlander, *The Political Life of Medicare* (Chicago: University of Chicago Press, 2003), 32; John A. Talbott and Robert E. Hales, eds., *Textbook of Administrative Psychiatry: New Concepts for a Changing Behavioral Health System*, 2nd ed. (Washington: American Psychiatric Publishing, 2001), 12-13.

17 Dear and Wolch, *Landscapes of Despair*, 65-66, 140-2.

18 Margaret W. Linn and Shayna Stein, "Nursing Homes as Community Mental Health Facilities," 267-71, in Rochefort, *Handbook on Mental Health Policy in the United States*.

19 Linn and Stein, "Nursing Homes as Community Mental Health Facilities," 278-9.

20 Grob, *Mad Among Us*, 265-7, 289-90; Grob, *From Asylum to Community*, 267-9.

21 Frederic G. Reamer, "The Contemporary Mental Health System: Facilities, Services, Personnel, and Finances," 25-26, in Rochefort, *Handbook of Mental Health Policy in the United States*.

22 Dear and Wolch, *Landscapes of Despair*, 65-66, 140-2.

23 David Mechanic and David A. Rochefort, "Deinstitutionalization: An Appraisal of Reform," *Annual Review of Sociology*, 16:1 [1990], 301.

24 U.S. Census Bureau, "Historical National Population Estimates: July 1, 1900 to July 1, 1999," http://www.census.gov/popest/archives/1990s/popclockest.txt, last accessed October 29, 2006.

25 Reamer, "The Contemporary Mental Health System," 27-29.

26 Reamer, "The Contemporary Mental Health System," 27-29.

27 Rochefort, "Mental Illness and Mental Health as Public Policy Concerns," 15.

28 Grob, *Mad Among Us*, 265-7, 289-90; Grob, *From Asylum to Community*, 269-70.

29 Grob, *Mad Among Us*, 290-1; Linn and Stein, "Nursing Homes as Community Mental Health Facilities," 271-2, in Rochefort, *Handbook on Mental Health Policy in the United States*.

30 Plaut and Rubenstein, "State Care for the Mentally Ill," 197.

31 Cameron, "A National Community Mental Health Program," 138-9.

32 Grob, *Mad Among Us,* 292-4.

33 Bromet and Schulberg, "Special Problem Populations: The Chronically Mentally Ill, Elderly, Children, Minorities, and Substance Abusers," 68-69.

34 Grob, *Mad Among Us,* 294-5.

35 Julian Leff and Noam Trieman, "Long-stay Patients Discharged From Psychiatric Hospitals," *British Journal of Psychiatry* 176(3)[2000]:217-22. See also Graham Thornicroft, Paul Bebbington, and Julian Leff, "Outcomes for Long-Term Patients One Year After Discharge From a Psychiatric Hospital," *Psychiatric Services* 56:11[Novembger 2005], 1416-22, where the average age of the discharged group was 67.3 years.

36 Bromet and Schulberg, "Special Problem Populations," 69-70.

37 Grob, *Mad Among Us,* 295-8.

38 U.S. Senate, *To Protect the Constitutional Rights of the Mentally Ill,* 154.

39 Cameron, "A National Community Mental Health Program," 137.

40 Dear and Wolch, *Landscapes of Despair,* 97.

41 Armour, "Mental Health Policymaking in the United States: Patterns, Process, and Structures," 184-5.

42 Howard H. Goldman, "The Obligation of Mental Health Services to the Least Well Off," *Psychiatric Services* 50[1999]:5:659-60.

43 Rochefort, "Mental Illness and Mental Health as Public Policy Concerns," 7; David A. Rochefort and Bruce M. Logan, "The Alcohol, Drug Abuse, and Mental Health Block Grant: Origins, Design, and Impact," 143-56, 161-2, 184-5, in Rochefort, *Handbook on Mental Health Policy in the United States.*

44 Goldman, "The Obligation of Mental Health Services to the Least Well Off," 5:659-63.

Chapter 13: The Right to Treatment (1960-1975)

1 Morrissey, "The Changing Role of the Public Mental Hospital," 317-21, in Rochefort, *Handbook on Mental Health Policy in the United States.*

2 *Dusky* v. *U.S.,* 362 U.S. 402 (1960).

3 Keilitz, "Legal Issues in Mental Health Care: Current Perspectives," 374-6.

4 Morton Birnbaum, "The Right to Treatment," *American Bar Association Journal,* 46[May, 1960]:499.

5 Birnbaum, "The Right to Treatment, 502-3.

6 U.S. Senate, *To Protect the Constitutional Rights of the Mentally Ill,* 12, 131, 147-8, 205-6.

7 U.S. Senate, *To Protect the Constitutional Rights of the Mentally Ill,* 152.

8 Joint Commission on Mental Illness and Health, *Action for Mental Health,* 140-55.

9 David L. Bazelon, "The Right to Treatment: The Court's Role," *Hospital and Community Psychiatry* 20:5 [May, 1969], 129.

10 Bazelon, "The Right to Treatment: The Court's Role," 130.

11 Isaac and Armat, *Madness in the Streets,* 128-32; Ennis, *Prisoners of Psychiatry,* 99-108; *Wyatt* v. *Stickney,* 344 F.Supp. 373 (M.D.Ala. 1972).

12 Grob, *Mad Among Us,* 274-5.

13 *Lake* v. *Cameron,* 364 F.2d 657 (D.C.Cir. 1966).

14 Brooks, *Law, Psychiatry and the Mental Health System,* 730-2.

15 *In re Gault,* 387 U.S. 1 (1967).

16 *O'Connor* v. *Donaldson,* 422 U.S. 563 (1975).

17 Steven P. Segal and Pamela Kotler, "Community Residential Care," 252-4, in Rochefort, *Handbook on Mental Health Policy in the United States;* William B. Hawthorne, Elizabeth E. Green, Todd Gilmer, Piedad Garcia, Richard L. Hough, Martin Lee, Linda Hammond, and James B. Lohr, "A Randomized Trial of Short-Term Acute Residential Treatment for Veterans," *Psychiatric Services* 56[November, 2005]1379-86.

Chapter 14: The Right to Due Process (1960 – 1980)

1 Brooks, *Law, Psychiatry and the Mental Health System*, 752-3.

2 Brooks, *Law, Psychiatry and the Mental Health System*, 753-5.

3 Brooks, *Law, Psychiatry and the Mental Health System*, 753-6.

4 Paul S. Appelbaum, "The Draft Act Governing Hospitalization of the Mentally Ill: Its Genesis and Its Legacy," *Psychiatric Services* 51:[February 2000]190.

5 Brooks, *Law, Psychiatry and the Mental Health System*, 820-2.

6 William Vizzard, "The Gun Control Act Of 1968," *St. Louis University Public Law Review*, 18:1[1999]: 79-97 n. 77; 27 CFR § 478.11.

7 *Greenwood* v. *U.S.*, 350 U.S. 366 (1956).

8 *U.S. Senate, To Protect the Constitutional Rights of the Mentally Ill*, Hearings before the Subcommittee on Constitutional Rights of the Committee on the Judiciary, United States Senate (88th Cong., 1st sess.), 22, 26-28, 39, 46, 64.

9 U.S. Senate, *To Protect the Constitutional Rights of the Mentally Ill*, 38-39, 41, 47, 66, 126, 132, 144, 163-4.

10 U.S. Senate, *To Protect the Constitutional Rights of the Mentally Ill*, 14, 36-37, 46.

11 U.S. Senate, *To Protect the Constitutional Rights of the Mentally Ill*, 182.

12 U.S. Senate, *To Protect the Constitutional Rights of the Mentally Ill*, 160.

13 U.S. Senate, *To Protect the Constitutional Rights of the Mentally Ill*, 152.

14 U.S. Senate, *To Protect the Constitutional Rights of the Mentally Ill*, 192-3.

15 U.S. Senate, *To Protect the Constitutional Rights of the Mentally Ill*, 189-90.

16 U.S. Senate, *To Protect the Constitutional Rights of the Mentally Ill*, 190-1.

17 M.F. Abramson, "The Criminalization Of Mentally Disordered Behavior: Possible Side-Effect Of A New Mental Health Law," *Hospital and Community Psychiatry*, 23[1972]:101-105.

18 Brooks, *Law, Psychiatry and the Mental Health System*, 756-8.

19 Lynn Vincent and Robert Stacy McCain, *Donkey Cons: Sex, Crime, and Corruption in the Democratic Party* (Nashville, Tenn.: Nelson Current, 2006), 181-2.

20 Bruce J. Ennis, *Prisoners of Psychiatry* (New York: Harcourt Brace Jovanovich, 1972), viii.

21 Ennis, *Prisoners of Psychiatry*. 5-17.

22 Brooks, *Law, Psychiatry and the Mental Health System*, 344-9.

23 Ennis, *Prisoners of Psychiatry*, 208-9.

24 Ennis, *Prisoners of Psychiatry*, 66-86, 109-27.

25 Ennis, *Prisoners of Psychiatry*, 45-65.

26 Larry Fisher-Hertz, "City host to several big trials," Poughkeepsie *Journal*, August 15, 2004; "Paonessa Dies at Sing Sing," Gloversville (N.Y.) *Leader-Republican*, January 16, 1953.

27 *People* v. *Alfred Curt Von Wolfersdorf*, 66 Misc.2d 904 (N.Y. 1971).

28 Isaac and Armat, *Madness in the Streets,* 109-11.

29 *Maniaci* v. *Marquette University*, 50 Wisc.2d 287, 184 N.W.2d 168 (1971).

30 *Baxstrom* v. *Herold*, 383 U.S. 107 (1966).

31 E. Fuller Torrey, *The Insanity Offense: How America's Failure To Treat The Seriously Mentally Ill Endangers Its Citizens* (New York: W.W. Norton, 2008), 76-78.

32 *Lessard* v. *Schmidt*, 349 F.Supp. 1078, 1083 (E.D.Wisc. 1972).

33 *Lessard* v. *Schmidt*, 349 F.Supp. 1078, 1085 (E.D.Wisc. 1972).

34 *Lessard* v. *Schmidt*, 349 F.Supp. 1078, 1086 (E.D.Wisc. 1972).

35 *Lessard* v. *Schmidt*, 349 F.Supp. 1078, 1088 (E.D.Wisc. 1972).

36 *Lessard* v. *Schmidt*, 349 F.Supp. 1078, 1090 (E.D.Wisc. 1972).

37 *Lessard* v. *Schmidt*, 349 F.Supp. 1078, 1089, 1090 (E.D.Wisc. 1972).

38 *Lessard* v. *Schmidt*, 349 F.Supp. 1078, 1091, 1092, 1093, 1094 (E.D.Wisc. 1972).

39 *Lessard* v. *Schmidt*, 349 F.Supp. 1078, 1089, 1092 fn.18 (E.D.Wisc. 1972).

40 Isaac and Armat, *Madness in the Streets*, 127.

41 Brooks, *Law, Psychiatry and the Mental Health System,* 606.

42 M.F. Abramson, "The Criminalization Of Mentally Disordered Behavior: Possible Side-Effect Of A New Mental Health Law," *Hospital and Community Psychiatry*, 23[1972]:101-105.

43 J. Monahan, "The Psychiatrization of Criminal Behavior: A Reply," *Hospital & Community Psychiatry,* 24[1973]:105-107.

44 David Kolb, ed., *New Perspectives on Hegel's Philosophy of Religion* (Albany, N.Y.: State University of New York Press, 1992), 181 n. 13.

45 Isaac and Armat, *Madness in the Streets*, 135-7.

46 Ennis, *Prisoners of Psychiatry*, 84.

47 Ennis, *Prisoners of Psychiatry*, 83-94.

48 *O'Connor* v. *Donaldson*, 422 U.S. 563, 577 (1975).

49 Isaac and Armat, *Madness in the Streets*, 136-7; Peele, Gross, Arons, and Jafri, "The Legal System and the Homeless," 264-5.

50 *O'Connor* v. *Donaldson*, 422 U.S. 563, 583-5 (1975) (J. Burger, conc.)

51 *Addington* v. *Texas*, 441 U.S. 418, 420, 421 (1979).

52 *Vitek* v. *Jones*, 445 U.S. 480, 492, 493, 494, 495 (1980).

53 *Vitek* v. *Jones*, 445 U.S. 480, 496 (1980); *Washington* v. *Harper*, 494 U.S. 210, 216 (1990).

Chapter 15: The Right to Refuse Treatment (1969 – present)

1 Isaac and Armat, *Madness in the Streets*, 113-17; D.L. Rosenhan, "On Being Sane in Insane Places," *Science* 179[January 19, 1973]:250-8.

2 Adam Winkler, "Fatal in Theory and Strict in Fact: An Empirical Analysis of Strict Scrutiny in the Federal Courts," *Vanderbilt Law Review*, 59[2006]:798-801, available at http://ssrn.com/abstract=897360, last accessed March 14, 2008. This is something of an oversimplification; there at least three different types of strict scrutiny. Richard H. Fallon, Jr., "Strict Judicial Scrutiny," *UCLA Law Review*, 54[2007]:1267-1337, available at http://www.uclalawreview.org/volumes/54/_pdf/5.1-4.pdf, last accessed March 14, 2008, provides a detailed examination of the history and flaws of strict scrutiny.

3 Winkler, "Fatal in Theory and Strict in Fact," 793-871.

4 Isaac and Armat, *Madness in the Streets,* 115-17.

5 Grob, *Mad Among Us*, 288-9.

6 Braddock, "A National Deinstitutionalization Study," 225.

7 Ennis, *Prisoners of Psychiatry*, 109-27.

8 Isaac and Armat, *Madness in the Streets*, 137-9.

9 Isaac and Armat, *Madness in the Streets*, 142-4.

10 Brooks, *Law, Psychiatry and the Mental Health System*, 877; "Insane Persons. In General. Inmate of State Institution for the Criminally Insane May Recover Damages for Inordinate Length of Incarceration Due to Lack of Proper Psychiatric Care," *Harvard Law Review*, 82: 8[June, 1969], 1771-1777.

11 Isaac and Armat, *Madness in the Streets*, 142-4.

12 *Superintendent Of Belchertown State School* v. *Saikewicz*, 370 N.E.2d 417, 432, 373 Mass. 728, 754 (1977).

13 *Guardianship Of Roe Matter Of*, 421 N.E.2d 40, 51, 383 Mass. 415, 434 (1981).

14 *Guardianship Of Roe Matter Of*, 421 N.E.2d 40, 52, 383 Mass. 415, 435 (1981)

15 *Guardianship Of Roe Matter Of*, 421 N.E.2d 40, 52, 53, 383 Mass. 415, 436 (1981).

16 *Guardianship Of Roe Matter Of*, 421 N.E.2d 40, 53, 54, 55, 383 Mass. 415, 437, 438, 439 (1981).

17 *Guardianship Of Roe Matter Of*, 421 N.E.2d 40, 54, 55, 383 Mass. 415, 441, 442 (1981).

18 *Guardianship Of Roe Matter Of*, 421 N.E.2d 40, 56, 383 Mass. 415, 441, 442 (1981).

19 *Guardianship Of Roe Matter Of*, 421 N.E.2d 40, 57, 58, 383 Mass. 415, 441, 443, 444 (1981).

20 *Guardianship Of Roe Matter Of*, 421 N.E.2d 40, 58, 383 Mass. 415, 445, 446 (1981).

21 *Guardianship Of Roe Matter Of*, 421 N.E.2d 40, 59, 60, 383 Mass. 415, 448, 449 (1981).

22 Isaac and Armat, *Madness in the Streets*, 149.

23 Peele, Gross, Arons, and Jafri, "The Legal System and the Homeless," 269; Erin O'Connor, "Is Kendra's Law A Keeper? How Kendra's Law Erodes Fundamental Rights Of The Mentally Ill," *Brooklyn Journal of Law and Public Policy,* 344-5, discusses *Rivers* v. *Katz*, 495 N.E.2d 337 (N.Y. 1986), which ruled that the state could administer medications to patients only if the patient was a danger to himself or others, or lack the capacity to make the decision himself.

24 *Washington* v. *Harper,* 494 U.S. 210, 219 (1990).

25 *Washington* v. *Harper,* 494 U.S. 210, 223, 224 (1990).

26 *Washington* v. *Harper,* 494 U.S. 210, 224 (1990).

27 *Riggins* v. *Nevada*, 504 U.S. 127, 136, 138 (1992).

28 Isaac and Armat, *Madness in the Streets*, 150-2; Keilitz, "Legal Issues in Mental Health Care: Current Perspectives,"377-8.

29 Ingo Keilitz, "Legal Issues in Mental Health Care: Current Perspectives," 367, in Rochefort, *Handbook on Mental Health Policy in the United States.*

Chapter 16: California Marches Off The Cliff (1967 – 2001)

1 Cal. Welfare & Institutions Code § 5000 (2007).

2 Cal. Welfare & Institutions Code § 5008(h) (2007).

3 Carol A. B. Warren, *The Court of Last Resort: Mental Illness and the Law* (Chicago: University of Chicago Press, 1982), 22.

4 Jackson K. Putnam, *Jess: The Political Career of Jesse Marvin Unruh* (Lanham, Md.: University Press of America, 2005), 208.

5 Putnam, *Jess*, 209-210.

6 Warren, *The Court of Last Resort*, 22-24.

7 *Conservatorship of Cabanne*, 223 Cal. App. 3d 199, 272 Cal. Rptr. 407, 1990 Cal. App. LEXIS 901 (1990).

8 *Conservatorship of Margaret L.,* 89 Cal. App. 4th 675, 107 Cal. Rptr. 2d 542, 2001 Cal. App. LEXIS 419, 2001 Cal. Daily Op. Service 4490, 2001 Daily Journal DAR 5460 (2001).

9 *Conservatorship of Roulet,* 20 Cal. 3d 653; 574 P.2d 1245, 143 Cal. Rptr. 893, 1978 Cal. LEXIS 194 (1978).

10 *In re S.*, 19 Cal. 3d 921; 569 P.2d 1286; 141 Cal. Rptr. 298; 1977 Cal. LEXIS 176 (1977); *In re Gault*, 387 U.S. 1 (1967); *In re E.,* 15 Cal. 3D 183, 538 P.2d 231; 123 Cal. Rptr. 103; 1975 Cal. LEXIS 225 (1975) addresses slightly different procedural questions from *In re S.* but comes to similar conclusions.

11 *Conservatorship of Smith*, 187 Cal. App.3d 903, 232 Cal. Rptr. 277; 1986 Cal. App. LEXIS 2309 (1986).

12 *In re Qawi*, 32 Cal. 4th 1, 81 P.3d 224; 7 Cal. Rptr. 3d 780; 2004 Cal. LEXIS 1; 2004 Cal. Daily Op. Service 85; 2004 Daily Journal DAR 111 (2001).

13 Group for the Advancement of Psychiatry, *Forced into Treatment: The Role of Coercion in Clinical Practice* (Washington: American Psychiatric Press, 1994), 31.

14 Jerome V. Vaccaro and Gordon H. Clark, *Practicing Psychiatry in the Community: A Manual* (Washington: American Psychiatric Press, 1996), 118; American Psychiatric Association, *Issues in Community Treatment of Severe Mental Illness* (Washington: American Psychiatric Press, 1999), 12.

15 Stephen B. Seager, *Street Crazy: America's Mental Health Tragedy* (Redondo Beach, Cal.: Westcom Press, 2000), 193.

Chapter 17: Ron & Orthomolecular Treatment

1 Harold D. Foster, *What Really Causes Schizophrenia* (Victoria, B.C.: Trafford Publishing, 2003), 26.

2 P.J. Harrison and D.R. Weinberger, "Schizophrenia genes, gene expression, and neuropathology: on the matter of their convergence," *Molecular Psychiatry* 10:[2005]44, http://www.nature.com/mp/journal/v10/n1/pdf/4001558a.pdf, last accessed August 25, 2007; Jule Klotter, *"The Beginnings of Orthomolecular Psychiatry.*(Vitamin B-3 and Schizophrenia)(Review)," *Townsend Letter for Doctors and Patients* [April 2001]:124; Jonathan E. Prousky, "The orthomolecular treatment of schizophrenia: a primer for clinicians," *Townsend Letter: The Examiner of Alternative Medicine* 283]Feb-March 2007]: 86-101; Lawrence Galton, "Why Young Adults Crack Up," The Huxley Institute for Biosocial Research, http://www.schizophrenia.org/crackup.html, last accessed August 25, 2007.

Chapter 18: Homelessness & Urban Decay (1975 – present)

1 Dennis P. Culhane, Edmund F. Dejowski, Julie Ibañez, Elizabeth Needham, Irene Macchia, "Public Shelter Admission Rates in Philadelphia and New York City: The Implications of Turnover for Sheltered Population Counts," *Housing Policy Debates*, 5:2[1994], 108.

2 Dear and Wolch, *Landscapes of Despair*, 175.

3 Isaac and Armat, *Madness in the Streets*, 4; Steven A. Holmes, "Bureau Won't Distribute Census Data on Homeless," *New York Times*, June 28, 2001, http://www.nytimes.com/2001/06/28/national/28CENS.html?ex=1179115200&en=fdd16863 1eb9e2c1&ei=5070, last accessed May 12, 2007.

4 Culhane, Dejowski, Ibañez, Needham, Macchia, "Public Shelter Admission Rates in Philadelphia and New York City," 109-110.

5 Isaac and Armat, *Madness in the Streets*, 4; Steven A. Holmes, "Bureau Won't Distribute Census Data on Homeless," *New York Times*, June 28, 2001, http://www.nytimes.com/2001/06/28/national/28CENS.html?ex=1179115200&en=fdd16863 1eb9e2c1&ei=5070, last accessed May 12, 2007; Culhane, Dejowski, Ibañez, Needham, Macchia, "Public Shelter Admission Rates in Philadelphia and New York City," 110.

6 Dear and Wolch, *Landscapes of Despair*, 175-6; Levine and Haggard, "Homelessness as a Public Mental Health Problem," in Rochefort, *Handbook on Mental Health Policy*, 294-9, 306.

7 Isaac and Armat, *Madness in the Streets*, 4-6.

8 H. Richard Lamb, ed., *The Homeless Mentally Ill. A Task Force Report of the American Psychiatric Association* (Washington: American Psychiatric Association, 1984), xiii, describes the concept of deinstitutionalization "as basically a good one" but the book overall examines in detail how it grew the homeless population.

9 Isaac and Armat, *Madness in the Streets*, 4-6.

10 Bachrach, "Mental Health Services," 16-19; A. Anthony Arce and Michael J. Vergare, "Identifying and Characterizing the Mentally Ill Among the Homeless," 78-86, in Lamb, *Homeless Mentally Ill*.

11 Dear and Wolch, *Landscapes of Despair*, 180-5.

12 Bachrach, "The Homeless Mentally Ill and Mental Health Services," 34-35; Robin Herman, "Woman Refuses Aid, Dies In Carton On Street," *New York Times*, January 27, 1982.

13 Bachrach, "Mental Health Services," 14.

14 Isaac and Armat, *Madness in the Street*, 2.

15 Grob, *Mad Among Us*, 302-3.

16 Margot Hornblower, "Down and Out—But Determined," *Time*, November 23, 1987.

17 Josh Barbanel, "Joyce Brown Obtains a Ban On Medicine," *New York Times*, January 16, 1988.

18 Josh Barbanel, "Homeless Woman Sent to Hospital Under Koch Plan Is Ordered Freed," *New York Times*, November 13, 1987.

19 "American Notes New York City," *Time*, March 21, 1988; Josh Barbanel, "Joyce Brown Panhandles Again," *New York Times*, March 10, 1988; Isaac and Armat, *Madness in the Streets*, 256-60.

20 Nicholas Rango, "Exposure-Related Hypothermia in the United States: 1970-79," *American Journal of Public Health*, 74:10[October, 1984] 1159-60; Centers for Disease Control and Prevention, National Center for Health Statistics. Compressed Mortality File 1979-1998. CDC WONDER On-line Database, compiled from Compressed Mortality File CMF 1968-1988, Series 20, No. 2A, 2000 and CMF 1989-1998, Series 20, No. 2E, 2003, ICD-9 E901.

21 Grob, *Mad Among Us*, 258-9.

22 Grob, *From Asylum to Community*, 249-51.

23 Grob, *Mad Among Us*, 261-5; Rochefort, "Mental Illness and Mental Health as Public Policy Concerns," 6; Grob, *From Asylum to Community*, 242-3.

24 Faris and Dunham, *Mental Disorders in Urban Areas*, 151-77.

25 Grob, *From Asylum to Community*, 243.

26 Grob, *Mad Among Us*, 301-2; David A. Rochefort and Bruce M. Logan, "The Alcohol, Drug Abuse, and Mental Health Block Grant: Origins, Design, and Impact," 159, in Rochefort, *Handbook on Mental Health Policy in the United States*.

27 Grob, *Mad Among Us*, 302.

28 Gregory Jaynes, "Urban Librarians Seek Ways To Deal With 'Disturbed Patrons'," *New York Times*, November 24, 1981.

29 Chip Ward, "America Gone Wrong: A Slashed Safety Net Turns Libraries into Homeless Shelters," *AlterNet*, April 2, 2007, http://www.alternet.org/story/50023/, last accessed April 15, 2007.

30 *Kreimer* v. *Morristown*, 765 F.Supp 181 (D.N.J. 1991).

31 *Kreimer* v. *Morristown*, 958 F.2d 1242 (3d Cir. 1992).

32 John Cichowski, "Some riders wear suits, some file them," *The Record*, March 15, 2005, http://www.northjersey.com/page.php?qstr=eXJpcnk3ZjczN2Y3dnFlZUVFeXkyNjcmZmdiZWw3Zjd2cWVlRUV5eTY2NjYwODkmeXJpcnk3ZjcxN2Y3dnFlZUVFeXk5, last accessed April 15, 2007.

Chapter 19: Indoor Tragedies (1975 – present)

1 Eve Bender, "Wisconsin Court Rejects Attempt To Narrow Commitment Law," *Psychiatric News*, 37:24]December 20, 2002], 13.

2 Michelle Roberts, "Free to Die," Portland *Oregonian*, December 30, 2002, http://olive-1.live.advance.net/special/shadows/index.ssf?/special/shadows/oregonian/20021230_lede.html, last accessed May 7, 2007.

3 Michelle Roberts, "County watches woman starve herself to death; state leaves supervisors' missteps unpunished," Portland *Oregonian*, December 29, 2002, http://olive-1.live.advance.net/special/shadows/index.ssf?/special/shadows/oregonian/20021229_reed.html, last accessed May 7, 2007.

4 Bachrach, "Mental Health Services," 15-16.

5 Dear and Wolch, *Landscapes of Despair*, 205-46.

6 H. Richard Lamb, "Deinstitutionalization and the Homeless Mentally Ill," 56-57, in Lamb, *Homeless Mentally Ill*.

7 Bachrach, "Mental Health Services," 28-29.

8 Irene Shifren Levine, "Service Programs for the Homeless Mentally Ill," 174-86, in Lamb, *Homeless Mentally Ill*; Rochefort, "Mental Illness and Mental Health as a Public Policy Concern," 11-12.

9 Irene Shifren Levine, "Service Programs for the Homeless Mentally Ill," 174-86, in Lamb, *Homeless Mentally Ill*; Sheila Rule, "2,000 More Beds for the Homeless Planned in City," *New York Times*, November 24, 1983; Howard Blum, "Creedmoor Homeless Plan Disputed," *New York Times*, December 6, 1983; Joseph B. Treaster, "Long-Term Residence Planned for Mentally Ill," *New York Times*, January 29, 1984.

10 Lamb, *Homeless Mentally Ill*, 8-9.

Chapter 21: Crime (1972 – present)

1 Donald T. Lunde, *Murder and Madness* (San Francisco: San Francisco Book Co., 1976), 49-52. Lunde evaluated Frazier's mental state for the court.

2 Lunde, *Murder and Madness*, 49-52.

3 Lunde, *Murder and Madness*, 53-56. Lunde also evaluated Kemper's sanity for the courts.

4 Lunde, *Murder and Madness*, 63-81. Lunde evaluated Mullin's sanity for the courts.

5 "Slaughter in a School Yard," *Time*, January 30, 1989, 29.

6 AP, "Police Still Unraveling Trail Left by Woman in Rampage," *New York Times*, May 22, 1988, http://query.nytimes.com/gst/fullpage.html?res=940DE2DA1231F931A15756C0A96E9482 60&sec=health&spon=&pagewanted=1, last accessed April 24, 2007.

7 Jaxon Van Derbeken, Bill Wallace, and Stacy Finz, "L.A. Suspect Dreamed of Killing: History of erratic behavior, ties to neo-Nazi group," San Francisco Chronicle, August 12, 1999, A1, http://www.sfgate.com/cgi-bin/article.cgi?file=/chronicle/archive/1999/08/12/MN48243.DTL, last accessed April 29, 2007.

8 Jim Yardley, "DEATHS IN A CHURCH: THE OVERVIEW, An Angry Mystery Man Who Brought Death," *New York Times*, September 17, 1999, http://query.nytimes.com/gst/fullpage.html?res=990DEEDC123CF934A2575AC0A96F9582 60&sec=health&spon=&pagewanted=all, last accessed April 29, 2007; "Tapes, letters reveal gunman's chilling actions, thoughts," CNN, September 17, 1999, http://www.cnn.com/US/9909/17/church.shooting.02/, last accessed April 29, 2007.

9 Maria Sudekum Fisher, "Mall shooter used dead woman's home while she was still inside," Topeka [Kans.] *Capital-Journal*, May 3, 2007, http://cjonline.com/stories/050307/kan_167236210.shtml, last accessed May 28, 2011.

10 Maria Sudekum Fisher, "Mall gunman planned to 'cause havoc'," Houston *Chronicle*, May 1, 2007, http://www.chron.com/disp/story.mpl/nation/4763148.html, last accessed May 28, 2011; Kansas City *Star*, May 2, 2007, Eric Adler, "Case points up a crisis in care," Kansas City *Star*, May 1, 2007, A1.

11 Christine Vendel, "WARD PARKWAY SHOOTER: 24-year-old Northland man was killed in December 1981: Logsdon had killed before," Kansas City *Star*, May 9, 2007, A1.

12 Bill Miller, "Capitol Shooter's Mind-Set Detailed," *Washington Post*, April 23, 1999, http://www.washingtonpost.com/wp-srv/national/longterm/shooting/stories/weston042399.htm, last accessed April 24, 2007.

13 Martin Kasindorf, "Woman kills 5, self at postal plant," *USA Today*, February 1, 2006, http://www.usatoday.com/news/nation/2006-01-31-postal-shooting_x.htm, last accessed April 24, 2007; Jim Maniaci, "'Crazy as a loon'," Gallup [N.M.] *Independent*, February 2, 2006, http://www.gallupindependent.com/2006/feb/020206shtrhme.html, last accessed April 24, 2007.

14 "Close the loophole Cho sneaked through," Hampton Roads *Virginian-Pilot*, April 25, 2007, http://content.hamptonroads.com/story.cfm?story=123471&ran=40263, last accessed April 25, 2007; Dr. Michael Welner, "Cho Likely Schizophrenic, Evidence Suggests," ABC *News*, April 17, 2007, http://abcnews.go.com/Health/VATech/story?id=3050483&page=1, last accessed April 24, 2007..

15 Austin Fenner, Kirsten Fleming, and Dan Mangan, "'I am shooting—have a nice day'," *New York Post*, April 7, 2009, http://www.nypost.com/p/news/national/item_GuHhWgg8gQRGSopO39fyFO;jsessionid=83 8260AAD90A3678AA8F7BC080B42526, last accessed May 21, 2011.

16 Tim Steller, "Man linked to Giffords shooting rampage called 'very disturbed'," *Arizona Daily Star*, January 8, 2011, http://azstarnet.com/news/local/crime/article_91db5db4-1b74-11e0-ba23-001cc4c002c0.html, last accessed May 21, 2011.

17 Craig Harris and Michael Kiefer, "Judge finds Jared Loughner incompetent to stand trial," *Arizona Star*, May 25, 2011, http://www.azcentral.com/arizonarepublic/news/articles/2011/05/25/20110525gabriel-giffords-shot-jared-loughner-competncy-hearing.html, last accessed May 26, 2011.

18 "Gunman's Rampage in France Leaves 14 Dead," *Los Angeles Times*, July 13, 1989, http://articles.latimes.com/1989-07-13/news/mn-4502_1_half-hour-rampage, last accessed May 27, 2011.

19 David Lester, *Mass Murder: The Scourge of the 21st Century* (Hauppage, N.Y.: Nova Science Publishers, 2004), 106.

20 "Teen-Age Gunman Kills Himself and 12 Others in France," *New York Times*, September 25, 1995, http://www.nytimes.com/1995/09/25/world/teen-age-gunman-kills-himself-and-12-others-in-france.html, last accessed May 27, 2011.

21 James Graff, "Politics Under the Gun," *Time*, March 31, 2002, http://www.time.com/time/magazine/article/0,9171,221091,00.html, last accessed May 27, 2011.

22 Nick Caistor, "Profile of a Teenage Killer," *BBC News*, April 28, 2002, http://news.bbc.co.uk/2/hi/europe/1956206.stm, last accessed May 27, 2011; "18 Dead in German School Shooting," *BBC News*, April 26, 2002, http://news.bbc.co.uk/2/hi/europe/1952869.stm, last accessed May 27, 2011.

23 "Brazil School Shooting: Twelfth Child Dies," *SkyNews*, April, 8, 2011, http://news.sky.com/skynews/Home/World-News/Video-Brazil-School-Shooting-12-Children-Killed-In-Rio-De-Janeiro-By-Gunman-In-Worst-Ever-Spree/Article/201104215968639?lpos=World_News_Carousel_Region_4&lid=ARTICLE_1 5968639_Video%3A_Brazil_School_Shooting_12_Children_Killed_In_Rio_De_Janeiro_By _Gunman_In_Worst_Ever_Spree, last accessed May 21, 2011.

24 "Safety council to investigate gun laws," *DutchNews.nl*, April 12, 2011, http://www.dutchnews.nl/news/archives/2011/04/safety_council_to_investigate.php, last accessed May 21, 2011; "Schutter was al eerder suicidaal," *NOS Nieuws*. April 10, 2011, http://nos.nl/artikel/232127-schutter-was-al-eerder-suicidaal.html, last accessed May 21, 2011.

25 UPI, "AROUND THE NATION; Courtroom Gunman Is Freed in Bail," *New York Times*, April 13, 1986, http://query.nytimes.com/gst/fullpage.html?res=9A0DE6DF1339F930A25757C0A96094826 0&n=Top%2fReference%2fTimes%20Topics%2fSubjects%2fB%2fBail, last accessed April 24, 2007.

26 Jeremy Hay, "Son held in slaying of mother in RP," Santa Rosa (Cal.) *Press-Democrat*, April 19, 2007, http://www1.pressdemocrat.com/apps/pbcs.dll/article?AID=/20070419/NEWS/704190344/1 033/NEWS01, last accessed April 24, 2007.

27 "Experts: Mentally ill face criminal stigma," Stockton (Cal.) *Record*, November 24, 2005, http://www.recordnet.com/apps/pbcs.dll/article?AID=/20051124/NEWS01/511240312, last accessed January 15, 2011.

28 Jaxon Van Debeken, "Slasher Suspect Had Violated His Previous Probation: Authorities lost track of case," *San Francisco Chronicle*, November 13, 1998, http://www.sfgate.com/cgi-bin/article.cgi?f=/c/a/1998/11/13/MN86295.DTL&hw=Joshua+Rudiger&sn=005&sc=586, last accessed April 24, 2007.

29 Jaxon Van Debeken, "'Vampire Slasher' Gets 23-to-Life Prison Term," *San Francisco Chronicle*, February 19, 2000, http://www.sfgate.com/cgi-bin/article.cgi?f=/c/a/2000/02/19/MN106182.DTL&hw=Joshua+Rudiger&sn=001&sc=1000 , last accessed April 24, 2007.
30 Michael A. Fuoco, "Baumhammers' attorney to argue mental infirmity," Pittsburgh *Post-Gazette*, May 1, 2000, http://www.post-gazette.com/regionstate/20000501baumhammers2.asp, last accessed April 24, 2007.
31 Jim McKinnon, "Baumhammers' father protests death penalty," Pittsburgh *Post-Gazette*, November 10, 2001, http://www.post-gazette.com/regionstate/20011110baumhammers1110p4.asp, last accessed April 24, 2007.
32 Frank Trippett, "The Madman on the Ferry," *Time*, July 21, 1986, http://www.time.com/time/magazine/article/0,9171,961814,00.html, last accessed May 13, 2007.
33 Jim O'Grady, "Officials Decide to Release Man Who Killed 2 With Sword," *New York Times*, March 26, 2000, http://query.nytimes.com/gst/fullpage.html?sec=health&res=9506E5DC123DF935A15750C0A9669C8B63, last accessed May 13, 2007.
34 Laurie Goodstein and William Glaberson, "The Well-Marked Roads to Homicidal Rage," *New York Times*, April 10, 2000.
35 Treatment Advocacy Center, "Preventable Tragedies," http://treatmentadvocacycenter.org/problem/preventable-tragedies-database, last accessed June 7, 2012.
36 U.S. Department of Justice, Office of Justice Programs, Bureau of Justice Statistics, "Homicide trends in the U.S.," http://www.ojp.usdoj.gov/bjs/homicide/hmrt.htm#longterm, last accessed April 24, 2007.
37 Clayton E. Cramer, "Is Gun Control Reducing Murder Rates?", *Shotgun News*, August 21, 2000, 18-19; Jens Ludwig and Phillip J. Cook, "Homicide and Suicide Rates Associated With Implementation of the Brady Handgun Violence Prevention Act," *Journal of the American Medical Association* 284:5 [August 2, 2000] 585-591; Jeffrey A. Roth and Christopher S. Koper, "Impacts of the 1994 Assault Weapons Ban: 1994-96," NCJ 173405, (Washington: National Institute of Justice, 1999), 1, available at http://www.ncjrs.org/pdffiles1/173405.pdf, last accessed April 24, 2007.
38 Bernard E. Harcourt, "From the Asylum to the Prison: Rethinking the Incarceration Revolution," *Texas Law Review*, 84[2006]:1766-75.
39 Bernard E. Harcourt, "From the Asylum to the Prison: Rethinking the Incarceration Revolution - Part II: State Level Analysis," (March 2007). University of Chicago Law & Economics, Olin Working Paper No. 335; University of Chicago, Public Law Working Paper No. 155. Available at SSRN: http://ssrn.com/abstract=970341.
40 Steven P. Segal, "Civil Commitment Law, Mental Health Services, and US Homicide Rates," *Social Psychiatry and Psychiatric Epidemiology*, November 10, 2011, http://kendruo law.org/national-studies/commitmenthomiciderates.pdf, last accessed June 7, 2012.
41 Goldhamer and Marshall, *Psychosis and Civilization*, 40-41.
42 Randolph A. Roth, "Spousal Murder in Northern New England, 1776-1865," 72, in Christine Daniels and Michael V. Kennedy, eds., *Over the Threshold: Intimate Violence in Early America* (New York: Routledge, 1999).
43 See Ulrich, *A Midwife's Tale*, 291-306, and North, *The History of Augusta*, 208-14, for a detailed account of the 1806 Purrinton murders, in which James Purrinton used a knife to murder his wife and seven of his eight children (one survived the attack), then committed suicide. Disturbingly similar is the case of William Beadle, of Wethersfield, Connecticut. In 1782, Beadle murdered his entire family (wife and four children) by knocking them unconscious with an ax, then slitting their throats. He then killed himself by firing two pistols at his head, simultaneously. Steven Mintz, *Moralists and Modernizers: America's Pre-Civil War Reformers* (Baltimore: Johns Hopkins University Press, 1995), 6; Royal Ralph Hinman, *A Catalogue of the Names of the Early Puritan Settlers of the Colony of Connecticut...* (Hartford, Conn.: Case, Tiffany, & Co., 1852), 165-7. Beadle was protecting them from ensuing poverty, his capital having been destroyed by the Revolution. George

Simon Roberts, *Historic Towns of the Connecticut River Valley* (Schenectady, N.Y.: Robson & Adee, 1906), 153-6.

44 Brown, *The Transfer Of Care*, 133-7; Thomas M. Arvanites, "The Mental Health and Criminal Justice Systems: Complementary Forms of Coercive Control," 138-41, in Allen A. Liska, ed., *Social Threat and Social Control* (Albany, N.Y.: State University of New York Press, 1992).

45 Arthur Zitrin, Anne S. Hardesty, Eugene I. Burdock, and Ann K. Drossman, "Crime and Violence Among Mental Patients," *American Journal of Psychiatry* 133[2]:142-9 (1976).

46 Larry Sosowsky, "Crime and Violence Among Mental Patients Reconsidered in View of the New Legal Relationship Between the State and the Mentally Ill," *American Journal of Psychiatry* 135[1]:33-42 (1978).

47 Larry Sosowsky, "Explaining the Increased Arrest Rate Among Mental Patients: A Cautionary Note," *American Journal of Psychiatry* 137[12]:1602-5 (1980).

48 H. Richard Lamb and Linda E. Weinberger , "Persons With Severe Mental Illness in Jails and Prisons: A Review," *Psychiatric Services* 49:483-92 (1998).

49 Jeanne Y. Choe, Linda A. Teplin, and Karen M. Abram, "Perpetration of Violence, Violent Victimization, and Severe Mental Illness: Balancing Public Health Concerns," *Psychiatric Services* 59:153-164, [February 2008].

50 Eric B. Elbogen and Sally C. Johnson, "The Intricate Link Between Violence and Mental Disorder: Results From the National Epidemiologic Survey on Alcohol and Related Conditions," *Archives of General Psychiatry* 2009:66(2):152-161.

51 Jeffery W. Swanson, *et al.*, "A National Study of Violent Behavior in Persons With Schizophrenia," *Archives of General Psychiatry* 63[2006]:490-9. This study has significant limitations because the data came out of a sample used for a drug test, and thus excluded those with limited decision-making abilities, those with certain physical health problems— and included only those that were "suboptimal" in their current treatment. In addition, the study relied heavily on self-reporting of violence by schizophrenics—a subject where even healthy people might be inclined to lie or shade the truth.

52 Paul Eugene Bowers, *Clinical Studies in the Relationship of Insanity to Crime* (Michigan City, Ind.: The Dispatch Press, 1915), provides a detailed discussion of the relationship, asserting that large numbers of those imprisoned for crimes were mentally ill, "feebleminded," or otherwise suffering from mental problems.

53 Lamb and Weinberger, "Persons With Severe Mental Illness in Jails and Prisons: A Review."

Chapter 22: The Pendulum Swings Back

1 Keilitz, "Legal Issues in Mental Health Care: Current Perspectives," 368-70.

2 Keilitz, "Legal Issues in Mental Health Care: Current Perspectives," 368-70.

3 Marvin S. Swartz and Jeffrey W. Swanson, "Involuntary Outpatient Commitment, Community Treatment Orders, and Assisted Outpatient Treatment: What's in the Data?" *Canadian Journal of Psychiatry,* 49:9[September 2004], 586.

4 N.C. Gen. Stat. § 122C-263(d)(1)(c) (1997), quoted in Bruce J. Winick, Ken Kress, and Michael L. Perlin, "Therapeutic Jurisprudence and Outpatient Commitment Law: Kendra's Law as Case Study," *Psychology, Public Policy, and Law* 9:189.

5 Winick, Kress, and Perlin, "Therapeutic Jurisprudence and Outpatient Commitment Law," 9:188.

6 Winick, Kress, and Perlin, "Therapeutic Jurisprudence and Outpatient Commitment Law," 9:188-9.

7 Sally L. Satel, "Real Help for the Mentally Ill," *New York Times*, January 7, 1999; O'Connor, "Is Kendra's Law A Keeper?" 322 n. 33.

8 Robert D. McFadden, "New York Nightmare Kills a Dreamer," *New York Times*, January 5, 1999.

9 Amy Waldman, "Woman Killed in a Subway Station Attack," *New York Times*, January 4, 1999.

10 N. R. Kleinfield with Kit R. Roane, "Subway Killing Casts Light On Suspect's Mental Torment," *New York Times*, January 11, 1999.

11 Michael Cooper, "Suspect Has a History of Mental Illness, but Not of Violence," *New York Times*, January 5, 1999.

12 Michael Cooper, "Suspect Has a History of Mental Illness, but Not of Violence," *New York Times*, January 5, 1999.

13 Michael Winerip, "Bedlam on the Streets," *New York Times*, May 23, 1999.

14 "METRO NEWS BRIEFS: NEW YORK; Hospital Stay Revealed For Man in Train Killing," *New York Times*, March 31, 1999.

15 N. R. Kleinfield with Kit R. Roane, "Subway Killing Casts Light On Suspect's Mental Torment," *New York Times*, January 11, 1999.

16 "After Kendra Webdale's Death," *New York Times*, January 8, 1999.

17 "A Signature for 'Kendra's Law'," *New York Times,* August 28, 1999.

18 New York State Office of Mental Health, *Kendra's Law: Final Report on the Status of Assisted Outpatient Treatment*, March 2005, 1.

19 O'Connor, "Is Kendra's Law A Keeper?" 334-6.

20 New York State Office of Mental Health, *Kendra's Law*, 2.

21 New York State Office of Mental Health, *Kendra's Law*, 7.

22 O'Connor, "Is Kendra's Law A Keeper?" 362.

23 New York State Office of Mental Health, *Kendra's Law*, 8.

24 New York State Office of Mental Health, *Kendra's Law*, 10-15.

25 New York State Office of Mental Health, *Kendra's Law*, 16-19.

26 Winick, Kress, and Perlin, "Therapeutic Jurisprudence and Outpatient Commitment Law," 9:194-5.

27 Winick, Kress, and Perlin, "Therapeutic Jurisprudence and Outpatient Commitment Law," 9:197-8.

28 Paul S. Appelbaum, "Law & Psychiatry: Ambivalence Codified: California's New Outpatient Commitment Statute," *Psychiatric Services* 54 [January 2003] 26-28.

29 Treatment Advocacy Center, "Every Brother, Everyone Deserves Better," October 17, 2008, http://www.treatmentadvocacycenter.org/index.php?option=com_content&task=view&id=604&Itemid=97, last accessed November 4, 2008.

30 C.W. Nevius, "Slaying on Russian Hill," San Francisco *Chronicle*, January 29, 2008, D1.

31 Rosanna Esposito, Valerie Westhead, and Jim Berko, "Florida's Outpatient Commitment Law: Effective but Underused," *Psychiatric Services* 59:3[2008], 328.

32 Swartz and Swanson, "Involuntary Outpatient Commitment," 586.

33 Swartz and Swanson, "Involuntary Outpatient Commitment," 587.

34 Swartz and Swanson, "Involuntary Outpatient Commitment," 388-9.

35 Robert A. Brooks, "Psychiatrists' Opinions About Involuntary Civil Commitment: Results of a National Survey," *Journal of the American Academy of Psychiatry and the Law* 35:2[2007], 223-4.

36 Brooks, "Psychiatrists' Opinions About Involuntary Civil Commitment," 224-5.

37 Eve Bender, "Wisconsin Court Rejects Attempt To Narrow Commitment Law," Psychiatric News, 37:24 [December 20, 2002], 13.

38 *State of Wisconsin* v. *Dennis H.*, 647 NW2d 851 (Wisc. 2002).

39 *State of Wisconsin* v. *Dennis H.*, 647 NW2d 851 (Wisc. 2002).

Chapter 24: We Can Pay Now Or We Can Pay Later

1 George W. Dowdall, *The Eclipse Of The State Mental Hospital: Policy, Stigma, And Organization* (Albany, N.Y.: State University of New York Press, 1996), 43-46.

2 See Richard D. Schneider, Hy Bloom, and Mark Heerema, *Mental Health Courts: Decriminalizing the Mentally Ill* (Toronto: Irwin Law, 2007) for an overview.

3 Lynne Lamberg, "Efforts Grow to Keep Mentally Ill Out of Jails," *Journal of the AMA* 292:5 [August 4, 2004] 555-6; James J. Stephan, *State Prison Expenditures, 2001* (Washington: Bureau of Justice Statistics, 2004), NCJ 202949, 1.

4 Lamberg, "Efforts Grow to Keep Mentally Ill Out of Jails," 555.

5 Shawn Vestal, "Killer told doctor he'd use guns, bombs," Spokane (Wash.) *Spokesman-Review,*   May   21,   2011, http://www.spokesmanreview.com/breaking/story.asp?ID=9972, last accessed May 28, 2011.

6 Paula M. Ditton, Bureau of Justice Statistics, "Mental Health and Treatment of Inmates and Probationers," (Washington: U.S. Department of Justice, 1999), NCJ 174463.

7 Ming T. Tsuang, Sarah I. Tarbox, Levi Taylor, and William S. Stone, "The Treatment of Schizotaxia," in William S. Stone, Stephen V. Faraone, and Ming T. Tsuang, eds., *Early Clinical Intervention and Prevention in Schizophrenia* (Totowa, N.J.: Humana Press, 2004), 294.

BIBLIOGRAPHY

"18 Dead in German School Shooting," *BBC News*, April 26, 2002.

Abdolmaleky, Hamid Mostafavi, Kuang-hung Cheng, Stephen V. Faraone, *et al.* "Hypomethylation of *MB-COMT* promoter is a major risk factor for schizophrenia and bipolar disorder." *Human Molecular Genetics* 15:21 (2006) 3132-45.

Abramson, M. F. "The Criminalization Of Mentally Disordered Behavior. Possible Side-Effect Of A New Mental Health Law." *Hospital and Community Psychiatry*, 23[1972]:101-105.

Acts of a General Nature, Enacted, Revised and Ordered to be Reprinted, At the First Session of the Twenty-Ninth General Assembly of the State of Ohio. (Columbus, Ohio: Olmsted & Bailmache, 1831), 29:224.

Adler, Eric. "Case points up a crisis in care." Kansas City *Star*, May 1, 2007, A1.

"Advocate Radical Change in Mental Health Care for Black Patients." *Jet*. May 20, 1971, 47.

Agnew, D. Hayes, Alfred Stille, Lewis P. Bush, Charles K. Mills, Roland G. Curtin. *History and Reminiscences of the Philadelphia Almshouse and Philadelphia Hospital.* (Philadelphia: Detre & Blackburn, 1890).

American Psychiatric Association. *Issues in Community Treatment of Severe Mental Illness.* (Washington: American Psychiatric Press, 1999).

Andrews, Linda Wasmer, ed. *Encyclopedia of Depression.* (Santa Barbara, Cal.: Greenwood Press, 2010).

Appelbaum, Paul S. "The Draft Act Governing Hospitalization of the Mentally Ill: Its Genesis and Its Legacy." *Psychiatric* Services 51:[February 2000]190-194.

_____. "Law & Psychiatry: Ambivalence Codified: California's New Outpatient Commitment Statute." *Psychiatric Services* 54 [January 2003]26-28.

Arce, A. Anthony and Michael J. Vergare. "Identifying and Characterizing the Mentally Ill Among the Homeless." 75-89, in Lamb, *Homeless Mentally Ill.*

Armour, Philip K. "Mental Health Policymaking in the United States: Patterns, Process, and Structures." In Rochefort, *Handbook of Mental Health Policy in the United States.*

Arsenault, Louise, Mary Cannon, Richie Poulton, Robin Murray, Avshalom Caspi, Terrie E. Moffitt, "Cannabis Use In Adolescence And Risk For Adult Psychosis: Longitudinal Prospective Study," *British Medical Journal* [November 23, 2002], 325:1212-1213.

Arsenault, Louise, Mary Cannon, John Witton, Robin E. Murray, "Causal Association Between Cannabis and Psychosis: Examination of the Evidence," *British Journal of Psychiatry* [2004] 184:110-117

Bachrach, Leona L. "The Homeless Mentally Ill and Mental Health Services: An Analytical Review of the Literature," 30-31, in Lamb, *Homeless Mentally Ill,* 11-53.

Bartlett, Peter and David Wright, eds. *Outside the Walls of the Asylum: The History of Care in the Community: 1750-2000.* (New Brunswick, N.J.: Athlone Press, 1999).

Baxter, W.E. American Psychiatric Association. "Central Inspection Board (1947-1960) ARCHIVES FINDING AID." (1985)

Bazelon, David L. "The Right to Treatment: The Court's Role." *Hospital and Community Psychiatry,* 20:5 [May, 1969], 129-35.

Bender, Eve. "Wisconsin Court Rejects Attempt To Narrow Commitment Law." *Psychiatric News,* 37:24]December 20, 2002], 13.

Benton, Josiah Henry. *Warning Out in New England: 1656-1817.* (Boston: W.B. Clarke Co., 1911).

Birnbaum, Morton. "The Right to Treatment." *American Bar Association Journal,* 46[May, 1960]:499-505.

Blackwood, Douglas H.R., Ben J. Pickard, Pippa A. Thomson, Kathryn L. Evans, David J. Porteous, and Walter J. Muir. "Are Some Genetic Risk Factors Common to Schizophrenia, Bipolar Disorder and Depression? Evidence from DISC1, GRIK4 and NRG1." *Neurotoxicity Research* 11:1 (2007) 73-83.

Bowers, Paul Eugene. *Clinical Studies in the Relationship of Insanity to Crime.* (Michigan City, Ind.: The Dispatch Press, 1915).

Braddock, David. "A National Deinstitutionalization Study." *State Government.* Autumn 1977, 220-6.

Brattleboro (Vt.) Vermont Asylum for the Insane. *The Vermont Asylum for the Insane: Its Annals for Fifty Years.* (Battleboro, Vt.: Hildreth and Fales, 1887).

Brennand, Kristen J., Anthony Simone, Jessica Jou, *et al.* "Modelling Schizophrenia Using Human Induced Pluripotent Stem Cells." *Nature* 473[May 12, 2011]:221-7.

Briggs, Lloyd Vernon. *History of the Psychopathic Hospital, Boston, Massachusetts.* (Boston: Wright & Potter Printing Co., 1922).

Brooking, Julia I., Susan A. H. Ritter, and Ben L. Thomas, eds. *A Textbook of Psychiatric and Mental Health Nursing.* (New York: Churchill Livingstone, 1992).

Brooks, Alexander D. *Law, Psychiatry and the Mental Health System.* (Boston: Little, Brown & Co., 1974).

Brooks, Robert A. "Psychiatrists' Opinions About Involuntary Civil Commitment: Results of a National Survey," *Journal of the American Academy of Psychiatry and the Law* 35:2[2007], 219-28.

Brown, Phil. *The Transfer Of Care: Psychiatric Deinstitutionalization And Its Aftermath.* (Boston: Routledge & Kegan Paul, 1985).

Buswell, Henry F. *The Law of Insanity In Its Application to the Civil Rights and Capacities and Criminal Responsibility of the Citizen.* (Boston: Little, Brown & Co., 1885).

Caistor, Nick. "Profile of a Teenage Killer," *BBC News,* April 28, 2002.

Cameron, James M. "A National Community Mental Health Program: Policy Initiation and Progress," 121-42. In Rochefort, *Handbook on Mental Health Policy in the United States.*

Campbell, Robert Jean. *Campbell's Psychiatric Dictionary.* 8th ed. (New York: Oxford University Press, 2004).

Castel, Francoise, Robert Castel, and Anne Lovell. *The Psychiatric Society.* (New York: Columbia University Press, 1982).

Choe, Jeanne Y., Linda A. Teplin, and Karen M. Abram. "Perpetration of Violence, Violent Victimization, and Severe Mental Illness: Balancing Public Health Concerns." *Psychiatric Services* 59:153-164, [February 2008].

Committee on Health Care for Homeless People, U.S. Institute of Medicine. *Homelessness, Health, and Human Needs* (Washington: National Academy Press, 1988).

Coppersmith, W. Louis. "Deinstitutionalization in Pennsylvania." *State Government,* Autumn 1977, 227-30.

Cramer, Clayton E. "Is Gun Control Reducing Murder Rates?" *Shotgun News,* August 21, 2000, 18-19.

Crane, George E. "Tardive Dyskinesia in Patients Treated with Major Neuroleptics: A Review of the Literature." *American Journal of Psychiatry* 124:8 [February 1968 Supp.] 39-48.

Culhane, Dennis P., Edmund F. Dejowski, Julie Ibañez, Elizabeth Needham, Irene Macchia, "Public Shelter Admission Rates in Philadelphia and New York City: The Implications of Turnover for Sheltered Population Counts," *Housing Policy Debates,* 5:2[1994], 107-140.

Daniels, Christine and Michael V. Kennedy, eds. *Over the Threshold: Intimate Violence in Early America* (New York: Routledge, 1999).

de Young, Mary. *Madness: An American History of Mental Illness and Its Treatment.* (Jefferson, N.C.: McFarland & Co., 2010).

Ditton, Paula M. Bureau of Justice Statistics, "Mental Health and Treatment of Inmates and Probationers," (Washington: U.S. Department of Justice, 1999), NCJ 174463.

Donohoe, Marie L. "A Social-Service Department in a State Hospital." *Mental Hygiene* 6:1 [January, 1922] 306-11.

Dowdall, George W. *The Eclipse Of The State Mental Hospital: Policy, Stigma, And Organization.* (Albany, N.Y.: State University of New York Press, 1996).

Elbogen, Eric B. and Sally C. Johnson. "The Intricate Link Between Violence and Mental Disorder: Results From the National Epidemiologic Survey on Alcohol and Related Conditions." *Archives of General Psychiatry* 2009:66(2):152-161.

Ennis, Bruce J. *Prisoners of Psychiatry.* (New York: Harcourt Brace Jovanovich, 1972).

Esposito, Rosanna, Valerie Westhead, and Jim Berko, "Florida's Outpatient Commitment Law: Effective but Underused," *Psychiatric Services* 59:3[2008], 328.

Farabee, Dale H. and Lillian Press. "Legislative Perspective on Public Mental Health Programs." *State Government*, Autumn 1977, 203-207.

Faris, Robert E. L. and H. Warren Dunham. *Mental Disorders in Urban Areas: An Ecological Study of Schizophrenia and Other Psychoses.* (New York: Hafner Publishing Co., 1960).

Field, Edward, ed. *State of Rhode Island and Providence Plantations at the End of the Century: A History.* (Boston: Mason Publishing Co., 1902).

Fisher, Maria Sudekum. "Mall shooter used dead woman's home while she was still inside." Topeka [Kans.] *Capital-Journal*, May 3, 2007.

_____, "Mall gunman planned to 'cause havoc'." Houston *Chronicle,* May 1, 2007.

Fitzgerald, Mike, Paul Hamos, John Muncie, and David Zeldin, eds. *Welfare in Action.* (London: Routledge & K. Paul, 1977).

Franklin, Benjamin. *Some Account of the Pennsylvania Hospital From Its First Rise to the Beginning of the Fifth Month, Called May, 1754.* (Philadelphia: United States' Gazette, 1817).

Goldhamer, Herbert and Andrew W. Marshall. *Psychosis and Civilization: Two Studies in the Frequency of Mental Disease.* (Glencoe, Ill.: The Free Press, 1953).

Goldman, Howard H. "The Obligation of Mental Health Services to the Least Well Off" *Psychiatric Services* 50[1999]:5:659-63.

Graff, James. "Politics Under the Gun." *Time,* March 31, 2002.

Grieco, Robert and Laura Edwards. *The Other Depression: Bipolar Disorder.* (New York: Taylor & Francis Group, 2010).

Grob, Gerald N. *From Asylum to Community: Mental Health Policy in Modern America.* (Princeton, N.J.: Princeton University Press, 1991).

_____. *Mental Illness and American Society, 1875-1940.* (Princeton University Press, 1983).

Group for the Advancement of Psychiatry. *Forced into Treatment: The Role of Coercion in Clinical Practice.* (Washington: American Psychiatric Press, 1994).

"Gunman's Rampage in France Leaves 14 Dead," *Los Angeles Times*, July 13, 1989.

Harcourt, Bernard E. "From the Asylum to the Prison: Rethinking the Incarceration Revolution." *Texas Law Review* 84[2006]:1751-86.

_____. "From the Asylum to the Prison: Rethinking the Incarceration Revolution Part II: State Level Analysis." (March 2007). U of Chicago Law & Economics, Olin Working Paper No. 335. Available at SSRN: http://ssrn.com/abstract=970341.

Harris, Isham G. "Commitment of the Insane, Past and Present, in the State of New York." *New York State Journal of Medicine* 7:12 [December, 1907] 487-91.

Harrison, George Leib. *Legislation on Insanity: A Collection of All the Lunacy Laws of the States and Territories of the United States to the Year 1883, Inclusive...* (Philadelphia: privately printed, 1884).

Harrison, P.J. and D.R. Weinberger. "Schizophrenia genes, gene expression, and neuropathology: on the matter of their convergence." *Molecular Psychiatry* 10:[2005]40-68.

Henquet, Cécile, Marta Di Forti, Paul Morrison, Rebecca Kuepper and Robin M. Murray, "Gene-Environment Interplay Between Cannabis and Psychosis," *Schizophrenia Bulletin* [August 22, 2008] 34:6:1111-1121.

Hinman, Royal Ralph. *A Catalogue of the Names of the Early Puritan Settlers of the Colony of Connecticut...* (Hartford, Conn.: Case, Tiffany, & Co., 1852).

Hobson. J. Allan and Jonathan A. Leonard. *Out Of Its Mind: Psychiatry in Crisis.* (Cambridge, Mass.: Perseus Publishing Group, 2001).

Horwitz, Allan V. *Creating Mental Illness.* (Chicago: University of Chicago Press, 2002).

Hurd, Duane Hamilton. *History of Middlesex County, Massachusetts...* (Philadelphia: J.W. Lewis & Co., 1890).

_____. *History of Norfolk County, Massachusetts*.... (Philadelphia: J.W. Lewis & Co., 1884).

Institute of Medicine. Division of Mental Health and Behavioral Medicine. National Institute of Mental Health. *Mental Health Services in General Health Care: Coordinated Mental Health Care in Neighborhood Health Centers*. (Washington: National Academy of Sciences, 1979).

International Schizophrenia Consortium. "Common polygenic variation contributes to risk of schizophrenia and bipolar disorder." *Nature* 460[August 6, 2009] 748-52.

Isaac, Rael Jean and Virginia C. Armat. *Madness In The Streets: How Psychiatry And The Law Abandoned The Mentally Ill*. (New York: The Free Press, 1990).

Jarvis, Edward. "Law of Insanity, and Hospitals for the Insane in Massachusetts." *Monthly Law Reporter* 22:[November 1859]365-409.

Joint Commission on Mental Illness and Health. *Action for Mental Health: Final Report of the Joint Commission on Mental Illness and Health*. (New York: Basic Books, 1961).

Jolley, G., S. R. Hirsch, E. Morrison, A. McRink, and L. Wilson, "Trial of brief intermittent neuroleptic prophylaxis for selected schizophrenic outpatients: clinical and social outcome at two years," *British Medical Journal* 837:1136 [October 13, 1990], http://www.bmj.com/content/301/6756/837.abstract , last accessed May 14, 2011.

Keilitz, Ingo. "Legal Issues in Mental Health Care: Current Perspectives." In Rochefort, Handbook on Mental Health Policy in the United States, 363-83.

Knobler, Stacey *et al. The Infectious Etiology of Chronic Diseases: Defining the Relationship, Enhancing the Research, and Mitigating the Effects*. (Washington: National Academies Press, 2004).

Kolb, David, ed. *New Perspectives on Hegel's Philosophy of Religion*. (Albany, N.Y.: State University of New York Press, 1992).

Kotowicz, Zbigniew. *R.D. Laing and the Paths Of Anti-Psychiatry*. (London: Routledge, 1997).

Laing, R.D. *The Divided Self*. (New York: Pantheon Books, 1960).

Lamb, H. Richard. *The Homeless Mentally Ill: A Task Force Report of the American Psychiatric Association* (Washington: American Psychiatric Association, 1984).

Lamb, H. Richard and Linda E. Weinberger. "Persons With Severe Mental Illness in Jails and Prisons: A Review." *Psychiatric Services* 49:483-92 (1998).

Lamberg, Lynne. "Efforts Grow to Keep Mentally Ill Out of Jails," *Journal of the AMA* 292:5 [August 4, 2004] 555-6.

Leff, Julian and Noam Trieman. "Long-stay Patients Discharged From Psychiatric Hospitals," *British Journal of Psychiatry* 176(3)[2000]:217-22.

Lester, David. *Mass Murder: The Scourge of the 21st Century.* (Hauppage, N.Y.: Nova Science Publishers, 2004).

Levine, Irene Shifren. "Service Programs for the Homeless Mentally Ill," 174-86, in Lamb, *Homeless Mentally Ill.*

Levine, Irene Shifren and Haggard, Loretta K. "Homelessness as a Public Mental Health Problem," in Rochefort, *Handbook on Mental Health Policy.*

Linn, Margaret W. and Shayna Stein. "Nursing Homes as Community Mental Health Facilities." In Rochefort, *Handbook on Mental Health Policy in the United States,* 267-92.

Liska, Allen A. ed. *Social Threat and Social Control.* (Albany, N.Y.: State University of New York Press, 1992).

Lubow, Robert and Ina Weiner, eds. *Latent Inhibition: Cognition, Neuroscience, and Applications to Schizophrenia.* (Cambridge, Eng.: Cambridge University Press, 2010).

Ludwig, Jens and Philip J. Cook. "Homicide and Suicide Rates Associated With Implementation of the Brady Handgun Violence Prevention Act." *Journal of the American Medical Association* 284:5 [August 2, 2000] 585-591.

Lunde, Donald T. *Murder and Madness.* (San Francisco: San Francisco Book Co., 1976).

Marietta, Jack D. and G.S. Rowe. *Troubled Experiment: Crime and Justice in Pennsylvania, 1682-1800.* (Philadelphia: University of Pennsylvania Press, 2006).

Massachusetts Commission on Lunacy. *Report on Insanity and Idiocy in Massachusetts.* (Boston: William White, 1855).

Matejkowski, Jason C., Sara W. Cullen, and Phyllis L. Solomon, "Characteristics of Persons With Severe Mental Illness Who Have Been Incarcerated for Murder," *Journal of the American Academy of Psychiatry and the Law* 36:1[2008]74-86, http://www.jaapl.org/cgi/reprint/36/1/74, last accessed May 14, 2011.

McGrath, John, Joy Welham, James Scott, *et al.* "Association Between Cannabis Use and Psychosis-Related Outcomes Using Sibling Pair Analysis in a Cohort of Young Adults," *Archives of General Psychiatry* 67:5 [May 2010] 440-447.

[1] J.P. McEvoy, "The Costs of Schizophrenia," *Journal of Clinical Psychiatry,* 68 Suppl. 14:4-7 (2007), abstract available at http://www.ncbi.nlm.nih.gov/pubmed/18284271, last accessed June 9, 2012.

Mechanic, David. "Toward the Year 2000 in U.S. Mental Health Policymaking and Administration." In Rochefort, *Handbook on Mental Health Policy in the United States,* 477-501.

Menninger, Roy W. and John Case Nemiah, eds. *American Psychiatry After World War II (1944-1994).* (Washington: American Psychiatric Press, 2000).

Merrill, Deane. "Estimated Population of American Colonies, 1630-1780." http://merrill.olm.net/mdocs/pop/colonies/colonies.htm,   last   accessed September 10, 2009.

Mintz, Steven. *Moralists and Modernizers: America's Pre-Civil War Reformers.* (Baltimore: Johns Hopkins University Press, 1995).

Morison, Alexander. *Cases of Mental Disease, With Practical Observations on the Medical Treatment for the Use of Students.* (London: Longman & Co., 1828).

Morrissey, Joseph P. "The Changing Role of the Public Mental Hospital." In Rochefort, *Handbook on Mental Health Policy in the United States*, 311-38.

Morton, Thomas G. "Reminisces of Early Hospital Days." *Philadelphia Medical Times,* December 26, 1885.

New York Hospital Society, *Charter of the Society of the New-York Hospital and the Laws Relating Thereto, with the By-laws and Regulations of the Institution, and Those of the Bloomingdale Asylum for the Insane.: With the By-laws and Regulations of the Institution, and Those of the Bloomingdale Asylum for the Insane* (New York: Daniel Fanshaw, 1856).

North, James W. *The History of Augusta, From the Earliest Settlement to the Present Time...* (Augusta, Me.: Clapp & North, 1870).

O'Malley, Padraig, ed. *Homelessness: New England and Beyond.* (Amherst, Mass.: University of Massachusetts Press, 1992).

Overholser, Winfred. "Mental Hygiene." *Proceedings, American Philosopical Society* 90:4[September 1946] 259-64.

"Paonessa Dies at Sing Sing," Gloversville (N.Y.) *Leader-Republican*, January 16, 1953.

Peele, Roger, Bruce Gross, Bernard Arons, and Mokarram Jafri, "The Legal System and the Homeless," 273-4, in Lamb, *Homeless Mentally Ill,* 261-78.

People v. *Alfred Curt Von Wolfersdorf,* 66 Misc.2d 904 (N.Y. 1971).

Pinel, Philippe, D. D. Davis trans. *A Treatise on Insanity, In Which Are Contained the Principles of a New and More Practical Nosology of Maniacal Disorders.* (Sheffield, Eng.: W. Todd, 1806).

Plaut, Eric A. and Susannah Rubenstein. "State Care for the Mentally Ill: A Brief History." *State Government.* Autumn 1977, 192-7.

Prichard, James Cowles. *A Treatise on Insanity and Other Disorders Affecting the Mind.* (Philadelphia: E.L. Carey & A. Hart, 1837).

Providence (R.I.) City Council. *The Early Records of the Town of Providence.* (Providence, R.I.: Snow & Farnham, 1899).

Putnam, Jackson K. *Jess: The Political Career of Jesse Marvin Unruh.* (Lanham, Md.: University Press of America, 2005).

Reamer, Frederic G. "The Contemporary Mental Health System: Facilities, Services, Personnel, and Finances." In Rochefort, *Handbook of Mental Health Policy in the United States,* 21-42.

Rinkel, Max, H. Jackson DeShon, Robert W. Hyde, and Harry C. Solomon, "Experimental Schizophrenia-Like Symptoms," *American Journal of Psychiatry* 108:8:572-578 [February, 1952].

Roberts, George Simon. *Historic Towns of the Connecticut River Valley.* (Schenectady, N.Y.: Robson & Adee, 1906).

Rochefort, David A. "Mental Illness and Mental Health as Public Policy Concerns." in David A. Rochefort, ed., *Handbook on Mental Health Policy in the United States* (Westport, Conn.: Greenwood Press, 1989), 3-20.

_____, ed. *Handbook on Mental Health Policy in the United States* (Westport, Conn.: Greenwood Press, 1989).

Rochefort, David A. and Bruce M. Logan. "The Alcohol, Drug Abuse, and Mental Health Block Grant: Origins, Design, and Impact." In *Handbook on Mental Health Policy in the United States* (Westport, Conn.: Greenwood Press, 1989), 143-71.

Romero, George. *The Rescue.* (Arcadia, Cal.: Lotus Vision Publishing Co., 2010).

Roth, Jeffrey A. and Christopher S. Koper. "Impacts of the 1994 Assault Weapons Ban: 1994-96." NCJ 173405, (Washington: National Institute of Justice, 1999).

Ryan, Frank P. "Human Endogenous Retroviruses In Health And Disease: A Symbiotic Perspective." *Journal of the Royal Society of Medicine,* 97:560-565 (December 2004).

Sankey, William Henry Octavius. *Lectures on Mental Diseases.* (London: John Churchill and Sons, 1866).

Sarason, Irwin G. and Barbara R. Sarason. *Abnormal Psychology: The Problem of Maladaptive Behavior.* 10th ed. (Upper Saddle River, N.J.: Prentice-Hall, 2002).

Scheff, Thomas J. *Being Mentally Ill: A Sociological Theory,* 3rd ed. (Hawthorne, N.Y.: Aldine de Grutyer, 1999).

Schneider, Richard D., Hy Bloom, and Mark Heerema. *Mental Health Courts: Decriminalizing the Mentally Ill.* (Toronto: Irwin Law, 2007).

Segal, Steven P. "Civil Commitment Law, Mental Health Services, and US Homicide Rates," *Social Psychiatry and Psychiatric Epidemiology,* November 10, 2011, http://kendras-law.org/national-studies/commitmenthomiciderates.pdf, last accessed June 7, 2012.

Segal, Steven P. and Pamela Kotler. "Community Residential Care." In Rochefort, *Handbook on Mental Health Policy in the United States*, 237-65.

Shipton, Clifford K. *New England Life in the Eighteenth Century.* (Cambridge, Mass.: Harvard University Press, 1995).

Smith, J. and Andre Moncourt. *The Red Army Faction: A Documentary History.* (Oakland, Cal.: PM Press, 2009).

Sosowsky, Larry. "Crime and Violence Among Mental Patients Reconsidered in View of the New Legal Relationship Between the State and the Mentally Ill." *American Journal of Psychiatry* 135[1]:33-42 (1978).

_____. "Explaining the Increased Arrest Rate Among Mental Patients: A Cautionary Note." *American Journal of Psychiatry* 137[12]:1602-5 (1980).

Speidel, Carl Caskey. "Studies of Living Nerves. VI. Effects of Metrazol on Tissues of Frog Tadpoles....," *Proceedings of the American Philosophical Society* 83[1940]:349-78.

State of New York. *Seventeenth Annual Report of the State Board of Charities.* (Albany: Weed, Parsons & Co., 1884).

_____. State Commission in Lunacy. *Ninth Annual Report.* (Albany: Wynkoop Hallenbeck Crawford Co., 1898).

State of Pennsylvania. *Official Documents, Comprising The Department And Other Reports Made To The Governor, Senate And House Of Representatives Of Pennsylvania.* (Harrisburg, Penn.: Edwin K. Meyers, 1893).

Stefansson, Hreinn, Roel A. Ophoff, Stacy Steinberg, et al., "Common variants conferring risk of schizophrenia," *Nature* 460[August 6, 2009] 744-8.

Stone, William S., Stephen V. Faraone, and Ming T. Tsuang, eds. *Early Clinical Intervention and Prevention in Schizophrenia.* (Totowa, N.J.: Humana Press, 2004).

Swartz, Marvin S. and Jeffrey W. Swanson. "Involuntary Outpatient Commitment, Community Treatment Orders, and Assisted Outpatient Treatment: What's in the Data?" *Canadian Journal of Psychiatry,* 49:9[September 2004], 585-91.

Talbott, John A. and Robert E. Hales, eds. *Textbook of Administrative Psychiatry: New Concepts for a Changing Behavioral Health System,* 2nd ed. (Washington: American Psychiatric Publishing, 2001).

Taubes, Tanaquil. "'Healthy Avenues of the Mind': Psychological Theory Building and the Influence of Religion During the Era of Moral Treatment," *American Journal of Psychiatry* 155:8[August 1998], 1001-1008.

"Teen-Age Gunman Kills Himself and 12 Others in France," *New York Times,* September 25, 1995.

Thomas, Benjamin Franklin. *The Town Officer: A Digest of the Laws of Massachusetts In Relation to the Powers, Duties and Liabilities of Towns, and Town Officers.* (Worcester, Mass.: Warren Lazell, 1849).

Thornicroft, Graham. Paul Bebbington, and Julian Leff, "Outcomes for Long-Term Patients One Year After Discharge From a Psychiatric Hospital," *Psychiatric Services* 56:11[Novembger 2005], 1416-22.

Torrey, E. Fuller. *The Insanity Offense: How America's Failure To Treat The Seriously Mentally Ill Endangers Its Citizens.* (New York: W.W. Norton, 2008).

Torrey, E. Fuller and Judy Miller. *The Invisible Plague: The Rise of Mental Illness from 1750 to the Present* (New Brunswick, N.J.: Rutgers University Press, 2001).

Tourney, Garfield. "A History of Therapeutic Fashions in Psychiatry, 1800-1966." *American Journal of Psychiatry* 124:6 [December 1967] 784-96.

Tucker, Jonathan B. ed. *Toxic Terror: Assessing Terrorist Use of Chemical and Biological Weapons.* (Cambridge, Mass.: MIT Press, 2000).

Tuke, D. Hack. *The Insane in the United States and Canada* (London: H.K. Lewis, 1885).

Ulrich, Laurel Thatcher. *A Midwife's Tale: The Life of Martha Ballard, Based on Her Diary, 1785-1812.* (New York: Vintage Books, 1991).

U.S. Senate. *To Protect the Constitutional Rights of the Mentally Ill.* Hearings before the Subcommittee on Constitutional Rights of the Committee on the Judiciary, United States Senate. (88th Cong., 1st sess.).

Vaccaro, Jerome V. and Gordon H. Clark. *Practicing Psychiatry in the Community: A Manual.* (Washington: American Psychiatric Press, 1996).

Vardy, M. M. and S. R. Kay, "LSD psychosis or LSD-induced schizophrenia? A multimethod inquiry." *Archives of General Psychiatry* 40:8:877-83 [August 1983], abstract available at http://www.ncbi.nlm.nih.gov/pubmed/6870484, last accessed May 14, 2011.

Vendel, Christine. "WARD PARKWAY SHOOTER. 24-year-old Northland man was killed in December 1981: Logsdon had killed before." Kansas City *Star*, May 9, 2011, A1.

Vestal, Shawn. "Killer told doctor he'd use guns, bombs." Spokane (Wash.) *Spokesman-Review*, May 21, 2011.

Waln, Jr., Robert. "An Account of the Asylum for the Insane, established by the Society of Friends, near Frankford, in the vicinity of Philadelphia." *Philadelphia Journal of Medical and Physical Science* [1825] 10:225-52.

Warren, Carol A. B. *The Court of Last Resort: Mental Illness and the Law.* (Chicago: University of Chicago Press, 1982).

Watkins, Tom H. *The Hungry Years: A Narrative History of the Great Depression in America.* (New York: Macmillan, 2000).

White, William A. *Outlines of Psychiatry*, 2nd ed. (New York: The Journal of Nervous and Mental Disease Publishing Co., 1909).

Winick, Bruce J., Ken Kress, and Michael L. Perlin. "Therapeutic Jurisprudence and Outpatient Commitment Law: Kendra's Law as Case Study." *Psychology, Public Policy, and Law* 9:183-209.

Zammit, Stanley, Peter Allebeck, Sven Andreasson, Ingvar Lundberg, and Glyn Lewis, "Self reported cannabis use as a risk factor for schizophrenia in Swedish conscripts of 1969: historical cohort study." *British Medical Journal*

325:1199   [November   23,   2002],   abstract   available   at
http://www.bmj.com/content/325/7374/1199, last accessed May 14, 2011.

Zitrin, Arthur, Anne S. Hardesty, Eugene I. Burdock, and Ann K. Drossman,
    "Crime and Violence Among Mental Patients." *American Journal of
    Psychiatry* 133[2]:142-9 (1976).

Zwelling, Shomer S. *Quest For A Cure: The Public Hospital In Williamsburg,
    1773-1885.* (Williamsburg, Va.: Colonial Williamsburg Foundation, 1985).

The Cover

The cover photograph by C. G. P. Grey shows a homeless man in New York City, taken August 4, 2005, released under the Creative Commons Attribution license. Cover layout and book formatting by Clayton E. Cramer.

CPSIA information can be obtained at www.ICGtesting.com
Printed in the USA
LVOW12s0105261213

366875LV00007B/32/P